The World
of Obituaries

The World of Obituaries

Gender across Cultures and over Time

Mushira Eid

Wayne State University Press
Detroit

Manufactured in the United States of America.
06 05 04 03 02   5 4 3 2 1

Library of Congress Cataloging-in-Publication Data

Eid, Mushira.
    The world of obituaries : gender across cultures and over time / Mushira Eid.
        p. cm.
    Includes bibliographical references and index.
    ISBN 0-8143-2755-9 (alk. paper)
    1. Women—Obituaries—History—20th century. 2. Obituaries—Social aspects.
3. Sexism in language. 4. Arabic language—Sex differences. 5. English language—
Sex diferences. 6. Persian language—Sex differences. 7. Women in mass media.
I. Title.
HQ1122 .E35 2002
902.72—dc21   2001002030

To the memory of my father,
Abou Bakr Eid,
whose life has inspired mine
and whose sudden death has taken me
on a journey of acceptance

Contents

Acknowledgments

This work has been supported by two faculty development grants from the College of Humanities at the University of Utah. I wish to thank the college and the university for their support. I also wish to thank colleagues, friends, and research assistants who in their different capacities contributed to this work. First and foremost is Shohreh Gholsorkhi (University of Utah, later Princeton University), who served as my primary resource person on the Persian obituaries (data collection and translation). She also worked on the English obituaries and some Arabic as well. We worked together for many years on this project, and her contribution has been invaluable. Nayer Fallahi (University of Utah) was my resource person for the 1998 obituaries. I thank her for her time, effort, and enthusiasm for the project. For additional consultation on Persian obituaries, I thank my colleagues Soheila Amirsoleimani and Michel Mazzaoui at the University of Utah. I also thank them for their moral support and for listening when I needed to talk. Others have helped in data collection as well, particularly Valerie Smith and Tessa Hauglid. Basima Bezirgan at the University of Chicago Library and Suad Muhammad Gamal at Washington University have provided me with library resources, information, and support during the sabbatical years I spent in Chicago and St. Louis, and I thank them both. For help with statistics, I wholeheartedly thank Soleiman Abu Badr (University of Utah) for his time, patience, and advice, which helped make this a better volume. I am also indebted to the late Nawal El Mahallawi (*Al-Ahram*), who provided me with information and resources I could not have accessed on my own. Her encouragement and support will be missed.

A Note on Transliteration

I have adopted a simplified transliteration system to write Arabic and Persian names and titles in English. The simplification is intended to avoid diacritics, as much as possible, but more important, it is intended to reflect the way names and titles are likely to be written by speakers of these languages today, with some modification. (A note is included in appendix A for the transliteration of titles.) In the transliteration of names, sounds not found in English are given their closest counterparts. The name *Mahmoud,* for example, includes the Arabic *ḥ* "*ḥaaʾ,*" which is represented by *h.* The hamza (ʾ) and the ayn (ʿ) are not represented in names, primarily because they break up the sequencing of letters in English. My own last name, for example, includes an initial ayn in Arabic, which is not written in English. I followed this strategy unless the name would be misinterpreted without it. Otherwise the transliteration system of consonants is familiar to those working with languages of the Middle East. The representation of vowels is more likely to be inconsistent. Long vowels are sometimes written as sequences of two vowels, for example, *ou* in *Mahmoud,* but sometimes by just a vowel as in my own first name, *Mushira,* where the vowel *i* is long. In the transliteration of Quranic verses, however, pronunciation details are included and long vowels are represented as sequences of two identical vowels. I have also used the Egyptian Arabic pronunciation of *jiim* (*j*) as *giim* (*g*) in all names and titles in the text. This pronunciation predominates in Egypt now; *jiim* is rarely heard even in news broadcasts and other official meetings. However, in tables and graphs I have retained the *jiim* in titles, particularly those shared with Persian, to reflect this shared source. Likewise, Persian words derived from Arabic have also been transliterated to reflect the Arabic source, as explained in appendix A.

Introduction: Gender, Language, and the Obituaries

One is not born, but rather becomes, a woman.
—Simone de Beauvoir, *The Second Sex*

I felt the dead more steadfast in seeking their rights
than the living. The departed want us to take every
opportunity we have to carry out the sacred mission
they have placed on our shoulder.
—Huda Shaarawi, 1937[1]

People's initial responses to hearing that I work with obituaries fall into one of two categories: "How macabre! Why not do something with the living?" or "How interesting! I love reading the obituaries." Both are almost always followed by requests for further information: "What made you think of that?" or "What are you doing with them?" Both are a reflection of our attitudes toward death and dying: fear or resentment, as in the first reaction, acknowledgment or acceptance, as in the second. By way of introducing the research and the volume as a whole, I start by answering these questions.

I have had a lifelong fascination with obituaries. As a young adult in Cairo, Egypt, I would turn to the obituary pages first before reading other sections of the newspaper. A wealth of information appeared to be included in these pages about people and their families—who they are, what they do, and where they live. I recall doing the same thing with English newspapers later on, but I also recall thinking English newspaper obituaries were very different from their Arabic counterparts. Part of my motivation for undertaking this research has been to identify these differences and to understand their significance and cross-cultural implications.

My study of the obituaries, however, has been primarily motivated by gender-related issues and has been inspired by a class I taught in 1987 at the University of Utah on language and gender in cross-cultural perspective.

The topics included sexism in language and other gender inequities expressed through language. Since newspaper obituaries constitute a linguistic form in which both women and men are represented, they emerged as possible candidates for the study of gender-related differences in language, both cross-culturally and historically.[2]

I also recall in the context of debates on gender equity an eye-opening statement I had at some point heard or read, which I have later come to associate with Simone de Beauvoir and is quoted above. Contrary to traditional wisdom, one is not born a woman; it is something one becomes. If so, how does one become a woman (or a man for that matter), and what does it mean to be one? What does this mean in the world of the obituaries and perceptions of gender constructed therein? As I began this research, I asked myself: What makes one a woman, rather than a female, in the obituaries? What makes one a man, rather than a male? Can such questions be asked to begin with in the context of obituaries? As a result I found myself asking questions about equity, about the construction of gender, about public versus private space and the sharing of that space by the sexes both physically and linguistically, about visibility, and about power relations in both private and public domains. These questions led me along different paths and opened up various avenues of research.

I found myself looking at literary texts, research on language and gender, debates over representations of women and men in textbooks, fairy tales, television shows and advertisements, and a host of other areas. I finally had the courage to ask myself: why not the obituaries? After all, they can be viewed as a genre of a sort. They are texts written by individuals within a certain cultural context for a certain purpose. As such they conform to a certain format and reflect aspects of the social context within which they are written—its values and perhaps its attitudes toward death, its people and perhaps how they view themselves and, by implication, their perception of gender. But is that all they can be? Can obituaries, for example, have their own conventions? Can they create a world of their own relatively independent of the social reality beyond them? What sort of world would that be? Who populates it? How does it differ from the social reality outside it? I found myself engaged in a debate reminiscent of the Sapir-Whorf hypothesis about language: Does it reflect or create (perceptions of) social reality? Although I do not intend to engage in that debate, I believe language does both. I raise this question in relation to obituaries.

When one reads a newspaper's obituary pages, one expects women and men to be closely, if not equally, represented. This expectation was not confirmed by my reading of the Arabic obituaries, and in particular the 1938 obituaries in the Egyptian newspaper *Al-Ahram*. My initial reading left me cold, disappointed, and confused. Because very few women were mentioned as deceased or as survivors, the obituary pages appeared to reflect a society without women. My attempt to understand this initial impression and the factors contributing to it is yet another reason behind my undertaking this research. Unfortunately, a closer reading of these obituaries only disconfirmed the underlying assumption that women and men have equal access to the obituary pages. Women, in some parts of the world more so than in others, have been denied equal access to the public domain, even in death. My study of the 1938 Egyptian obituaries (Eid 1994a) establishes a bias, both quantitative and qualitative, in favor of men. Women's identity has been suppressed, hidden, or made invisible, whereas men's is never questioned and, depending on the interpretation of these results, men's identity may have even been glorified through their representation in the obituary pages. Thus the world created through the 1938 Egyptian obituaries may be a true reflection of its gendered social reality with its inequitable allotment of public space. It was, after all, "a man's world." Is it still?

This initial realization led to a number of inquiries, which I formulate in terms of two major research questions. The first deals with this perceived invisibility of women in the obituaries and its cross-cultural significance. If we examine the obituary pages from 1938 to the present, would we find "invisibility" to be a characteristic of gender inequity across cultures? The second deals with the extent to which such inequities may have changed or been maintained over time. If change has occurred, what form has it taken and what may have caused it?

To address the cross-cultural issue, I have selected for the purpose of this study three different languages and their corresponding cultures: Arabic (Egypt), English (United States), and Persian (Iran). Linguistically, English and Persian are more closely related, both being Indo-European, but Arabic is Semitic. Culturally, Arabic and Persian represent predominantly Islamic cultures, whereas English represents a predominantly Judeo-Christian culture. But cultural contacts between speakers of Arabic and Persian have over the centuries made the languages "culturally related" with a common (Arabic) script, shared vocabulary items, and similar linguistic structures.[3]

These choices are diverse enough to allow for sufficient differences and similarities to emerge.

To address the historical issue, I have selected a period of fifty years, 1938–88, to cover in this research. Obituaries have been collected for a month (thirty days) at ten-year intervals (1938, 1948, 1958, etc.) from each language. This period is long enough to reflect change, if change has taken place. But 1988 also represents the year I began the data collection process. More than ten years have passed since then. Therefore, I provide results of the analysis of 1998 obituaries as well in chapter 6. Details on data collection, including sources and methodology, are described in chapter 1.

But to measure gender (in)equity and change in the obituaries, it is necessary to determine first how gender is constructed in them and to consider the issue of obituaries as a source of information—the why-study-the-obituaries question and the type of information obituaries include that would allow for the study of gender identity and its change over time. This is addressed in chapter 1 through a survey of obituaries sampled from all three languages and an overview of the framework of analysis and initial hypotheses entertained.

The survey illustrates areas pertinent to the construction of gender identity in the obituaries. As texts, the obituaries construct individuals' identities through the symbolic use of language. Three linguistic variables emerge as symbolic of what I call "basic" and "acquired" identities—Name, Title, and Occupation. Although all three can be said to represent identities given or acquired during a person's lifetime, names are basic identities and as such they differ dramatically from the other two: all human beings are given (or have) names, but not all are given (or have) titles or occupations. A detailed discussion of the variation found in the obituary pages in terms of deceased identification by name, title, and occupation is found in chapters 3 through 5. To assess the impact of sex, of different cultures, and of different times on the variation both independently and relative to each other, I rely on quantitative analysis and basic statistical tests for distributional significance.

The relationship between language and gender equity in the obituaries can be placed within a conceptual framework based on the (sociolinguistic) principle that language is a choice, and linguistic choices, like sociocultural or political choices, not only reflect the context in which they are made but also serve to reproduce or change it (Eid 1994b). "The individual," as Le Page and Tabouret-Keller (1985:181) have argued, "creates for himself [or herself] the patterns of his [her] linguistic behavior so as to resemble those of the group or groups with which from time to time he [she] wishes to be identified, or so as to be unlike those from whom he [she] wishes to be distinguished." Such a model of linguistic agency, as one might call it, implies that linguistic choices are acts with political and social implications and with potential for both political and social change. According to Trevor Pateman (1975), "It is not unimportant that a person uses 'chick' nor unimportant that he stops using it. Every act reproduces or subverts a social institution (in the above case, relations between men and women)."[4]

As a text, an obituary is created through linguistic choices made not by the individual it represents (unless the deceased had written his or her obituary ahead of time or had specified its content, which is not the usual practice) but by a member (or, sometimes, members) of the deceased's family. Like other writers and speakers, the obituarist creates a text that is conveyed through linguistic choices. On that basis, obituaries are said to reflect social perceptions and attitudes of the sociocultural context within which they are written, conveyed through the writers—the creators—of the obituaries and their representations of others.

Before we embark on the analysis of identities constructed in the obituary pages, we first ask how concepts of equity, visibility, and space-sharing are related.

Gender inequity—like other inequities based on race, ethnicity, class, or religion—takes different shapes and forms, both linguistic and nonlinguistic. Regardless of the source, its overall effect is exclusion, either direct by not allowing a group in some space—organizations, professions, or texts—or indirect by creating a negative image of that group so its members are ultimately excluded. Research on gender issues has been focused on the documentation and explanation of such inequities as well as proposals to rectify them. The exclusion of one sex group (typically women) from textbooks, for instance, or from employment in some field (armed forces) is an example of the first type, since their inclusion but in a negative or demeaning role is an example of the second. Likewise in sociolinguistics literature, arguments about the use of the generic *man/he* can be viewed as an example of the first type: these terms are no longer understood as being "generic." The use of sexist and demeaning language when speaking to or of women is an example of the second.[5] Space and visibility then have become criteria by which to measure gender (in)equity in both language and society.

How would these two measures of inequity (relative group exclusion and creation of negative group image) apply to the obituaries? Chapter 2 provides the necessary background. Two nonlinguistic variables, obituary size and population distribution (of the deceased), are analyzed as measures of gender equity defined in terms of the relative space occupied by the sexes in overall obituary space and in the space occupied by each culture group. The effect of time on the occupation of space by the sexes and by individual cultures is also assessed. The results show different effects from the three independent variables Sex, Culture, and Time, and combinations thereof. Since chapter 2 is focused on space-sharing and visibility in the obituaries, it also includes a brief survey of these issues as they apply to women and men outside the obituaries in the three cultural contexts examined.

Three major lines of thought then run through the volume. One develops the world of the obituaries on its own, demonstrating some fascinating differences within that world. Another relates it to the world outside it, partly to understand the obituary world itself, including the people who populate it, and partly to understand the world outside its domain. A third attempts to model the results within a space-sharing conceptual frame of analysis. Chapter 7 pulls these ideas together with its focus on the obituaries as textual space linked to the space beyond them through the obituarists as author, the newspapers as medium, and the readers as audience.

Throughout the volume, the analysis of the obituaries is placed within the context of women's movements in the three cultures and other major sociocultural and political events that may have impacted the social perception of gender roles and change therein. These, however, are explored only for their potential relevance to the results obtained in terms of explanatory value and contextual background, and their relevance to the overall purpose of relating the two worlds: the world of the obituaries and the world outside it. But do such events necessarily imply a corresponding effect on the obituaries and the people represented in them? The answer is for the reader to find in the pages of this volume.

Part I

Preliminaries

Chapter 1
Obituaries across Cultures

[The] growing good of the world is partly dependent
on unhistoric acts; and that things are not so ill with
you and me as they might have been is half owing to
the number who lived faithfully a hidden life, and rest
in unvisited tombs.

—George Eliot, *Middlemarch*

When I saw men honor the memory of Bahithat al-
Badiya and praise her virtues, I cast away my selfishness
in sorrowing over my brother and called upon my
sisters to perform their duty to Bahithat al-Badiya. We
conducted a eulogy for her at the Egyptian University.
The women requested that I lead it, and thus I took
to the rostrum for the first time in my life. . . . I used
to look to her whenever I felt the need for her unique
patriotism and courage. I used to talk to her inside
myself. I heard her voice in my conscience.

—Huda Shaarawi, 1937[1]

I. OBITUARIES AS SOURCE OF INFORMATION

Obituaries are in a sense society's final public tribute to its dead, and
as such they reflect aspects of the social perception—hence identification—of
people. This final tribute, viewed as a cultural variable, takes different forms
in different cultures. Most popular perhaps in many cultures are eulogies for
the deceased presented (and at times published) by family members, friends,
and colleagues. Elegiac poetry may be popular in some cultures (such as pre-
Islamic Arabia), but tombstone inscriptions may be more popular in others
(for example, European culture). Newspaper obituaries constitute another
such form; these are what I study in this volume.

Newspaper obituaries may be written by the family of the deceased or by newspaper staff independent, for the most part, of the family. Newspapers distinguish between the two types simply because family-written obituaries are paid for by the family (and possibly friends of the deceased), whereas staff-written obituaries are usually considered news items. Some English-language newspapers reserve the term "obituary" for staff-written obituaries and use such terms as "death notices," "death announcements," and the like for family-written ones. Arabic and Persian-language newspapers do not make such a linguistic distinction but restrict the obituary pages to the family-written type and consider staff-written obituaries to be news items published in other pages of the newspaper in accordance with the importance of the deceased. When presidents or major (literary, political, sports, art, etc.) figures die, their death is usually reported as a news item on the front page, whereas less prominent people get written up in other pages. The prominence of such figures, however, and the fact that their death is already reported as news does not preclude a family-written obituary as well.[2] Staff-written obituaries of relatively less prominent people are included in some newspapers—for example, the *New York Times*—on the same page as family-written obituaries. Some others—for example, the Egyptian *Al-Ahram* and the Iranian *Ettela' at*—may insert a one- or two-line statement at the end of an obituary to express condolences to the families. (See obituary 29 in section 2 of this chapter.)

Variation exists among both family- and staff-written newspaper obituaries across cultures and over time. British newspaper obituaries have undergone a drastic change during the past twenty years or so. They are described in an article in *The Economist* as constituting "a genre that is changing and developing into something of a cult: obituaries as entertainment."[3] Prior to the 1980s, they were "as solemn as the classified death notices that accompanied them. But since the mid-1980s they have become a source of daily fascination and delight." From the 1960s onward as the British press became more intrusive in its reporting on the living, these habits extended to the coverage of the dead as well—admittedly "still moderated by a degree of reserve." In the mid-1980s, "when a general, structural upheaval overtook the British quality press, provoking sharp new competition for market share and a search for editorial edge, the unexploited potential of obituaries as a source of human interest was recognized, and the obituarists came into their own" (64). Thus British (unsigned) newspaper obituaries are no longer limited to the rich and the famous. They have extended their coverage to include "circus performers, jazz musicians, squires, poets, eccentrics and rogues" (64). Their style is described as being "anecdotal, discursive, yet elegantly concise; learned, touching, and, in a kindly way, often extraordinarily funny" (64). The article quotes the obituary of the playwright William Douglas-Home in its reference to his mother's false teeth: "[They] once 'flew out of her mouth as she shook hands with an admiral' " (68).

Not all newspaper obituaries, however, are as "entertaining" as the British ones. The majority may be characterized as matter-of-fact, describing the accomplishments of the deceased and focusing on both the personal and professional attributes by which the writer of the obituary hopes the deceased would be remembered. In a study of the image of librarians in the obituaries, Gunnar Knutson (1981) describes the *New York Times'* treatment as "objective" and not reflecting "the familiar stereotypes" projected in other areas of the mass media. He concludes that when compared with corresponding accounts in library journals, the *New York Times'* treatment turns out to be "superior." It presents "a more organized factual presentation" whereas the library journals "convey a better sense of the personality of the subject" (95).

Because of what they are, obituaries provide a wide range of information and thus lend themselves to various types of research on documentation, social perception, and group identity. Betty Jarboe (1989), for example, considers the obituaries to be important as a means of documenting information not only for the ordinary citizen but for the famous as well. For the ordinary citizen it provides valuable biographical data and is often "the only printed source for obtaining information about an individual." For the famous "whose lives are eventually recorded in print, the obituary is important for its contemporary viewpoint" (vii). The article in *The Economist* mentioned above predicts that "the daily obituary columns will provide a mosaic of social history as valuable to future scholars as John Aubrey's "Brief Lives" (considered by today's practitioners to be an admirable model of obituary style) is to modern students of the 17th century."[4] Knutson's study provides a content analysis of one hundred obituaries of prominent librarians recorded in the *New York Times* from 1884 to 1976. He identifies eleven categories upon which to base his analysis of how librarians have been portrayed in the media through obituaries.[5]

As an object of study, staff-written newspaper obituaries have many advantages. They are, as noted by Knutson, "formal pieces, designed to eulogize important community and national figures" (11). Hence, for a study like his dealing with media perception and representation of a certain professional group, they provide "a unique method of measuring professional status and image." Obituaries simply record a person's death and list that person's notable achievements. And because they are usually written on brief notice, most likely with no thought of how they may be used in the future, they reflect values and belief systems unobstructed by point of view or opinion. There is also little structural variation within staff-written obituaries. According to Knutson, typically in a newspaper obituary, a professional identification is made in the first paragraph followed by an account of the person's life devoted to significant events and positions held by the individual (12). This makes the obituaries similar enough for the purpose of comparison, but they also remain unique items depending on the writer and the life story of the deceased.

What about family-written obituaries? They differ in significant ways from staff-written obituaries, but they are also similar to them in many ways. In a staff-written obituary, the newspaper decides who is important enough to receive attention, what details of the person's career and personal life are to be reported and emphasized, and how the piece is to be formatted and presented to the public. With a family-written obituary, however, a newspaper does not typically make decisions about who is to be included in the pages, the space devoted to the obituary, what it would include in terms of content, or what specific style should be used.[6] Since these obituaries are both written and paid for by the family, they are treated in many newspapers as classified ads, printed in most cases exactly as received by the newspaper.

Nevertheless, variation in formatting and presentation exists across newspapers, and sometimes within the same newspaper. English-language newspapers in the United States appear to have standardized their format for presenting family obituaries. This is particularly true of newspapers of large cities, such as New York or Chicago. Both the *New York Times* and the *Chicago Tribune,* for example, have their family obituaries listed in alphabetical order. The issues of the *New York Times* examined had no pictures of the deceased, and the obituaries were on the whole relatively short. (The median length of the *New York Times* obituaries I studied is 8.6 lines.) A newspaper from a smaller metropolitan area, such as the *Salt Lake Tribune,* shows more variation in terms of format. It includes pictures for what appear to be a majority of deceased. The obituaries tend to be longer and include more information and detail than those of the larger cities. As a result, a paper like the *Salt Lake Tribune* can probably publish a smaller number of obituaries.[7]

Like staff-written obituaries, family-written obituaries show little structural variation. Their purpose is to announce a person's death, identify the deceased and his or her family, and provide information about the funeral and other services. There is, however, variation in terms of how the deceased and his or her family are identified both within and across cultures. In some cases the obituaries include detailed biographical information about the deceased including, for example, dates and places of birth and marriage (the *Salt Lake Tribune*); in others the obituary is used as an opportunity for the family to express their feelings about the departure of a beloved one (Persian *Ettela'at*). A more detailed discussion of obituary content is provided in the next section when we sample obituaries from all three newspapers.

Despite their differences, both staff- and family-written obituaries are concerned with the identification of people. My decision to use only family-written obituaries was determined by the nature and purpose of the research. Because of his concern with the predominantly negative image of librarians in the mass media, Knutson, for example, chose—and appropriately so—the staff-written obituaries as representative of one such area in the media. He also chose these because of their potential for objectivity. His purpose was to show that some areas of the mass media are not biased in their representation of librarianship; and when they are not, a specific image of librarians emerges which, he suggests, is characterized by a set of eleven categories. Choosing family-written obituaries would not have served the purposes of his research. First, they are not controlled by the mass media and therefore are not reflective of its biases, or lack thereof. Second, family-written obituaries are not necessarily focused on professional achievements and skills of the deceased. Third, and as a result, they could not serve the purpose for which the research was designed, partly because they could not be compared with obituaries of these same librarians published in professional journals—an important point for Knutson's analysis and his comparison of representation of a profession by itself versus its representation by the media.

The purpose of the present study is much better served by analyzing family-written obituaries. It attempts to assess how ordinary people are represented and to access information that lies beyond the conscious awareness of ordinary people writing the obituaries. Newspaper staff are subject to newspaper editorial policies on content and style (for example, those covering nonsexist language in the United States); death notices written and paid for by the family (or whoever is putting them in the newspaper) are not. Since family-written obituaries have as their primary purpose the announcement of death so that friends, family, and colleagues can pay their respects to the deceased and his or her family, they are more likely to be personal and reflect the way people are, or perhaps were, actually identified in their everyday interactions—in short, how they are known to others and perceived by them.

What type of information, then, can be obtained from family-written obituaries (henceforth, "obituaries")? How can this information impact the assessment of gender-related differences in language and issues of gender (in)equities and change? To address these questions and illustrate points made thus far about the obituaries as a linguistic and cultural form, I examine a sample of obituaries from the three languages, selected primarily from 1938 and 1988. The discussion is intended to introduce the reader to the content and style of obituaries from the three cultures and over the time span covered. It also brings into focus areas where gender inequities are expected, thereby identifying the major variables analyzed in later chapters.

2. SAMPLING THE OBITUARIES

2.1 Egypt

If you were a woman who died in Egypt in 1938, how would your obituary have read? It could have read like that of the deceased in our first sample.[8]

(1) Passed into God's mercy the **wife** of the late Mustafa *beh* Ismail; **mother** of *Mr.* Ali Ismail, teacher at Applied Engineering [School], Ismail Sirri, an engineer in the municipal council, Abdel Hamid Sirri, account representative of the Egypt Naval Operations Company, [mother of] the wife of *Mr.* Kamel Taha, assistant director at the Roads [Department]; and **relative** of Hasan Kamel Sirri, chief engineer in the Survey [Department], and Mohammad Tawfiq Sirri *beh,* former Justice of the Court. Funeral procession held today at 4:00 P.M. from her house #289 Malika Nazli St. Condolences limited to funeral procession. [OB#55; March 12, 1938]

But who is *she,* and what do we know about her? Very little; we do not even know her name. We know her husband's name, her sons' names, occupations, and places of employment; we know two of her relatives and their occupations; we also know that she happens to be the mother of Mr. Taha's wife (that is, his mother-in-law) and that Mr. Taha is an assistant director of what may be the U.S. equivalent of the Department of Public Works. We also know the time and place of the funeral procession. There is plenty of information here—not about *her* but about *them:* male members of her family whose achievements are celebrated with pride in *her* obituary. These achievements are represented in this particular obituary by jobs and other indicators of social and economic stature as reflected by titles such as *beh*.[9] In addition to the men, two women are mentioned in this obituary—the deceased and her daughter—but neither is identified by her own name. We cannot tell who they are unless we first identify their husbands. Thus the two women in this obituary seem to have no identity independent of their husbands.

Our friend without a name in this first obituary is in some ways better-off, and in other ways worse-off, than some other women we shall meet in this sampling of the obituaries. She is better-off in that her daughter is mentioned in her obituary, albeit through the husband, but worse-off in that her name is not mentioned. A better scenario for 1938 Egypt is obituary 2, where the deceased is given a name and a title.

> (2) Passed into God's mercy at her estate at the Qanatir *Mrs.* Zeinab *hanim* El-Esawi, **mother** of Suleiman Suleiman Berto; **mother-in-law**[10] of Ibrahim *beh* Amin, inspector at the [Department of the] Interior; **grandmother** of Ahmed Amin, the wife of Abdel Muhsin Wahbi, the wife of Mahmoud Abu Shuhba, the engineer. . . . [OB#53; March 12, 1938]

Zeinab Elesawi is identified by her name, but her female offspring are not. We deduce she has a daughter because she is the mother-in-law of Ibrahim *beh* Amin, and her granddaughters are identified by their husbands. The men here, like those in obituary 1, have their names, titles, and occupations mentioned, perhaps also to glorify their achievements.

It is harder to tell whether our friend below from 1938 is better- or worse-off than the previous two.

> (3) Passed into God's mercy last night the deceased *Mrs.* Zakia Quta **widow** of the late Baghus Quta; **mother** of *avocato* Hanna Quta, George *effendi* Quta, Naoum *effendi* Quta, Costantine *effendi* Quta, *Dr.* Aziz Quta, and *avocato* Ilias Quta. Funeral procession today at 4:30 P.M. from her home

> at #6 Egyptian Antikkhana Street to the Roman Catholic
> Cathedral in Egypt [Cairo] in the Faggala [area] the Leon
> Basha Building. . . . [OB#54; March 12, 1938]

Zakia Quta has her name mentioned along with those of her husband and children, but otherwise hers is an all-male obituary. The absence of any mention of female survivors may just be a coincidence: Zakia Quta may not have had any female offspring or siblings. This conclusion seems reasonable in view of the length (short) of the obituary and the fact that only the immediate offspring are mentioned. Nevertheless, her obituary makes us question whether female survivors had an equal opportunity for representation in the obituaries as their fellow males.

Obituaries 2 and 3, in which a woman is identified by her name, introduce two other issues: the use of last names and religious affiliation. Zakia Quta has the same last name as her husband and children, which is unusual in Egypt where there is not an established tradition of name change upon marriage for either women or men.[11] In general, for family members to have the same last names the husband and wife would most likely be paternal cousins, thus sharing the same last name of their sibling fathers.[12] Alternatively, the shared last name may simply be a coincidence. In some cases the wife is called by her husband's name socially, particularly in situations where the social relationships involved originated through the husband, but with no legal name change. In such a case the woman may be identified in the obituary by this "social name," if that is how she would have been socially known to others.

The other issue raised by Zakia Quta's obituary is religious affiliation and the effect it may have on the identification of the deceased. It is clear that Zakia Quta is Christian because the services were held at the Roman Catholic Church in Cairo. The obituary also reveals some non-Arabic influences, particularly in the use of the term *avocato,* Italian for "lawyer," instead of the Arabic term *muḥami.* Some survivors' names sound non-Egyptian (for example, Costantine), suggesting perhaps a Levantine family origin, a reasonable assumption in view of the patterns of settlement in Egypt, particularly in the nineteenth and early twentieth centuries.

The examples given thus far have all involved married women. How would you have been identified if you were an unmarried woman who died in Egypt in 1938? If you were lucky, you would have been identified with your first name and your father's name (both his first and last), just as you would have been identified during your lifetime. This was the case with Victoria Mikhail Khouri in obituary 4, where non-Egyptian links are even clearer than in Zakia Quta's obituary.

(4) The hand of death has regretfully plucked the youth bud of the late *Miss* Victoria Mikhail Khouri, **sister** of the honorable *khawagas* Fouad Khouri and his siblings; and **relative** of the families of Khouri, Tarabulsi, and Quzma in Mansoura, Tanta, Sinbillawen, Syria, and America. Funeral starts today from her family's home on Abbas Street at 3:30 P.M. to the Roman Orthodox Church in Mansoura. May God envelop her with His Grace and may her family have patience and consolation. [OB#62; March 13, 1938]

You could have also been identified with your first name only, the rest of your name being deduced from your father's name. This would have most likely been true for those who died at a young age, as happened to Afifa.

(5) The hand of death has plucked with regret the youth bud of the late *Miss* Afifa **daughter** of the late Roufail *effendi* Farag; **sister** of Hanna Roufail, chief engineer at the Border Police, and Farag Roufail at the University; **relative** of the honorable Girgis Farag of the Alexandria Court. . . . [OB#24; March 5, 1938]

Finally, you could have been treated like the vast majority of women in the 1938 obituaries and identified through the closest male relative: father, brother, uncle, or even a male cousin, as was the fate of the nameless woman in obituary 6.

(6) Passed into the Mercy of God the *lady* **sister** of the honorable Mohamed *effendi* Atiya, chief clerk of the late Omar Sultan *basha*'s waqfs [religious endowments]. She will be buried in the family cemetery in the town of Anshas El Basal where condolences will be limited to the funeral in town. We ask for Mercy and Acceptance [into heaven] for her. [OB#69; March 14, 1938]

As the above obituaries suggest, your mother would have rarely, if ever, been mentioned; only fathers served to identify their daughters.

But what about men? How are they represented in the obituaries of 1938 Egypt? Male obituaries differ from female obituaries not in format or even in length; they differ in one respect—men are always identified by their names. For the most part, men are also identified by their titles and occupation, although there is variation, as can be seen from the way survivors are identified in the above obituaries. In obituary 1, for example, all the males have occupations mentioned, but only two have titles (*Mr.* for Kamel Taha, and *beh* for Mohammad Tawfiq Sirri). In obituary 2 some have titles and jobs; others have only one; and some have neither. In obituary 3 all the men have titles, some indicating social status like *effendi;* others indicating professions like doctor (*Dr.*) and lawyer (*avocato*); and others better described as being identified with honorific terms, such as *hadarat* (the honorables) in obituaries 5 and 6.

Obituaries of men in 1938 Egypt may resemble 7 and 8 below. In obituary 7 the deceased, Ali *beh* Khalifa Mahmoud, is identified with his title *beh* reflecting his high social status. Two other pieces of identification are given at the outset: his being head of the Mahmoud family in the Beheira Province, and his being a former member of the House of Representatives. Both pieces of information confirm not only his status but also the power that he and, by implication, his family enjoy. The rest of the obituary provides further confirmation of this status. The vast majority of his survivors have upper-class titles like *beh;* they occupy (or have occupied) powerful positions; they are politically involved in the Egyptian Wafd Party, so much so that the chairman of the party (Mustafa El-Nahhas *basha*) has sent a delegate to represent him at the funeral as a final tribute to the man and his family. The obituary, therefore, provides information about the status of this particular family—more correctly, the status of its male members since this very long (forty-five lines) obituary does not mention any women by name.

> (7) We lament with extreme sorrow the forgiven Ali *beh* Kha-
> lifa Mahmoud, head of the famous Mahmoud family in
> Beheira and former member of the House of Representa-
> tives; **father** of the honorables Khalifa Ali Mahmoud, student
> at the Egyptian University, and Mohammad Talat Khalifa,
> student at the American University; **brother** of the honor-
> able and respected Mohammad *beh* Khalifa Mahmoud, the
> mayor of El-Rahmaniya; **paternal cousin** of Khalifa *beh* El-
> Sayyed Mahmoud, Mohammad *beh* Mahmoud, Ahmad *beh*

Mahmoud, Hassan *beh* Mahmoud, Mahmoud *beh* Mahmoud, Ahmad *beh* Labib Mahmoud, and the rest of the Ma-
hamda family in El-Rahmaniya; **son of the sister** of *sheikh*
Fath Allah Hasan El-Wakil of the Samakhrat notables; **son
of the paternal sister** of the honorables and respected Abdel
Wahed *beh* El-Wakil, former member of the House of Representatives, Hafez *beh* El-Wakil of the Samakhrat notables,
Kamel beh El-Wakil, a Justice of the Court, *Mr.* Mohammad
beh Ahmad El-Wakil, the attorney, Mukhtar *beh* El-Wakil of
the Senate; **son of maternal sister** of *Dr.* Abdel Wahed *beh*
El-Wakil, Health Inspector of the Capital, Mohammad *effendi* Tayel Dabbous, former member of the House of Representatives, *Dr.* Ahmad Tayel Dabbous, Abdel Wahed *effendi*
Dabous; **brother-in-law** of the honorable *doctors* Kamel *beh*
El-Kholi, pathologist in Tanta, *Dr.* Abdel Raouf *beh* Hasan,
Director of the Mental Hospital in Helwan; **husband of the
sister** of Mohammad *beh* Ahmad El-Sherif, Ahmad *beh* Ahmad El-Sherif, Elsayed *beh* Ahmad El-Sherif, Hasan *beh* Ahmad El-Sherif. Funeral procession will be held today Thursday at 3:00 P.M. in El-Rahmaniya in an awesome celebration.
The Honorable and Distinguised Mustafa El-Nahhas *basha,*
President of the Egyptian Wafd Party, has delegated the honorable Mohammad *basha* Salman El-Wakil, Chairman of
the Wafd General Committee in the Beheira Province to
represent his excellency at the funeral procession. Memorial
ceremonies will be held at El-Rahmaniya. May God have
Mercy on the deceased and may He bestow patience and
consolation onto his family. [OB#11; March 3, 1938]

By contrast, the deceased in obituary 8 and his family appear to have a
different social status. He has no title, nor do any of his survivors. Only his
immediate offspring are mentioned, and the deceased is identified as being
related to the Sharqawi family. But most important, the deceased is identified
by his full name: the first, Abdel Kirim, and his father's first and last (Ahmad
El-Sharqawi); and he is also identified by his profession as a merchant (*tajir*).

(8) We lament with extreme regret the passing away of the late
     Abdel Kirim Ahmad El-Sharqawi, the merchant in Sohag;

father of Ahmad *effendi* El-Sharqawi; and **relative** of the Sharqawi family; after a life of 50 years which he spent in charity and piety. We ask for Mercy for him and for patience and solace for his family. [OB#128; March 25, 1938]

Obituaries from 1938, then, provide a wealth of information about the deceased and their survivors: who they were, where they were from, and the status their families may have enjoyed. But the obituaries also show there may be gender-related differences in the ways the deceased and their survivors are identified. Some of these ways are linguistic, for example, through the use of names and titles; others are nonlinguistic as, for example, the apparent exclusion (hence inequitable representation) of women. Linguistic and nonlinguistic differentiation between the sexes serves to create the effect that women are invisible, or perhaps "hidden" from the pages of the 1938 Egyptian obituaries. But were women indeed invisible in society? Or is this a creation of the obituary pages and, by implication, of the families who wrote the obituaries?

If you were a woman who died in Egypt in 1988, how would you have fared in the obituaries in relation to your 1938 predecessors? Obituaries 9 and 10 suggest that you could have been identified by your own name and possibly by your title and occupation as well; and so could your female survivors.

(9)   In the name of God, the Merciful and the Compassionate

"Glory to Him in Whose Hands is the dominion of all things and to Him will ye be all brought back."[13]

Under unexpected conditions, passed into God's mercy the flower of young scientists

Doctor Shadia Ezzat Ramadan
Associate Professor at the Faculty of Science, the University of Al-Azhar Girls' Section

daughter of the late *Mr.* Ezzat Ramadan, General Director at the Ministry of Education and cultural consultant abroad; **daughter** of the daughter of the late Mahrous Aggag of the Menufiya notables

Wife of Doctor
Abdel Razeq Abdel Rahman Abu Siʿda

Associate Professor at the Al-Azhar University Faculty of Science; **mother** of the children Nivin and Nancy and the infant Mohammad; **sister** of engineer Tareq, accountant Abla wife of *Mr.* Tareq Marzouq financial consultant at Marok Company, Dalal, an attorney at Al-Azhar University; **daughter** of the two families Ramadan and Aggag at Sabk El-Dahhak; **relative** of all the families at Sabk El-Dahhak, Minufiya Province, and the families of Abu Si'da, Abu El-Ata. . . . [OB#581; April 6, 1988]

Shadia Ezzat Ramadan is mentioned by her first (given) name and her father's full name in accordance with naming traditions in Egypt and other Arab countries. She is mentioned by her professional title (doctor) as well as her job (associate professor at Al-Azhar University). Her name is in boldface, but so is her husband's, who is listed after her parents. Her father is listed as her first survivor, and then her mother. Note, however, that her mother is not mentioned by name; she is identified as the daughter of Mahrous Aggag (hence, the clumsy translation in identifying the deceased as "daughter of the daughter of"[14]). All survivors, male and female, are mentioned by name. We are interested here in the deceased's siblings since her children are all young. She has three siblings: one brother, Tareq, and two sisters, Abla and Dalal. Although all are identified by their professions (engineer, accountant, and attorney, respectively), there are differences in the identification of the two women. Abla is also identified as *ḥaram* (wife of) Tareq Marzouq, with her husband's occupation and place of employment also identified, but Dalal has no husband mentioned. She is identified only by occupation and place of employment, suggesting that she is not married.

This obituary shows it would have been better to die in 1988 than in 1938 if you cared to have your name mentioned. In that year equity appears to have been achieved for a deceased woman and her female survivors. But has it really? The next example raises some questions.

(10) "Lying in anticipation of the resurrection"[15]

Kawkab Bisada Tadros
wife of *khawaga* Saman Abdel Sayyed, the merchant at Dishna; **mother** of the wife of the late Erian Shaker, wife of accountant Nabil Fawzi at Masr El-Gidida Housing Co.; **grandmother** of Zakaria and Sameh Erian, Safwat, Evelyn

and Maya Nabil; **sister** of *Mr.* Fawzi. . . . [OB#7; March 10, 1988]

Although the deceased is mentioned by her full name, with no titles or profession, the representation of female survivors in her obituary is mixed. Her daughters are not mentioned by name; they are identified by their husbands ("wife of"). Her female grandchildren, however, are mentioned by name: Evelyn and Maya—again suggesting that age and marital status may play a role in identifying women in 1988 Egypt.

Mothers may now be mentioned in conjunction with fathers in the identification of their deceased child. We noted this in obituary 9, though the deceased's mother was not identified by her name but as "daughter of" followed by her father's name. In obituary 11 below, the mother, Nadia Mustafa Suleiman, is fully identified—she is mentioned by name (first name followed by her father's name) and by her place of employment. The difference in the identification of these two mothers suggests that age may also play a role in the way women are identified. Younger women may be more likely to have their names mentioned. A comparison between the children of the mothers in obituaries 9 and 11 suggests that Nadia Suleiman in obituary 11 is much younger. The mother in obituary 9, whose name is not given, had already had grandchildren, and all her other children had completed their college education and were employed. But in obituary 11, Nadia Suleiman's deceased son was a college student, and her other son was only a high school student.

(11)   Funeral was held yesterday Friday 3/18/88 for the loss of the youthful

Walid Ahmad Mohammad Ahmad Khidr
Student at the Faculty of Information[16]
Cairo University

son of *Mr.* Ahmad Mohammad Ahmad Khidr and *Mrs.* Nadia Mustafa Suleiman at the Ministry of Foreign Affairs; **brother** of Tamer Ahmad Mohammad Ahmad Khidr, a high school student. . . . [OB#251; March 3, 1988]

The sample obituaries discussed thus far illustrate changes in the way women have been represented in obituaries. These include mention of the woman's first name, her occupation, place of employment, and professional titles. The identification of female survivors has likewise changed, and mothers are more likely to be mentioned in the identification of their children in 1988 than in 1938.

The identification of men, on the other hand, by name, title, and occupation does not seem to have changed since 1938. Men continue to be identified always by name, and perhaps even more than before by title and occupation. The change that has taken place in male representation is a change in types of titles and professions they hold, a reflection of the social change that has taken place in Egypt between 1938 and 1988.

One other change in the representation of men, which also relates to women, is that men can in 1988 be identified by a female survivor in much the same way that Dr. Shadia Ezzat Ramadan's husband in obituary 9 was identified. In her case the husband's name was put in bold and centered much like hers. Obituary 12 shows the same pattern, but this time the deceased is a male.

(12) "To God we belong and to Him is our return"[17]

Funeral was held yesterday in Ismailia for

**al-ḥagg al-sayyid Mohammad Khidr
of the Suez Canal Company
Husband of *al-ḥagga***

Sumayya Mohammad Guweid

father of *Professor Doctor* Mohammad at El-Qasr El-Aini, *Dr.* Yehia at the Ministry of Health, *engineer* Adel at the Ministry of Industry, *engineer* Mamdouh, *chemist* Gamal at the Drug Enforcement, *accountant* Muhsen at the Arab Contractors Co., *Mrs.* Salwa at the University of Suez Canal wife of Ahmad Atef Hasab Allah . . . ; **husband of the sister** of . . . *Mrs.* Khalil Guweid and *Mrs.* Atef El-Wabouri. . . . [OB#474; March 31, 1988]

Mohammad Khidr is identified by his wife, *al-ḥagga* Sumayya Mohammad Guweid, and her name, like his, is centered and in boldface.

The fifty-year period between 1938 and 1988 appears to have witnessed a dramatic change in the way women are represented in Egyptian obituaries—a change that may be reflective of the society as a whole and of its perception of women's roles and their status in the society. Women seem to have traveled a long way in the obituaries, and perhaps in society as well, starting with being almost hidden from public view in the 1938 obituaries to being fully represented by their own names and accomplishments in 1988, and even having their names used in the identification of deceased males in their families. A comparison with the representation of men suggests that gender-related differences may even be more impressive than originally anticipated. In subsequent chapters I test and substantiate claims made in this section by examining, through a systematic quantitative analysis, a much larger sample of obituaries.

2.2 United States

If you were a woman who died in the United States in 1938, your obituary could have looked like Lillian Blout's.

(13) **BLOUT**—Lillian, beloved wife of Eugene and devoted mother of Elkan R. Services Riverside Memorial Chapel, Amsterdam Ave and 76th St., Thursday, 11:30 A.M. [OB #385; March 9, 1938]

You would have been mentioned by your last name first because the *New York Times* likes to organize its obituaries alphabetically, which guarantees that your first name will also be included. If you were survived by a husband, his name would have been mentioned, since you are his "beloved wife," and so would the names of your children, who remember you as their "devoted mother." We can also safely conclude that "Blout" is Lillian's married name since neither husband nor son have their last names mentioned; all three must have the same last name. Other than information on the (very) immediate family, Lillian Blout's obituary includes details only about the location and time of services.

If you (or members of your family who were writing your obituary) would have cared to identify your family's (that is, your maiden) name, then your obituary would have looked more like that of Minnie Uhry.

(14) **UHRY**—Minnie (née Mendel), devoted wife of Jules Uhry, loving mother of Henry F., darling grandmother of Gustave, dear daughter of Hannah Mendel, dear sister of Celia Frank, Florence Israel, Jennie Gluck, Hannah Brunswick, Emanuel Mendel, Nat Mendel, and the late Queenie Federman.

Funeral services Riverside Memorial Chapel. . . . [OB#380; March 8, 1938]

The parenthetical "née Mendel" after Minnie's name indicates that she was born with the last name of Mendel. But, like the vast majority of women in the United States at that time, upon marriage she took her husband's name. Her husband, son, and grandson are mentioned in that order and then her mother, sisters, and brothers. Her sisters are all married, since none have Mendel as their last name; only her mother does. Women in Minnie's family are included in the obituary, and they are even mentioned before the men (unlike the case in many of the Egyptian obituaries). The survivors express their feelings toward Minnie by referring to her as "devoted wife," "loving mother," "darling grandmother," "dear daughter," and "dear sister."

Can we then conclude that all women would have been mentioned by their first name in American obituaries in 1938? William D'Oench's daughter was not so fortunate. Her father's obituary reads:

(15) **D'OENCH**—William, on Tuesday, March 8, 1938, husband of Nancy Berry D'Oench, father of *Mrs.* Gustav Pagenstcher. Services St. Louis, Mo., Thursday, March 10. [OB#430; March 10, 1938]

Like her Egyptian sisters, she is mentioned only as Mrs. Gustav Pagenstcher. It is not as clear then how a woman would typically have been mentioned in 1938 American obituaries. Arthur Carroll's obituary illustrates this beautifully.

(16) **CARROLL**—Arthur, on March 17, 1938, beloved husband of Ethel Roberta Jones and brother of Lauren Carroll and *Mrs.* J. T. Johnston Malt [?] Funeral services will be held at Fifth Avenue Presbyterian Church Chapel, 5th Ave and 55th St., Sunday March 20, at 3 P.M. [OB#780; March 19, 1938]

The obituary includes three women, each one mentioned differently—by maiden name (his wife); by the same last name (his presumably unmarried sister); and by married name (his married sister), who uses her husband's initials instead of her first name.

Does this confusion about naming women still exist in 1988? More options would have been available to you in 1988. You could have been mentioned, like a minority of women, with your first name and two last names (maiden and married), and possibly with titles and jobs. Your obituary could have been similar to that of Elisabeth Spens-Thomson.

> (17) **SPENS-THOMSON**—Elisabeth Frost Miner, AKA Lisbeth Miner and AKA Betty Popkin. On March 11, 1988 in Annapolis, MD. **Widow** of Sandy Thomson. Survived by **her son**, Will Spens (former N.Y.C. television reporter, of New York City) and **her daughter**, Shena. Photographer and writer. Researcher, 1942–1949, Time-Life, Inc. Numerous awards and certificates of appreciation: U.S.C.G., U.S. Power Squadron, Boating Writers International, A.A.R.P., Women in Communication, National Federation of Press Women. [OB#436; March 23, 1988]

Or you could have been described like Ricky (Rita) Levenson, whose obituary is like that of Elizabeth Spens-Thomson in that it reminds one of a vita.

> (18) **LEVENSON**—Ricky (Rita) Ph.D., New York City psychotherapist, former clinical supervisor at NYU, past associations with Mount Sinai Hospital, Washington Square Institute, and Montefiore Hospital, assistant professor John F. Kennedy University, San Francisco (1971–72), an active member of division 39, American Psychological Association. Died Mar 22, 1988. Survived by loving **niece** and **nephew** Barton and Dudley Levenson, **cousins** Barbara Fields and Eric Carmiel, and her family of friends. Memorial service Thursday, Mar 24th, 2:30 P.M., at Frank E. Campbell, 1076 Madison Ave at 81 Street. The family will be receiving at Frank E. Campbell, Wednesday Mar 23rd, from 7–9 P.M. [OB#771; March 23, 1988]

Both women have accomplishments and achievements, which some might think are given more prominence in their obituaries than are their families. We suspect that Ricky was not married, since no mention is made of husband or children, only nieces and nephews. Elisabeth was married; her hyphenated name is a good indicator even if she had not been identified as the widow of Sandy Thomson. But her obituary is interesting from yet another perspective. She seems to have been known by other names and could perhaps illustrate confusion in women's identities possibly attributable to name changes associated with marriage. Is Miner, for example, her maiden name? Thomson is obviously her late husband's last name. But where do the names Spens and Popkin come from? Other marriages?

Surviving married females could have been treated like those of Dr. Nunnemacher in obituary 19 and have had their maiden names put in parentheses. Alternatively, they could have had their names hyphenated, as in obituary 17. Either way there would still have been confusion: too many options, too much variation.

> (19) **NUNNEMACHER**—*Dr.* Rudolph F. Age 76, of Putnam Hill Road, Sutton, Massachusetts, died March 1, 1988 at Worcester Memorial Hospital. Dr. Nunnemacher was Professor Emeritus of Zoology and former Chairman of the Biology Department of Clark University. He leaves his **wife** Doris D. Adams-Nunnemacher, a **son** Robert Nunnemacher of Sutton, three daughters, Sattie (Nunnemacher) Robert and Dorothea (Nunnemacher) Palmer, both of Sutton, and Greti Nunnemacher of Milton, a **stepson** Edward R. Blake of Westboro, a **stepdaughter** Carrie A. Blake of Portsmouth, New Hampshire, a **brother** Herman Nunnemacher. . . . [OB#250; March 8, 1988]

If you were a man who died in the United States in 1938 or 1988, your name would have been rendered in the same way in both years; men's names do not change. But you could also have been mentioned with a title, if you had one. In 1938, for example, Gelber in obituary 20 was identified as a doctor. Your 1988 obituary would have also included your occupation and perhaps more information about your career, which would have made your obituary longer, as was the case with Nunnemacher's obituary (thirty-eight lines).

> (20) **GELBER**—*Dr.* Charles N., of 277 Park Ave., suddenly, on March 3, beloved **husband** of Edith M., dear **brother** of *Mrs.* Lillian Lindsay, **son** of the late Esther N. Reposing Riverside Memorial Chapel, 76th St. Amsterdam Ave. Services Sunday, March 6, at 1 P.M. Please omit flowers. [OB#155; March 4, 1938]

The English obituaries sampled here suggest more uniformity in terms of how the deceased are listed. The obituaries tend to be short and identify immediate family members: spouse, offspring, parents, siblings. The deceased is mentioned with terms of endearment in relation to the survivors. Women's identification through their names is quite diverse: some mentioned with no name, some mentioned with two last names, some with only one. Their identification with titles and professions seems to be more limited. One difference between 1938 and 1988 in obituary form is that those from 1988 tend to be longer and include more information about the deceased's professional activities.

There is, however, one way the deceased in the English obituaries appear to be identified without a name. Obituary 21 illustrates this point. The newspaper listing gives only the last name of the deceased, Smith. But the narrative of the obituary identifies him as Captain Cornelius H. Smith, thereby giving his full name and title (military rank).

(21) **SMITH**—At his residence, 303 Sylvan St., Rutherford, N.J., on March 1, 1938, Captain Cornelius H. Smith, beloved **husband** of Blanche A. and **father** of *Miss* Maud B. Smith, *Mrs.* James F. MacKnight and *Mrs.* Ellis W. Welch. Services will be held at John T. Collins, Inc., Funeral Home, 19 Lincoln Ave., Rutherford, N.J., Thursday afternoon, 3 o'clock. [OB#110; March 2, 1938]

If you were a woman who died in the United States in 1938 or 1988, there would have been a greater likelihood that your identity would be preserved for future generations than if you had died in Egypt. Your first name, given to you at birth and retained throughout your life, would not have been lost. But your last name would have been quite confusing, particularly if you had been married or divorced. Also, the content of your obituary may not have been on par with that of men's obituaries.

2.3 Iran

How much better or worse would you have fared in your obituary if you were a woman who died in Iran in 1938? You could have been listed like the deceased in obituary 22. She has no name, so we cannot directly refer to her, nor can we identify her in this brief survey.

(22) On the occasion of the passing away of the **mother** of *Messrs.*[18] Hussein Tehrani and Ahmad Tehrani, there will

be a *majlis fatiha* [memorial ceremony][19] in Mahmoudiya
Mosque on Monday 8 (tomorrow) from three hours to noon
till one hour to noon. [OB#8; March 27, 1938]

Like the Egyptian women mentioned earlier, she has no name; instead she is
the mother of two sons who are mentioned with their full names and a title
of formality or respect. The *majlis fatiha* would have been held in the mosque
so that the deceased's children could properly receive condolences there. Still,
in 1938 you would have been better-off dying in Iran than in Egypt—if you
wanted your name mentioned in your obituary. As obituary 23 shows, you
could have been mentioned by your first name but not your last.

(23)   Due to the unexpected death of the late Ezzatulmoluk, our
        sister, there will be a *majlis tazakur* on Friday 27 from
        afternoon till sunset in the house of the late *hajj* Imam Gholi
        in bazar Abbas Abad and another *majlis tazakur* on Saturday
        28 at the same house:

        Hussein Eshraqi, Hassan Eshraqi and Ali Akbar Eshraqi.
        [OB#6; March 6, 1938]

What difference would it have made to have been mentioned with or without
a last name? Such variation would be meaningful if it applies only to women,
as appears to be the case in Ezzatulmoluk's obituary; her brothers are all
mentioned by their last names. The same is true for other obituaries from
1938 Iran. The deceased in obituary 24 is not only mentioned by both first
and last names but with his religious titles, *hajj* and *sheikh,* as well.

(24)   On occasion of the passing away of the late *hajj sheikh*
        Ahmad Kani we announce a *majlis tarhim* . . . noon at the
        Mahmoudiya Mosque.

        Abul Qassem Kani   *hajj* Mohammad Ali Kani [OB#10;
        March 3, 1938]

Unfortunately it is hard to elaborate on how women were identified in
obituaries in 1938 Iran simply because of the limited number of women's
obituaries from that time.

        If you were a woman who died in Iran in 1988, you would definitely
have been mentioned by your name. But, like your American sisters, your
last name may have been problematic. Obituary 25 lists a second last name
for Zahra Beheshti in parentheses. Since Zahra is the mother of the three

children listed after the announcement and since the children's last names match her first last name, this could have been her maiden name and the one in parentheses, Simbar, must have been her married name. This analysis is confirmed for this family since her daughter Giti is likewise identified. Zahra's other daughter, Fakhri, must not have been married or, if she were married, perhaps she had decided for some reason not to identify her married name. A third alternative is that she could have been married to her paternal cousin, who would then have had her same last name.[20]

(25)   We announce the death of Zahra Beheshti (Simbar) our dear **mother** and the head of the Beheshti family. A *majlis khatm* will be held on Thursday 18 (tomorrow) in al-Javad Mosque:

Hushang Beheshti, Fakhri Beheshti, Giti Beheshti (Zandi), families of Zandi, Haqiqi, Farahmand. . . . [OB#44; March 8, 1978]

The two Iranian women in the obituaries below are also identified by their name. But unlike the family of Ezzatulmoluk, their families decided to identify them with a title as well. Whereas Touran-Zaman is identified with her marital title *banu* (Mrs.), Nusrat Assadat Mansouriyeh is identified by two different titles, *khanum* and *doktor,* a combination for which an English equivalent is hard to find. The social title conveys respect whereas the professional title identifies her professional status and acquired identity.

(26)   "All that is on earth must perish."[21]

With utmost sorrow the death of the blessed *banu* Touran-Zaman Muhajer Iravani (Pirani) is announced to her family and friends. A *majlis tarhim* will be held from 1:00 to 3:00 in the afternoon Thursday 12/9/[13]66 [Solar Hijri] at al-Javad Mosque located at Haftum Tir square.

Your attendance will make her soul happy and give relief to the family.

Mr. Pirani (**spouse**), Forugh, Haideh, Mersedeh, Ali Reza Pirani (**children**), *hajjeh* Naegar Niyazi (**mother**), *engineer* Houshang Iravani, Mahin Muhajer Iravani, Gholam Reza Kashani, . . . Families: Pirani, Tavoli, . . .

The Mosque of Aljavad will not let women in unless they have a thick[22] chador or proper Islamic attire. [OB#2; December 1, 1998]

(27) With utmost sorrow we announce the passing of *khanum Dr.* NUSRATUSSADAT MANSOURIYEH which happened in West Germany. For this reason there will be a *majlis tazakur* to be held from 2 to 4 in the afternoon on Monday 22 of Isfand [March] in Aljavad Mosque 25 Shahivar Square.

Families: Mansouriyeh, Shahidzadeh, Soha, Houshmandrad, and related families [OB#72; March 12, 1978]

Ettela' at gives its condolences to the families of the deceased for their loss.

Thus, a woman who died in Iran in 1988 with a title would have had her title mentioned in her obituary.

The last two obituaries in this survey represent the longest male and female obituaries collected. Obituary 28 is that of a member of the religious (Muslim) establishment in Iran, and obituary 29 is that of the mother of the famous poet, Mehdi Akhavan Salis.[23]

(28) "If a learned scholar dies, a gap in peace is created which nothing can fill."

With utmost sorrow due to the regretful passing away of the learned scholar, the honorable *hujatul-islam wal-muslimin* [His Reverence] *hajj mirza* Ali Rajai (Pir Samadi) Ardebili, we announce to all respected friends and neighbors, especially the respected religious leaders and followers of the blessed gateway of His Excellency Aba Abdillah al-Hussein (Peace Be Upon Him). The women's and men's *majlis tarhim* will be held on Friday 9/13/[13]66 [Solar Hijri] from 9 to 11 before noon in the Ardebili Mosque located in Galubandak in Chaleh Hesar Ali.

Alahghar Sayyed Ghani Ardebili, Alahghar Sayyed Mohsen Khalkhali, . . .

The Husseini Ardebili Organization, . . .

Families of: Asadnejad, Fadl Alizadeh, Khoshnevis. . . . [OB #23; December 3, 1988][24]

(29) My mother, a few nights ago (last Wednesday night), after she was relieved by our promises to her, I who was awake nights and toward the end listened to her last wishes, decrees, and orders, I was watchful of the health and even the breath of my dear invalid. I realized that it seemed tonight things were different. It crossed my mind and I said that after a lifetime (seventy some years) of hardship, suffering, and turmoil

how well you're resting in your bed chamber tonight
how easily sleep has taken you, mother, tonight

My wife, who has shouldered all the responsibilities and difficult nursing in the last illness of my mother all by herself—not like a daughter-in-law but better than a daughter—(and how heartfelt and kind, but these words do not convey the extent of my thanks to her) . . . [unreadable text] She said the predictions of the attending physician (this last attending physician) almost came true.

Yes, my mother (since whatever I have of talent I have from her), yes my mother, she was sleeping restful from life, had gone to the pleasant last sleep, and had said goodbye to our ugly world. I went to another room, impatient and crying. But let's move on.

Although I do not have an affinity for these types of ceremonies, in thanks to her and according to her wishes the *majlis tarhim* will be held in the Safi Ali Shah Temple Monday 12/22/36 from 6 to 8 in the afternoon.

I myself, Mehdi Akhavan Salis, who is the oldest son of that dear deceased invite those who want to pay their respects and those from the families of relatives who have provided a lot of service and help.

Etemad Golestani, Pour Farzin, Chavushi Pour. [OB#71; March 12, 1978]

Ettela'at gives condolences to the Akhavan Salis family for
their loss.

The two obituaries are entirely different in content and style. They
present the man as a public figure and an authority in his field and the woman
as a family person, simply a mother. He, it seems, will be remembered for his
being a religious leader, an authority on Islam *hujatu l-islam wa l-muslimin*. She
will be remembered as a human being suffering illness during her last days and
released from her suffering through her death. The fact that her son is a poet
makes her obituary a very personal and a poetic tribute to her life. Although it
might be argued, and rightly so, that this difference is purely coincidental, the
obituaries serve to crystallize stereotyped gender perceptions, images perhaps,
of sex roles as reflected in many societies and in the obituaries. It is also ironic
that Mehdi Akhavan Salis never identifies his mother by name. For it is not
who she is that mattered at the time, but his own feelings of pain and loss.
Expressions of personal emotions such as those expressed by Mehdi Akhavan
Salis are for the most part missing from the English and Arabic obituaries.
This is not to say that they are typical of Persian obituaries either.

2.4 Conclusion

Several observations can now be made about the obituaries and their
cultural contexts. First, the type of information included in the obituaries is
shared in all three cultures, but certain aspects are more salient in some than
in other cultures. Second, the obituary as a linguistic and cultural form does
change over time in terms of content, length, and sometimes format.

The Arabic and Persian obituaries, for example, are set in a frame of
religious language much more so than are the English obituaries. They tend to
quote a verse from a holy book or introduce the obituary in language borrowed
from religious ceremony. The Egyptian obituaries tend not to express personal
feelings toward the deceased (other than those evoked by the religious frame)
unless the deceased is young and death unexpected. The Persian and English
obituaries tend to express more feelings: the English by using such words as
"beloved," "devoted," and the like; the Persian by describing feelings of loss
felt by the family (writers of the obituary), whose names usually appear after
the text and at times by showing concern over the happiness of the departed
soul, soliciting help from friends and relative through their participation in
the ceremonies. The English obituaries tend to be more formulaic in their

expression of "feelings" than the Persian obituaries. The Arabic obituaries seem to be the longest and least personal of all.

All three cultures showed variation in women's identification by name, but not in men's. But in all three cultures, variation in identification by title and occupation was not sex typed. The Arabic obituaries appear to have more women without names than do the English or Persian obituaries. They also tend to use more titles than the Persian obituaries, and much more so than English obituaries.

To what extent are these observations true of the obituaries in general, and of those collected for this study in particular? To what extent do generalizations made here about naming practices and other forms of identification in the obituaries constitute true generalizations, first about the obituaries and second about the cultures they represent? To answer these questions, I turn to a discussion of the data collected and the framework within which they will be analyzed.

3. DATA AND FRAMEWORK OF ANALYSIS

3.1 Initial Hypotheses

I start from the position—the null hypothesis, if you will—that, everything else being equal, there should *not* in principle be a difference in the representation of women and men in the obituary pages. There is, for example, no reason why only obituaries of men would appear in a newspaper, since both women and men die and both sexes should have equal access to the obituary pages. Nor is there an a priori reason why a deceased woman, for example, would be represented in her obituary without her first name (just as daughter of, sister of, wife of) but a man would not. A man can equally well be identified as son of, brother of, or husband of and have no first name mentioned either. If upon examination of the obituaries, the data are shown to be biased in favor of one sex, the null hypothesis would be falsified and an explanation would be in order. This is precisely what happened in the course of this research.

To reiterate, this study examines linguistic and nonlinguistic variation, in the representation of the deceased (and survivors) in an attempt to answer two major research questions: how is gender inequity constructed in the obituaries, and what is the relationship between the obituaries as a genre and the sociocultural contexts, including time and place, within which they are written. These two serve as background against which to measure the results and frame the questions in each of the subsequent chapters of this book. They can be viewed as recurrent themes, a unifying principle.

To assess gender equity in the obituaries, different types of data have been collected to set up an empirical base from which generalizations can be drawn regarding the identification of women and men in the obituaries. Depending on the results from the analysis of these data, the role of sociocultural influences versus the independence of the obituaries from such influences can then come into focus in an attempt to set the "facts" obtained from the obituaries within a broader context of research and knowledge obtained from other disciplines. Of particular relevance here is information on the status of women and women's movements in the different cultures as well as major political and cultural events that may have affected the obituaries.

Three linguistic variables were chosen for the analysis: Name, Title, and Occupation. These represent two types of identities: basic and acquired. The initial sampling of the obituaries showed variation in these three forms of identification within each culture and across all three. Therefore, they are the dependent variables. My initial hypothesis regarding this variation predicted that there would indeed be statistically significant gender-based differences in all three cultures and that these differences would be significant from the cultural and historical perspectives as well. Three primary independent variables were set up: Sex, Language/Culture, and Year/Time. I predicted that more women would be identified without name, title, and occupation than men in each culture, that this variation would be stronger in Arabic and Persian obituaries than in English obituaries, and that Time would have a strong positive effect. Inequity would be reduced, but not necessarily eliminated, with respect to each dependent variable. As women acquire (public) identities independent of family, they would increasingly be identified through their acquired roles, which would ultimately translate into public identities. The obituaries, I expected, would be reflective of this social change. This position is outlined in the form of three major hypotheses.

Hypothesis A: The Gender Hypothesis

Because of gender inequities that have traditionally assigned women to positions and roles secondary to those of men, thereby limiting them to home and family, often depriving them of the freedom to choose and to participate as equal partners with men in life, both public and private, more women than men would be identified in the obituaries without name, title, and occupation.

Hypothesis B: The Culture Hypothesis

Culture, viewed as a set of shared values, traditions, and norms of behavior, has a very strong effect in accordance with distance that separates people from each other or ties that bind them together. The more (prolonged) the contact between peoples, the more likely they are to share aspects of "culture." Thus obituaries from Egypt (Arabic) and Iran (Persian) are expected to be more closely related to each other than they are to those from the United States (English).

Hypothesis C: The Change Hypothesis

As women become more involved in public life and acquire jobs and identities independent of their family, they would increasingly be identified by their names and by the titles and occupations they hold. The change would appear earlier among the survivors than the deceased, since they constitute a population "younger" in some sense than that of the deceased and are likely to have received more education in preparation for new occupational roles.

Two secondary hypotheses were also originally stipulated. One predicted an effect from religious affiliation and the other from geographical affiliation (locally defined) on the basis that group values affect identification of people, where group is defined as social or geographical. These, however, will not be explored here.[25]

Overall, the results confirm these initial expectations but, as will be shown in subsequent chapters, some unexpected results have also emerged. Before turning to a discussion of these results, I first provide a description of the data collection process including the sources, the data themselves, the coding system used in collecting the data, and problems arising during the process.

3.2 Data Collection

3.2.1 The Sources

The primary data come from three major newspapers highly respected in their respective cultures: *Al-Ahram* (Egypt), *Ettela' at* (Iran), and the *New*

York Times (United States). The choice was determined in part by the papers' availability on microfilm as far back as 1938 at a place easily accessible to the author and research assistants. The Arabic and Persian newspapers chosen are both available on microfilm at the University of Utah libraries; both are major, capital-city newspapers published in Cairo and Tehran, respectively; and both have international editions and are now available on the Internet.[26] Both enjoy tremendous prestige in their respective cultures, with wide circulation and geographical distribution. The status of their obituary pages is, therefore, expected to match this prestigious position. To ensure comparability of the data, the third newspaper had to satisfy the same criteria. The *New York Times* was chosen, although it is not technically a capital-city newspaper. All three newspapers can safely be said to provide coverage of geographical locations that go beyond their immediate localities of Cairo, Tehran, and New York, although these cities are identified as the location for a majority (or near majority) of obituaries.[27] In what follows I provide some background about each newspaper.

Al-Ahram

Publication of the Egyptian newspaper *Al-Ahram* started in 1875 and it became a daily newspaper in 1881. It is described as "Egypt's first important news journal" (Ayalon 1995:155, 150–51) with a circulation in 1937 reported at 45,000–50,000 (90,000 in 1947 when Egypt's total circulation for leading dailies was 200,000). William Rugh (1979:32) reports its estimated circulation in 1976 at 520,000, second to *Al-Akhbar* with 650,000.[28]

Since 1926, *Al-Ahram* has devoted one or two columns daily to publishing obituaries on its penultimate page. In a very limited number of issues, the whole page was devoted to obituaries. This happened for the first time in the January 30, 1947, issue. In recent years the obituary page has often been extended to two, and sometimes three, pages. According to *Al-Ahram* sources, obituaries are treated as classified ads paid for by the family, friends, or colleagues of the deceased.[29] Therefore, they are not subject to the newspaper's editorial policies but are printed exactly as submitted to the newspaper.

As far as cost is concerned, in 1988, for example, the newspaper charged nine Egyptian pounds (approximately $3.50) per line, where a line is defined as five words in nine-point type. All ads require a minimum of two lines but no maximum. If, as we show in the next chapter, the average obituary in 1988 was twenty-five lines long, this makes the average cost of an obituary about

225 Egyptian pounds ($87.50). Boldface and larger type involve additional cost, as does the use of pictures.

The obituary page of *Al-Ahram* has over the years acquired both importance and prestige: it is known in Egypt as the place where one looks every morning to find out who has died and where to go to pay respects to the family. Lutfi Elkholi, in his column *ijtihadat* (Opinions) published in *Al-Ahram* (October 10, 1997), describes the obituary page of that newspaper as "unique" in that it provides "a detailed historical record of the daily social life of the middle and upper classes through the effect death has on the Egyptian household." He refers to what he describes as "a century-old popular saying that states: A person whose obituary has not appeared in *Al-Ahram* has not died." By comparison, *Al-Akhbar*'s obituary page is much more limited. A comparison of 1988 obituaries showed *Al-Akhbar* had a much smaller clientele for its obituary pages. A total of 74 obituaries were found in one month of this newspaper's obituary pages which, when compared with the 716 collected from an equal number of days from *Al-Ahram,* serves to support the contention that the latter is the place where people go for obituaries.

Al-Ahram obituary pages include not only obituaries but also condolences given by friends, colleagues, or other family members as well as *shukr* (thank-you notices). The latter are usually given by the family of the deceased after the three formal mourning days are over to thank all who participated in the funeral and visited the family during the mourning period.[30] Often the *shukr* is used to make specific mention of important figures (possibly government officials or representatives) who may have attended the funeral. At times these may be included in the obituary itself if the funeral takes place before the obituary appears (see obituary 7).[31]

The *shukr* column can also provide interesting perspectives on the issue of gender representation. In an earlier paper, I provide a brief comparison between one obituary and the corresponding *shukr* provided by the family at the end of the three-day mourning period (Eid 2000). In that particular case the male members of the family took over this function on behalf of the family as a whole. The *shukr* coming from the female members of the family, in that case sisters of the deceased, was, as often happens, separate and addressed exclusively to women, those who had attended the ceremonies and provided consolation to the women of the deceased family.[32] Even today, despite changes in gender roles and despite the acceptance of women's inclusion and mention by name in the obituaries, some families have maintained this gender-based differentiation: they find it inappropriate, some say unthinkable, for the family *shukr* to come from women. Women may still not be allowed to formally take over the public representation of family.

The Egyptian obituaries appear in two different formats or styles, not due to newspaper policies but to traditions developed within the obituary pages. Both formats provide necessary information about the deceased, the funeral, and the survivors. One format, such as that in obituary 7, usually gives a more elaborate listing of the survivors. It is descriptive, perhaps narrative in style but does not specify who is announcing the death. The other format illustrated below does. Therefore, it can be more personal and potentially more discursive in style, as we have seen in some of the Persian obituaries where this format is much more popular. In the Egyptian obituaries this format was more popular in the earlier years (1938–48) but had almost disappeared by 1988.

(30) Hakim Mitri at the Defense, Sadeq Mitri, the lawyer, Rushdy and Zarif Mitri, the jeweler, Atalla Shehata [chief book-keeper], *Yuzbashi* Asʿad Rafla and his siblings, Amin Yacoub, Khilla Tawfiq at the Survey [Department], Abdel Malek Shenouda, Gamil Mikhail, Fahim Moawwad, Habib Butros and his siblings, Aziz Matta and his brother, Salama Morgan and his siblings, Lamei Aqladius and his siblings, Yacoub Bekhit, Husni Henawi, and the rest of the El-Sayegh family in Tema lament with extreme sorrow the head of their family the late

al-Muqaddis **Metri Shehata**

Father of the first two, and in-law and relative of the rest. Mourning ceremonies at Tema. May the deceased have mercy. [OB#20; March 12, 1948]

In obituary 30 the deceased is identified at the end; in the other more typical format, the identification is usually made at the beginning. This is not to say that in the discursive style the deceased cannot be identified at the beginning, for they are in some obituaries. This format, I suggest, was probably the original format introduced when the newspaper industry first emerged in Egypt, most likely under the influence of a European (probably French) source. Cultural ties with France have been maintained in Egypt for years, perhaps since the Bonaparte expedition (1798–1801), also accredited with the introduction of printing to Egypt, among other things. These ties have been strengthened during the nineteenth century for many reasons, both political and cultural. Historians (al-Sayyid Marsot 1985) describe increased contacts with Europe, particularly France, as Mohammad Ali *basha* (1769–1849) and his descendants struggled to build a modern state in Egypt and gain independence from the Ottoman government. They also attribute some of Egypt's financial problems, and eventually its downfall and occupation by the British, partly to the strong impression left by French culture on the rulers of Egypt in their attempt to emulate what they saw in France—a luxury that required lavish expenditures. Parts of modern Cairo, for example, are said to have been modeled after Paris (Abu-Lughod 1971). Since the early part of the nineteenth century, Egyptian students were sent to France for education and training. Furthermore, the occupation of Egypt by the British in 1882 contributed to an increased affinity with the French, since the British came to be viewed as the enemy. These and other factors point to a strong French influence on the culture of the elite and upper classes in Egypt during the nineteenth and early twentieth centuries.

This second obituary style is also used in French newspapers (*Le monde* 1987, for example) and is popular not only in the Iranian newspapers (possibly for the same reason) but also other Arabic-language newspapers from Lebanon and Tunis, two areas where influence from French language and culture has been strong.

Ettela᾽at

Ettela᾽at was first published in 1926. According to Mina Majidian (1981:21–22), it was the leading newspaper during the reign of Reza Shah (1925–41), with a circulation of 15,000. Its circulation increased rapidly, rivaled only by *Keyhan,* which held the highest circulation of Iranian dailies during the reign of Reza Shah's son, Mohammad Reza Shah.[33] Majidian also reports it to be the oldest Iranian daily newspaper to have survived until today with relatively few interruptions, and cites various reasons for its longevity (21). *Ettela᾽at* normally supports the government (Wilber 1976, Vreeland 1957); and its editors had close ties with the government (Arasteh 1969), hence the secret of its success. All these reasons saved the newspaper from being shut down by the government during periods of political instability and upheaval.

In 1938, *Ettela᾽at* did not have a page devoted to the obituaries. Only nine obituaries were found and they were located in boxed space interspersed with other classified ads, or at the bottom or lower left-hand corner of regular pages. By 1988, obituary space was extended to cover almost a whole page. The obituary page of *Ettela' at,* like that of *Al-Ahram,* now publishes entries (columns or subsections) related to other functions and ceremonies associated with death. It includes, for example, a section called *tasliyat* (condolences) devoted to public condolences offered to families or specific individuals (similar to the *na'y* column in *Al-Ahram*), *yadbut* (commemorations), and *sepas gozaree* (thanks). This section includes items such as *tashakur wa itizar* (thanks and apologies), where families thank those who have consoled them and apologize for any unintentional mistakes made in the obituaries, and *tawziih wa tashiih* (clarification and correction).

The Persian obituaries announce what appears to reflect different types of ceremonies for the dead. The majority announce a *majlis tarhim* (assembly convened for the blessing of the dead) in the later years grouped under one section titled *majalis tarhim* (plural form). Some families, however, announce *majlis tazakur* or *majlis zikr* (an assembly for the remembrance of the dead). In the earlier issues *majlis tarhim* and *majlis tazakur* appear to have been used interchangeably. Some announce a *majlis khatm* (mourning days in which the whole Quran is read in memory of the dead). A few announce a *majlis fatiha* (where the first verse of the Quran is read). Unfortunately I have not been able to determine if these are just terminological differences or if they actually reflect different ceremonies, perhaps attributed to differences in Shi'i versus Sunni Islamic practices. Little material is available on the subject of death ceremonies in either country. Consultations with six Iranians of different age groups and two other specialists on Iran produced negative answers here. Thus if a difference exists (or has existed), it seems not to be salient knowledge at this time. The English equivalents provided above are from Haïm's *New Persian English Dictionary* (1969).

This variation in naming the ceremonies and gatherings held in honor of the deceased suggests possible differences in practices related to mourning ceremonies between Egyptian and Iranian cultures. Although both are predominantly Islamic, the rituals appear to differ, as does women's participation in them. In Iran women attend these ceremonies when held in a mosque, provided the women are appropriately dressed. Obituary 26, for example, specifies that mosque regulations prevent women from entering unless they are dressed in "a thick chador or proper Islamic attire." In Egypt women (particularly of the upper classes) do not participate in the prayers and other rituals held at the mosque. Ceremonies are typically sex segregated: women receive consolation in the privacy of the home whereas men receive it in public as well, thus reinforcing the dichotomy between private and public spheres.

New York Times

The first issue of the *New York Times* appeared in 1851, which makes it the oldest of the three newspapers under study. The status of the *New York Times* and in particular its obituary pages has already been discussed earlier within the context of other obituary-based research (Knutson 1981). Its circulation in 1982 was 935,000, the fourth largest in the United States after the *Wall Street Journal, New York Daily News, USA Today,* and *Los Angeles Times,* whose circulation exceeded one million for that year (Dunnett 1988).

The obituary pages of the *New York Times* include family-written obituaries (just called "deaths"), staff-written obituaries, and other death announcements received through wire services. I have checked their editorial policy regarding family-written obituaries to determine the extent to which the paper sets policy in this respect, particularly, if they had a policy on sexist language in the identification of people. Their guidelines only require that no obscene language be used and no mention be made of issues that could have legal implications. Other than that one is expected to use "common sense." The paper requires a minimum of four lines, at the rate of $18.40 per line in the weekday edition and $21.80 per line in the Sunday edition. The average size of the obituaries in 1988 was 8.6 lines, making the average cost of an obituary for that year about $158 calculated at the weekday rate.

The names of the deceased are listed in alphabetical order, last name first, with a separate list of all the deceased. This made it much easier to locate, collect, and file the English obituaries and to identify duplicates. The Arabic and Persian obituaries are not listed in the newspapers in any systematic way, and sometimes *shukr* and commemoration announcements are interspersed with the obituaries.

The three newspapers are comparable in many ways. They are all major daily newspapers highly respected in their respective cultures, with large circulation and geographical coverage, and they charge relatively high fees to run an obituary.[34] Their obituary pages include, in addition to family-written obituaries, sections related to other aspects of death announcements. The *New York Times,* but not *Al-Ahram* or *Ettela'at,* includes staff-written obituaries and wire service announcements of deaths. The other two newspapers include columns such as *shukr* and other forms of commemorations (for the passage of a week, forty days, and year).

3.2.2 The Data

Obituaries were collected for a period of one month (thirty days) at ten-year intervals (1938, 1948, 1958, 1968, 1978, 1988). For each year a "long list" was made of all obituaries found with a number assigned to each. In view of the variation in the number of obituaries obtained from each year and the relatively large numbers obtained, a short list was then developed of about 240 obituaries per culture to be used for a detailed analysis. These were randomly selected from each year's long list by excluding every n^{th} obituary number depending on the total number obtained from that year. Where the total number of obituaries for the year was less than the required 240, all the obituaries from that year were used. This happened in the Arabic obituaries in 1938 (148 obituaries total) and in the Persian obituaries in 1938 and 1948 (9 and 95 obituaries, respectively). Once the short lists were identified, information from each obituary was tabulated on a database by two research assistants. They worked on separate years, and at the end I checked the data

Table 1.1: Obituaries Collected by Culture and Time (Long List)

	1938	1948	1958	1968	1978	1988	Total
Arabic	148	287	379	560	790	742	2906
English	1268	1586	1595	1593	1131	1081	8254
Persian	9	95	202	304	301	248	1159
Total	1425	1968	2176	2457	2222	2071	12319

Table 1.2: Obituaries Selected by Culture and Time (Short List)

	1938	1948	1958	1968	1978	1988	Total
Arabic	148	239	237	236	238	239	1337
English	239	240	240	240	240	240	1439
Persian	9	95	202	238	241	239	1024
Total	396	574	679	714	719	718	3800

they had entered against the originals. The major part of the statistical analysis was done using Statview software.

But what would constitute an obituary for the purpose of this study? Would any death announcement in the obituary pages qualify? Before we proceed to a discussion of information extracted from each obituary and the coding system, I elaborate on my operational definition of an obituary.

For an obituary to be used in this study it had to meet a number of criteria. First, it had to identify only one deceased (that is, only single-person obituaries were used). Excluded were those announcing the death of more than one person, usually as a result of accidents (for example, a husband and wife, parent and child, etc.). Using such obituaries would have created problems in identifying the sex of the deceased since there could have been more than one. Alternatively, the obituary would have had to have been listed in accordance with the number of deceased mentioned in it. This multiple listing would have affected the count and confused the results. Second, the obituary had to mention a family or relative. Obituaries with no relatives mentioned were excluded, as were those written by friends or coworkers.

The reasons for these restrictions were partly dictated by the purpose of the research and partly by efficiency and time constraints. Since this research was not intended to be a study of the obituary pages as such, the precise number of obituaries a newspaper publishes would not have been terribly useful. More important for this research was the availability of sufficient numbers of women and men identified as deceased and survivors in what I expected to be their everyday form of identification, perhaps modified slightly to reflect the occasion and the medium in which the identification would appear (the obituary pages). Obituaries with no survivors or relatives were excluded for similar reasons but primarily because they would have reduced the number of people entered for the analysis of the survivors, thereby reducing our efficiency in using the time allocated to data entry.[35]

For the purpose of this study then, an obituary had to be written by the family, identify only one deceased, and identify at least one related family or individual.

3.2.3 The Coding System

The information obtained from the short-listed obituaries is of three major types: information on the obituary itself, information on the identification of the deceased, and information on the identification of the survivors.

Three major files were created to correspond to each type: an obituary file, a deceased file, and a survivors' file. The coding system was originally based on information deemed potentially relevant on the basis of the Arabic obituaries. As work progressed on the project, certain aspects of the data could not be supplied by either the Persian or English obituaries. Because of the comparative nature of this project, I report in this section on information applicable to all three.[36] Other information, specifically religious affiliation and geographic location, not very useful for the comparative approach, is discussed when relevant to argumentation in subsequent chapters.

The Obituary File

The obituary file codes two types of information: information about the obituary itself (its identification and size) and information about the family including geographical location. The file consists of six fields: Year/Time, OB#, Date, Language/Culture, Total Lines, and Location.

YEAR / TIME

The identification of the obituary in the newspaper was based on a number it was assigned (OB#) and the Date (month and day) it appeared. This information serves to track the obituaries, but has no use in analysis. Year has been coded separately from Date since it constitutes an independent variable in the analysis (Time). It is coded for six categories representing the six time periods (1938–88) in order to assess the effect of time on the identification of women and men and eventually explain changes that may have taken place during this period. Year is also referred to as Time, particularly when it is used as an independent variable in the analysis.

LANGUAGE / CULTURE

Language identifies the obituary as to the culture or area to which it belongs: Arabic/Egypt, Persian/Iran, and English/United States. This coding was needed for cross-cultural referencing in assessing the effect of culture/language on the variation. Language and Culture are at times used interchangeably with no significance implied. Obviously "Language" refers to the linguistic form in which the obituary is written and the newspaper source in which it appears, and "Culture" to the (geographical) location of the language and its users. Thus, for the purpose of this volume the two terms "Arabic" and "Egyptian" obituaries are equivalent, as are "English" and "American" as well as "Persian" and "Iranian." This should not imply any intention to ignore the use of these languages in regions other than those investigated in this study. The term "culture," when not applied to the variables involved, is used in its usual meaning referring to traditions and practices of a group.

OBITUARY SIZE

Total Lines refers to obituary size measured in terms of number of lines of type. Two major reasons affected this decision to use numbers of lines as measurement of size instead of inches, for example. First, it is by number of lines that families are charged. Second, the width of obituary columns and type size are standard in each newspaper, except when boldface or larger type size is used, usually at an extra charge, to highlight the name of the deceased and other information deemed worthy of emphasis by the family.[37] Information regarding obituary size has been coded because of its relevance in a number of ways: as a test for possible gender-based status differentiation and accessibility to the obituary pages, and as an assessment of cross-cultural value or "meaning" obituaries may have and the possible reevaluation of that meaning over time.

Obituary size is also an indicator of family status and financial affluence—the longer the obituary the more expensive it becomes and, by implication, the more affluent the family who pays for it. Furthermore, in Egypt (and other Middle Eastern countries) a person's status (which includes worth and power) is often a function of family status and that of other families with whom they are interrelated by blood or marriage. The larger the family's network, the more power and status it would enjoy, and the more status it would bestow on its individual members.

In Egypt this often translates in the obituaries to long lists of survivors and families. A person's or a family's mention in an obituary is socially interpreted as a sign of "closeness," which puts the person mentioned in a position to receive 'azaa (condolences) and be counted among those to whom tribute is paid. In doing so, a mutual exchange of status is negotiated: the family of the deceased both receives and bestows status by association with other families and individuals.[38] Furthermore, by being mentioned in an obituary, the person and his or her family are in a sense obligated to attend the 'azaa (mourning ceremonies) and the males of the family are obligated to attend the funeral and the services to receive condolences. This in turn increases the number of attendants at both funeral and home ceremonies, thereby adding to the importance of the family and the deceased.

If obituaries function as status indicators in addition to their basic role as death announcements, we would expect a great deal of variation in obituary length. This is because families will differ in the size of their networks, the importance they attach to them, and their financial ability to accommodate these two forces.

The Persian and English obituaries differ in their length from the Arabic. None of the English and Persian obituaries surveyed earlier has the elaborate descriptions of survivors that the Arabic obituaries have. They tend to be shorter and mention immediate family members. Thus, the "meaning" or value they are assigned in their respective cultures is, as I hope to show in the next chapter, also different.

The Deceased File

Information coded about the deceased involved coding for Name, Sex, Title, Occupation, and Religion.

NAME

A yes/no system was used in coding information about names: "yes" if the deceased's first (given) name was mentioned, "no" if it was not.

SEX

The sex of the deceased was coded as either female or male. No problems were encountered in making this identification. First, names tend to be identifiable in their reference to females and males. Second, if a name happens to be ambiguous as to the sex of its referent, the information can be determined in other ways, sometimes linguistically through the syntax and morphology of the language, other times through kinship terms.

Kinship terms in all three languages, however, would have been sufficient to indicate the sex of the deceased. Although English has no morphological gender distinction in nouns, adjectives, or verbs, the relation of the deceased to the survivors is reflected in kinship terms, thus coding the gender of the deceased: *wife/husband, mother/father, sister/brother*. Secondary relations such as *cousin* are ambiguous, but these were never the only relations mentioned in an English obituary. In Persian, with the exception of *hamsar* (spouse) and *farzand* (child), kinship terms also reveal the sex of the person identified: *madar/pedar* (mother/father), *dukt/pesar* (daughter/son), *hamshireh* (also *khahar*)/*baradar* (sister/brother). Some Persian words of Arabic origin retain their gender distinction: for example, women's names that end in *-eh;* some descriptive terms such as *marhoumeh* (fem.)/ *marhoum* (masc.) (the late); and kinship terms of Arabic origin: *valed-eh/ valed* (mother/father), *zoj-eh/zoj* (wife/husband). In Arabic these kinship terms mark female terms through the suffix *-a(t)* instead: *walid-a/ walid* (mother/father); *shaqiq-a/ shaqiq* (sister/brother).

Arabic provides through its syntax and morphology additional clues to the sex of the deceased. Grammatical gender is marked on all categories associated with a noun (verbs, adjectives, and so on) through syntactic agreement processes. Thus sentences announcing the death would always reflect the gender of the deceased through the verb: *intaqalat* (fem.)/ *intaqala* (masc.) (passed away). Likewise, any descriptive term used in reference to the deceased would reveal one's sex through gender marking: *al-marhoum-a* (fem.)/ *al-marhoum* (masc.) (the late).[39]

TITLE

Title is coded as a yes/no category to indicate if a title has been used in the identification of the deceased. Titles were further subdivided into two types: professional and social titles, and a yes/no coding system was used for both fields. Each type of title had associated with it another field to code the actual title used. Title names were entered as found in the obituaries and subsequently categorized into broader headings. A total of five fields were therefore used to code this information: three yes/no (Title, Professional Title, and Social Title) and two for names of each sub-type.

Because of potential overlap between professional titles and occupations, a working definition of "title" was adopted, based on difference in word order position between titles and occupations relative to the name they qualify. Since in all three languages a title, like other terms of address, occurs before a name (for example, Ms. or Professor Jane Smith), I considered a professional term like Arabic *al-muhandis* (engineer) or English *senator* as a title when it occurred before the name but a profession when it occurred after. The post-name position indicates the job or position occupied whereas pre-name position indicates a title as in "Bill Clinton, President of the United States" versus "President Bill Clinton."

This word order criterion was applied only in the case of professional terms where the status of title versus profession was not clear. Terms whose titlehood was not in doubt were counted as titles regardless of their position. Arabic *basha, beh,* and *effendi* never occur before the name.[40] They usually occur between the first and last names or after the name: *Mohammad beh Abdel Aziz* or *Mohammad Abdel Aziz beh.* The English titles like *Ph.D.* or *MD* would also fall under this category.

OCCUPATION

Information about the occupation of the deceased was coded in two fields. The first uses a yes/no system to indicate whether or not an occupation has been mentioned as part of the identification of the deceased; the second codes the actual name of the occupation as a prelude to a more general categorization. The process went through three stages: recording actual name, recording occupation type or area (military, education), and then coding through some independent classification system. In the final stage I relied on the system used in the Egyptian government's Bureau of Statistics and on research on social stratification in Egypt, particularly Ibrahim (1982) and Ansari (1986). The classification system was applied to English and Persian obituaries as well, since not as many occupations were mentioned in these two nor were they as elaborate as those in the Arabic obituaries. (See chapter 5 for more details.)

Occupation can refer to the job name, the place of employment, the type of employment, or any combination thereof. An example of such a combination comes from an obituary in which one of the survivors is identified as: *Qaimmaqam Mohammad beh Aziz, Inspector at Misr Police. Qaimmaqam* is a military title, suggesting he is either a police or army officer; it is followed by *Mohammad,* his first name, which is followed by *beh* (a social title), then his last name. His occupation (inspector) follows, then his place of employment (Misr [Cairo] police force). The Persian and English mention of occupations is not as detailed; nor for that matter are all the Arabic occupations mentioned. (See earlier survey of obituaries.)

RELATIVE INFORMATION

Two other types of information were coded in the deceased's file although they pertain to relatives: one codes for whether or not a relative is used to identify the deceased; if so, information about that relative (name, title, occupation) and his/her relation to the deceased was also coded. This information was originally coded to determine how people mentioned without their own names would be identified, but it turned out to be not as relevant to either Persian or English, for reasons to be explained in chapter 3.

3.3 Conclusion

A variety of data have been collected for this research: data about the obituaries themselves as they appear in the newspapers; about the deceased and their survivors; about the geographic location with which the deceased and their families identify; and about the time and language/culture of the obituaries. The data collected have been diverse, originally expected to be available (parallel) in all three data sets for the comparative, cross-cultural focus of the research. Not all types of information could be extracted from the obituary pages of all three newspapers. Of relevance here are religious affiliation and location because of their contributive effect to perceptions of identity and their potential impact on practices involved in naming and identifying people.

The data involve three linguistic and two nonlinguistic variables. The linguistic variables are so called because they involve the representation of people in the obituaries through language, specifically, the use of linguistic forms (or labels) to symbolically represent identities associated with individuals, both deceased and surviving. Nonlinguistic variables are not symbolic representations, but numeric representations (measures of length and quantity), associated with the issue of space occupation, space in a text that by definition is a linguistic form.

These five then constitute the dependent variables in this study and represent the variation to be explained. The analysis that follows will assess the impact of Sex, Culture, and Time, independently and combined, on this variation. These three represent the sex of the person identified (female or male), the newspapers as cultural and linguistic contexts within which the obituaries are written (Egypt/Arabic, United States/English, and Iran/Persian), and the six time periods within which identification is made (1938, 1948, 1958, 1968, 1978, and 1988).

In doing the statistics for this research, I have relied on statistics manuals and textbooks particularly those designed for language and linguistics (Butler 1985; Woods, Fletcher, and Hughes 1986). I have also sought during the final stages the help of Dr. Soleiman Abu Badr from the University of Utah.

Chapter 2

Space and Visibility in the Obituaries

Don't put the seal of silence on my lips
I have untold tales to tell
Take off the heavy chain from my foot
I am disturbed by all of this.
> —Forugh Farrohzad, 1955, *Asir* "Captive"[1]

The woman used to spend her whole life within the
walls of her house not going out into the street except
when she was carried to her grave.
> —Bahithat al-Badiya [Malak Hifni Nasef], 1909,
> "A Lecture in the Club of the *Umma* Party"[2]

Equity within the context of the obituaries can be measured in terms of the relative space and visibility a group occupies in the obituary pages of the three newspapers under consideration. Space and visibility may be impacted by a number of (nonlinguistic) criteria or devices such as obituary size, repeated mention, and use of visibility-creating devices. If a consistent pattern can be established showing an uneven distribution in the use of such devices in relation to some group, one can then conclude that this group has been disfavored and has thus received unequal treatment within the obituary pages.

Visibility-creating devices may be script or position related. Script-related devices such as use of boldface, different type size, and / or capitalization—when consistently applied in relation to some group—would contribute to the increased visibility of that group. Likewise, if a certain location on a page is associated with visibility (thus a position-related device) and if that location is consistently reserved for one group, this would constitute a degree of favoritism toward that group. Media and marketing specialists, for example, have argued that in English the upper left-hand corner is the "most visible," whereas in Arabic and Persian it is the upper right-hand corner.[3] If so, then reserving these locations on a page for one group would also constitute a form of favoritism leading to inequity.

Unfortunately the impact of these two visibility-creating devices (script and position) could not be measured systematically for all three newspapers simply because they are not utilized in all three. Capitalization is possible only in English; Arabic and Persian both use Arabic script, which has no capitalization. Although the use of boldface and different type sizes is possible in all three, no variation in boldface was noted in the English obituaries, and type size was almost impossible to measure in any precise manner.[4] Likewise, the alphabetical listing adopted in the English obituary pages precluded studying page location.[5] As a result, the analysis of space and visibility presented in this chapter has been limited to the first two devices—obituary size and repeated mention (henceforth numerical representation)—since only these two recur in all three newspapers and could, therefore, be systematically measured for comparative purposes. A detailed discussion of these two follows in the next two sections.

Within the context of obituaries, then, equity in space and visibility is measured in terms of two nonlinguistic variables: obituary size and numerical representation. Accordingly, gender (in)equity is viewed as the result of bias, or lack thereof, that results from the application of these devices in relation to either sex group. The statistical analysis measures the effect of the three variables (Sex, Culture, and Time) on obituary size and numerical distribution of the deceased, and teases out interaction effects, if any, of the variables relative to each other. In each case I show the gender basis of the variation and discuss effects of Culture and Time.

I. GENDERING OBITUARY SPACE: OBITUARY SIZE

One of my initial hypotheses regarding gender equity in the obituaries was based on obituary size. If women and men receive different treatment in the obituary pages, one would expect longer obituaries for the more "prominent" sex; and if women have been denied equal access to this public domain (Eid 1994a, 1994b), then obituaries of women should be shorter than those of men. But first, what does obituary length really mean within the context of equity in the distribution of space between the sexes and in the degree of visibility attained by each in the obituary pages?

It is safe to assume that within the public domain of the news media, space and visibility are in general allotted to more "prominent" people and more "noteworthy" news items, as determined by those responsible for the production of news. The space allotted to a news item as well as its location (front page, for example) is considered a very good indication of the relative importance the news piece is expected to receive. Recall in this respect the death of Princess Diana in 1997, for example. Some would say the coverage (that is, space allotted to the event) throughout the media (television, radio, newspaper, and Internet) was an indication of the importance, hence "prominence," the media felt this news item deserved. Others would say the news coverage created, rather than just reflected, a worldwide perception of importance.

If we assume similar principles apply within the context of the obituary pages, it would follow that the amount of space a family decides to buy for an obituary may be an indication of the importance they attach to the announcement and the degree of visibility they wish to create for the event. Since families write obituaries within a cultural context that assigns various meanings (and thus significance) to the announcement in a newspaper of an individual's death, obituary size is likely to be affected by that cultural context. Obituaries are also written for an audience, which includes friends, family members, and colleagues of the deceased. The size of the obituary may therefore be viewed as a reflection of the stature of the deceased, the importance he or she may have achieved, and perhaps the importance the family wishes to attach to the event. Finally, since obituaries are paid for by the family, economic factors may also impact a family's decision regarding obituary length.

Not all of these factors are accessible for analysis, however. Decisions made by families at the time of death and the reasons (economic and psycho-perceptual) behind their decisions are not available to us. What is available for analysis is the information included in the text of the obituaries and the cultural context of place and time.

On the other hand, it may be argued that family-written obituaries of the type studied here are simply announcements of death, as they are called in some English-language newspapers, and have no meaning beyond that. To falsify this hypothesis (which is also the null hypothesis in this case), it is sufficient to show significant variation in obituary size across cultures and over time. For if obituaries were simply death announcements, there would be no reason for them to dramatically change in size over time and across cultures.

Three sets of questions are therefore asked in this section. The first addresses the association between obituary size and sex of the deceased and the extent to which treatment of the sexes can be said to be equitable based on obituary length. The question also relates to the issue of who writes the obituaries. Do families tend to write shorter obituaries when the deceased is a woman? If so, why? Do they, for example, find less to say about a deceased woman than a deceased man? Since men have traditionally been more involved in the public domain, they would have more accomplishments to be cited in their obituaries which, as published texts, belong to the public domain.

The second set of questions addresses the association between obituary size and culture. Do cultural differences, including newspaper culture represented in individual newspaper style and editorial policies, affect obituary length as a whole and as a measure of gender equity? The cultural / linguistic tradition in English of citing individuals' names in the obituaries alphabetically has already restricted the study of certain visibility devices (for example, page location). The next chapter further illustrates the impact this difference has on yet another aspect of the study, the naming of the deceased.

The third set of questions addresses the impact of time on obituary length in its relation to gender equity and to the meaning of obituaries within different cultural contexts. If obituary size changes over time, what direction does this change take? How does time affect the association of gender, culture, and obituary size? To what extent can the change be explained in terms of the changing (public) roles of women and men across the three cultures? Finally, why would such a change affect obituary size in the first place?

1.1 Statistical Analysis and Results

The statistical analysis that follows measures obituary length as the mean, or average, number of lines per obituary. To assess the significance of the three independent variables (Sex, Culture, and Time) on variation in obituary length, the data were subjected to a three-way analysis of variance (ANOVA). The results in table 2.1 under "main effects" show that Sex, Culture, and Time are all statistically significant ($p < .001$), and that there is no significant interaction among the three variables, as the results under "three-way interactions" show. Furthermore, the analysis under "two-way interactions" for each of the pairs Sex and Culture, Sex and Time, and Culture and Time shows no significant effect for the interaction in the first two pairs.

Thus obituary size is not significantly impacted by the sex of the deceased within culture groups or within time groups. Only the interaction in the third pair (Culture and Time) achieves a level of significance, suggesting that within culture groups change in obituary size is significant over time.

Since the interaction of Culture and Time achieved statistical significance, the data were further subjected to a modified LSD (Bonferroni) test. The results show that the mean differences between each pair of the three groups under Culture (Arabic, English, Persian) are significant ($p < .001$), as are the six year groups under Time (from 1938 to 1988). Tables 2.2 and 2.3 report the results, where a level of statistical significance was achieved.

All in all, then, the statistical results confirm the gender basis of variation in obituary size for the overall population of the obituaries but not necessarily within each culture group nor within these groups over time.

1.1.1 Discussion of the Results

The mean size of an obituary is 12.42 lines for all 3,800 deceased. The mean size of a female obituary is 11.87 lines (1,620 females); a male obituary averages 12.97 lines (2,180 males). Since the difference proved to be statistically significant, this result confirms my initial hypothesis that obituary

Table 2.1. Three-Way Analysis of Variance: Obituary Size by Sex, Culture, and Time (N = 3800)

Source of Variation	Sum of Squares	df	Mean Square	F
Main effects	103746.192	8	12968.274	240.814*
Sex	1114.451	1	1114.451	20.695*
Language	70936.089	2	35468.044	658.623*
Time	31695.652	5	6339.130	117.714*
Two-Way Interactions	7756.183	17	456.246	8.472*
Sex & Culture	167.332	2	83.666	1.554
Sex & Time	98.228	5	19.646	.365
Culture & Time	7464.770	10	746.477	13.862*
Three-Way Interactions	429.338	10	42.934	.797
Sex & Culture & Time	429.338	10	42.934	.797
Explained	111931.713	35	3198.049	59.368
Residual	202698.280	3764	53.852	
Total	314629.993	3799	82.819	

*$p < .001$ $R = .57$ $R^2 = .33$

Table 2.2. Obituary Size by Sex, Culture, and Time

		Average Size	Number of Obituaries
SEX	Female	11.87	1620
	Male	12.97	2180
	Total Population	12.42	3800
CULTURE	Arabic	18.31	1337
	English	8.61	1439
	Persian	10.39	1024
TIME	1938	9.27	396
	1948	9.53	574
	1958	10.36	679
	1968	12.76	714
	1978	13.74	719
	1988	17.19	718

Note: size = number of lines

Table 2.3. Obituary Size by Time and Culture

	1938	1948	1958	1968	1978	1988
Arabic	13.72	13.08	14.51	19.60	22.03	25.17
	(148)	(239)	(237)	(236)	(238)	(239)
English	6.7	6.89	7.53	7.67	9.92	12.93
	(239)	(240)	(240)	(240)	(240)	(240)
Persian	4.33	7.27	8.86	11.10	9.35	13.50
	(9)	(95)	(202)	(238)	(241)	(239)

Note: ( ) = the number of obituaries for each culture-by-year group

size would vary depending on the sex of the deceased; and since obituaries of men are longer, it also confirms favoritism toward men. Deceased men, through the length of their obituaries, occupy more space and achieve a higher level of visibility than deceased women. From the cultural perspective, the mean length for Arabic obituaries is 18.31 lines, English 8.61, and Persian 10.39. The average Egyptian obituary is more than double the size of the English; Persian falls in between, much closer to English than to Arabic. In light of the high level of statistical significance obtained for this distribution, we conclude that obituary space is not equally shared by all three cultures.

These results provide support for the idea that obituaries may have different meanings in different cultures and that this difference may indeed be signified by obituary size. I have suggested (Eid 1994a) on the basis of mere length and content that Egyptian obituaries may have acquired a significance beyond their being simply death announcements. The comparative analysis provided here extends this idea to suggest that cultures may assign different meanings to their obituaries, and thus the length of obituaries would vary for each culture. To get a better sense of what obituary size means in each culture and in relation to the sexes, I analyze obituary size along one other criterion, the median.[6]

The median length of all 3,800 obituaries is 10 lines, with 1,727 obituaries (more than half) above this ten-line mark. Of these, however, 698 are those of women and 1,029 of men, making the female-to-male percentage above the median 40 percent to 60 percent. This provides further support for the idea that deceased men are given more space and visibility in the obituaries than are deceased women. The significance of obituary size becomes even more interesting when the data are broken down by Culture. Many more deceased in the Arabic obituaries have obituaries longer than the overall median. The number (976) is almost double the Persian (421) and three times the English (330) (see figure 2.1). But, as we see in figure 2.2, the picture changes slightly when we look at the distribution of female and male obituaries above this mark independently in each individual culture.

Although in all three cultures more male than female obituaries fall above the ten-line median mark, the ratios differ. In both Arabic and Persian the percentage of female to male obituaries above this mark is the same (39 percent to 61 percent), although the actual numbers differ (Arabic: 382 females to 594 males; Persian: 163 to 258). The difference between the sexes is far less in English with a 46 percent to 54 percent female-to-male ratio (153 to 177). Overall, then, in all three cultures, the mean size of women's obituaries tends to fall below the overall mean, and the mean size of men's obituaries tends to fall above it. In all three cultures fewer women's obituaries fall above the median length of ten lines than do men's. Thus the generalization that emerges from analyzing the data in relation to both mean and median is that both Culture and Sex impact the variation in obituary size. Men have more space and visibility in the obituaries, and more Arabic obituaries are longer than the ten-line median than either English or Persian obituaries.

Before considering an explanation for these results, we turn to a discussion of the effect of Time, the third independent variable, on mean obituary

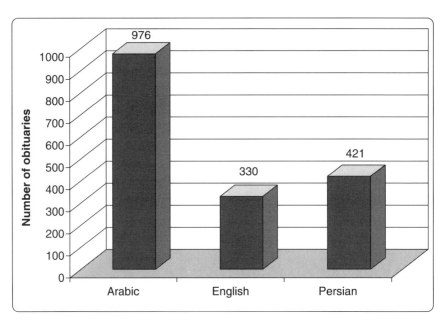

Fig. 2.1. Obituaries above the Median by Culture

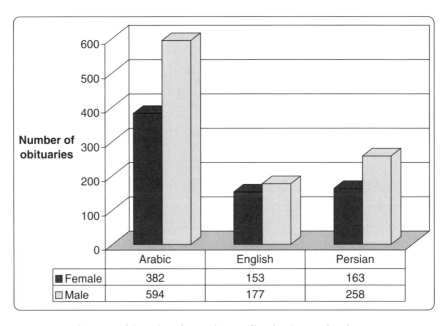

	Arabic	English	Persian
■ Female	382	153	163
□ Male	594	177	258

Fig. 2.2. Obituaries above the Median by Sex and Culture

length, first independent of Sex and of Culture, then combined with Culture. Only these analyses of time effects achieved statistical significance on obituary size (see table 2.1).

1.2 The Effect of Time on Obituary Size

The time data in table 2.2 are given in figure 2.3. The overall mean for each time period shows a consistent increase throughout the six time periods, albeit stronger in some than in others. During the decade 1938–48, for example, mean obituary length increased by only 0.26 lines whereas between 1978 and 1988 it increased by 3.45 lines, the highest increase for any period.[7]

A breakdown of obituary size data by both Time and Culture, reported in table 2.3 and represented in figure 2.4, shows an increase in obituary length in all three cultures, reaching its peak in 1988.[8] It also shows how striking cultural differences are. Most obvious perhaps is the way Arabic stands out, quite distant from English and Persian in mean obituary length throughout the six time periods. The figures for English and Persian obituaries, on the other hand, remain relatively similar, suggesting that in Egypt, obituaries have acquired a meaning and a cultural significance different from that in either the United States or Iran.

The consistent increase in obituary size may also be a reflection of the importance obituary pages acquire over time. As the obituary pages (and in some cases as the newspapers that publish them) gain status within a culture, obituary length would increase accordingly to reflect this change in perception. A comparison of the change across the three cultures shows stability in size during the first three years for Arabic and English obituaries. Arabic obituaries start to dramatically increase their size in 1968; for English, in 1978. Persian obituary size increases every year, except for 1978.

1.3 Contextualizing the Results: Obituary Culture

The explanation in this section relies on both newspaper development and cultural attitudes toward newspaper obituaries as part of what I call "obituary culture."

When newspapers are introduced into a community, they usually take time to establish themselves within that community before they can develop a successful pattern of circulation. Dunnett (1988:5) gives a number of factors

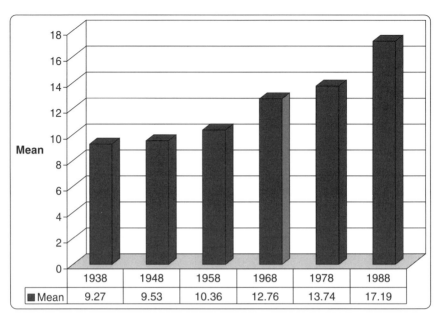

	1938	1948	1958	1968	1978	1988
■ Mean	9.27	9.53	10.36	12.76	13.74	17.19

Fig. 2.3. Obituary Size over Time

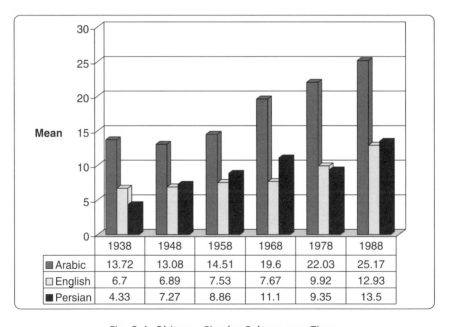

	1938	1948	1958	1968	1978	1988
■ Arabic	13.72	13.08	14.51	19.6	22.03	25.17
□ English	6.7	6.89	7.53	7.67	9.92	12.93
■ Persian	4.33	7.27	8.86	11.1	9.35	13.5

Fig. 2.4. Obituary Size by Culture over Time

important in creating a market for newspapers (particularly in the West). These include urbanization, economic growth, rising income, and compulsory education. He describes the newspaper industry as "a broker between readers and advertisers" since it "sells news and entertainment to readers and then sells those readers to advertisers" (3). In that sense, it sells what he calls "a joint product." If so, the development of an obituary page, or section, within a newspaper would fall under the second part of that formula. If families are viewed as advertisers—which they are since they pay for their product (the obituary) in order to reach a "market" of readers (families, friends, acquaintances of the deceased and their families)—they would use the newspaper medium for their advertisement only if it would serve their purpose. Thus it is only after the first part of the formula has been established, at least to some degree, and a readership has been realized for a newspaper that it can serve these families, the advertisers. The length of time this process takes varies depending on the factors Dunnett cites.

In Egypt and the United States, newspapers were established during the nineteenth century. But in Iran newspapers were not introduced until the early part of the twentieth century. *Ettela'at* was first published in 1926, and in 1938 it did not have an obituary page. By 1948, however, a section of a page was devoted to obituaries. *Al-Ahram* and the *New York Times,* on the other hand, had by 1938 developed a well-established obituary page, as explained in chapter 1.

This difference in newspaper development, and of these particular newspapers, as a medium for news transmission may be responsible for some of the differences in obituary size across the three sets of data. Since the English and Arabic newspapers had been established earlier and had already developed an obituary page prior to 1938, they would be expected to include more obituaries and, in the absence of other cultural considerations, perhaps longer ones as well. The differences illustrated in figure 2.4 between Arabic and English obituaries, on the one hand, and Persian, on the other, may be explained on this basis. One can argue that in English and Arabic the newspaper effect had in some sense disappeared by 1938 and the changes in obituary size we see later reflect cultural changes only, changes in social perception or value assigned to obituaries. The argument based on newspapers' development can also explain why Persian obituaries start out being the shortest, with a mean of 4.3 lines in 1938. In addition, political instability in Iran during the first half of the twentieth century resulted in newspapers and magazines often being shut down by the government (Majidian 1981; Sanasarian 1982; Paidar 1995).

Newspapers, it might also be argued, affect obituary size in yet another way: through their allotment of space to obituaries. The more space a newspaper assigns to its obituary section or page, the more likely it is for obituary size to increase as a result of exposure and additional value assigned to these pages and the obituaries they publish. The obituary size data, however, contradict this position. The 148 obituaries in the 1938 Arabic newspaper, for example, had an average length more than double that of the 240 English obituaries. Likewise, by 1948 the average length of the 95 Persian obituaries slightly exceeds that of the English obituaries, thus pointing again to cultural considerations that assign meaning to obituaries and their relative independence of the newspapers' assignment of space.

A more plausible argument would therefore attribute the change in obituary size to changes external to the obituary pages—to a mutual rather than a one-sided relationship of causality. The more a newspaper develops its reputation and respectability within a community, the more readership it gains. Readership, in turn, affects newspaper policies to some extent, particularly when it involves paid ads such as contributions to the obituary pages. When such pages are first set up in a newspaper, it takes time for them to establish their clientele. But once they do, increase in demand would most likely be reflected in a corresponding increase in the allotment of space by the newspapers to accommodate the demand. Lutfi Elkholi in his column cited earlier (*Al-Ahram,* October 4, 1997) addresses this issue in his assessment of the uniqueness of *Al-Ahram*'s obituary pages: "I believe *Al-Ahram* realized earlier than any other newspaper the value assigned to death [rituals][9] in Egyptian culture and civilization and in Egyptian people's lives, the need to announce it, commemorate it, and record it on paper just as it used to be recorded in ancient times on stone."

The reader may recall the question posed earlier regarding the effect of Time on obituary size: Does obituary size change over time and if so, why? We have essentially answered the question, showing through statistical analysis that it does. The explanations suggested here rely on the cultural contexts within which obituaries acquire their meaning, and thus their significance and length. An equally important consideration is the development of newspapers as a medium for the transmission of information—information that would eventually include the publication of death and funeral announcements, which would later develop into obituary sections or pages once a newspaper has established its readership and the culture has accepted it as a medium for the transmission of such news items.

We have not, however, been able to establish that Time has an effect on obituary size as a result of the sex of the deceased, since the analysis in table 2.2 does not establish a statistical significance. We conclude that there has not been a significant difference in change over time in the size of women's versus men's obituaries, thus no sex-differentiated time effect.

This then leaves two more questions to answer: first, why are women's obituaries shorter than men's cross-culturally and second, why are Arabic obituaries so much different from English and Persian obituaries in terms of their length? To answer these questions, we need to understand what obituary size means for each culture, what fills up obituary space, and if possible why families write obituaries for their deceased.

To answer the second question first, I suggest that obituaries vary in length depending on the value a culture places on them, specifically the degree to which they are perceived as being simply death announcements versus being something else, such as status symbols. The main purpose of an obituary is to announce the death of a family member, to announce the time and place of the services, and to identify members of the deceased's family so friends are able to attend and pay their respects. If this is so, then obituaries (for those cultures that utilize them) are universally perceived as "death announcements" or "funeral announcements," as they are sometimes called.

Obituaries, I propose, are part of what Habenstein and Lamers (1963: 758ff) call "the funeralization process" and describe as being a conservative social process, a set of activities that varies in its detail across cultures but is present in all cultures to address three universal needs created as a result of a death event: the need to dispose of the body; the needs of the departed "soul" or "spirit" which, according to the authors, is believed to have an "ongoing life" in most cultures; and the needs of the bereaved and members of the surviving family. It is within the context of this third need—and perhaps to a lesser extent the second—that I place the role of the obituaries and their relative length.

Obituaries are part of death ceremonies. They not only announce the event but also serve to publicize it through the wide circulation offered by newspapers. The religious and spiritual aspects of the ceremonies are believed in most cultures (the three under consideration included) to help the departed on his or her journey through various rituals, which often require the participation of family and friends (Habenstein and Lamers 1963). Newspaper obituaries make this participation possible. In some cultures, Egyptian and Iranian included, it is believed that the more people pray for the departed the better and easier is his or her journey (hence the importance of participation in the ceremonies from the perspective of the deceased). But the needs of the bereaved family members for support, for example, and for feeling that they have done the "right thing" (their duty toward the deceased) are also satisfied through this group participation in the ceremonies. Thus the process is both an individual and a group activity, and its success requires the participation of both.

The obituaries, then, allow for group participation through publicizing the event. Naturally the importance of their role increases in accordance with a heightened perception of what they can offer. If the primary role of the obituary is to announce the death and invite participation, its underlying role is to increase participation in the event. It is for this reason that I propose further that in some cultures obituaries acquire an additional role—as indicators of status.

This hypothesis predicts that cross-culturally, obituary size would cor-relate with a society's perception of the role obituaries have as death announce-ments only or as death announcements with an additional symbolic meaning. Obituary size will vary according to the perceived importance such additional meanings may have acquired not only across cultures but over time as well. Periods associated with unusual increase in obituary size, for example, 1958–68 and 1978–88, would be identified as periods where a change occurs in the social perception of the meaning of obituaries within the socioeconomic groups that use them.

Taking "announcement" and "status" as ends of a continuum, cultures fall at different points along this continuum. The Arabic obituaries represent the status end and English the death announcement end, with Persian falling somewhere in between but closer to the English than the Arabic end. This proposal would answer the second question regarding the divergence of Arabic obituaries vis-à-vis English and Persian obituaries. But whose "status" is reflected in an obituary? The individual, the family, or both?

In Egypt obituaries are really not "about" the deceased but about the family. The space an obituary occupies is not filled by information about the deceased (accomplishments, personalized information, or feelings of survivors) but with information about the deceased's family members, both immediate and extended, who are identified like the deceased by their names, titles, jobs or positions they occupy (or have occupied) in the public sphere, and by their families. In addition, the names of families related to the deceased also fill up obituary space in Arabic and Persian newspapers. By contrast, English obituary space is not filled with information about family, other than the names of immediate family members. In some cultures then obituaries may be more deceased oriented (English) than family oriented (Arabic), while in others they fall somewhere in between (Persian).

Variation in obituary size across cultures and over time is the result of interactions between obituary role (announcement versus status) and obituary orientation (deceased versus family). The less status oriented obituaries are (more announcement oriented), the more likely they are to be short and vice versa. But status may be family oriented or deceased oriented. Deceased- and status-oriented obituaries, for example, would devote the bulk of their space to covering the accomplishments of the deceased rather than the identification of their families.[10]

Assuming the above, four logically possible obituary types are predicted to occur: status- and deceased-oriented obituaries (+Status, +Deceased), neither status- nor deceased-oriented obituaries (-Status, -Deceased), status- but not deceased-oriented obituaries (+Status, -Deceased), and deceased- but not status-oriented obituaries(-Status, +Deceased). Obituary role and orientation are independent of each other due to the independence of their domains. Although both are theoretical constructs, obituary role links the obituaries to the social reality outside whereas obituary orientation is an analytical device applied in the analysis of the obituaries as texts, their content and structure. This framework can serve to explain differences noted so far and make further predictions to be tested later. But it ignores an important factor that affects obituary size in any culture—the economic or cost factor.

We now address our first question regarding the effect of the deceased's sex on obituary size, or why women's obituaries are shorter than men's. Families of the deceased, one might argue, have more to say about deceased men than deceased women. This is more likely to be true of deceased- than family-oriented obituaries. In fact the framework would predict that, all else being equal, the sex of the deceased would have less impact on obituary size in the family-oriented type where the focus is not so much on the deceased as it is on the family. Unfortunately, this prediction could not be tested because the interaction of Sex and Culture did not prove to be statistically significant. So although in all three cultures, regardless of obituary orientation, women's obituaries are shorter than men's,[11] the difference is not strong enough in any of the three to confirm or disconfirm predictions made from the interaction of obituary role and orientation. Sex differentiation in obituary size is universal, not culture differentiated.

Obituaries are also texts published in a public domain, namely, the newspapers. Insofar as they may have transcended their original role as death notices in some cultures, they have become more of a public than a private affair. Since the public domain has traditionally belonged to men, not women, it is not surprising that men's obituaries would be longer than women's. Traditionally men have been responsible for acquiring public status, which they convey onto their families, and it is through men that women have traditionally acquired public status and in some cultures access to public space.[12] Thus it would follow that in deceased-oriented obituaries, those of men would be longer.

The Persian obituaries are a good example of this. They tend not to list the deceased's accomplishments (not deceased-oriented) and tend to follow more closely the style of death announcements (not status-oriented). Yet obituaries of important people (for example, mayors, ministers) and religious leaders tend to include the titles, jobs, ranks, and positions they have occupied, among other details. As a result, their obituaries tend to be longer, thereby contributing to the overall length of men's obituaries. Women, on the other hand, have not occupied such leading positions for any prolonged period of time. The overall effect of such discrepancies in women's versus men's roles is that women's obituaries end up being shorter. The divergence in length between women's and men's obituaries is thus due to their divergent roles and status in the sociocultural structure, and in particular their occupation of public space and their role within that space.

Among status- and deceased-oriented obituaries (+Status, +Deceased), women's obituaries are expected to be shorter if indeed their accomplishments are not deemed as worthy of mention as those of men. The status orientation of this obituary type can, however, have a compensatory effect, resulting in intermediate-length obituaries as in the Persian obituaries. Neither status- nor deceased-oriented obituaries (-Status, -Deceased) are just death announce-ments. These would be the least sex differentiated, hence most favorable to women as their accomplishments in the public domain increase. In status-, non-deceased-oriented obituaries (+Status, -Deceased), the sex of the deceased is not as relevant and would therefore have little impact on obituary size, as in the Arabic obituaries. If women's obituaries are shorter here as well, other reasons would have contributed to this effect. Finally, in non-status-, deceased-oriented obituaries (-Status, +Deceased), individual accomplishments come into play, predicting longer obituaries for the more accomplished. But the negative status orientation associated with obituaries in such cultures would in a sense cancel out accomplishment effects. For if little value is associated with a commodity (here obituaries), its contribution in an accomplishment-oriented context is not very valuable. Thus, obituaries in this category may not show as much gender bias, as is the case in the English obituaries.

The interaction of obituary role and orientation as applied in the explanation of sex and culture differentiation in obituary size suggests that certain factors may mediate the effect of one or the other. It also has implications for change in obituary size. A change in the value or significance of obituaries in a culture would entail change in its typological classification as well. The classification of obituaries may therefore change over time within one obituary culture, defined here as one newspaper.

1.4 Conclusion

Variation in obituary size is not based on Sex alone. Culture has a significant effect as well, independent of Sex. Only Culture was found to have a significant effect on change in obituary size over Time. Change in obituary size beginning in 1968 is attributed to sociocultural value and significance assigned to obituaries as a result of both newspaper developments and possibly a change in the social perception of value a newspaper obituary may provide to the funeralization process. An obituary orientation-role model of analysis has been proposed to integrate possible cultural effects; and although some predictions could not be tested at this point, it is hoped the model would prove useful in other areas and studies of the obituaries, as we suggest in chapter 7.

The distribution of obituary space, measured in terms of number of lines, varies by Sex and by Culture. Women's obituaries occupy less space than men's, hence women's visibility is reduced within this public space. Arabic obituaries occupy the most space, followed by Persian, then English. A tentative (yet uniform) explanation for this distribution of space between the sexes and across cultures would attribute difference to the meaning (in the sense of importance or significance) of that space relative to the entity in question. From the cultural perspective, Arabic obituaries occupy the most space because of the relatively greater status orientation of obituaries in that culture and the historical importance of death rituals in Egypt since ancient times. From the gender perspective, men occupy more obituary space partly because public—including obituary—space is perceived as being more pertinent to men than women. Thus the public-versus-private-domain hypothesis is invoked as part of the explanation.

If a woman's domain is the home and if, as the quote from Bahithat al-Badiya at the beginning of this chapter suggests, at some point in time she was allowed to leave it only to go to her grave, it is not surprising that a woman's obituary, as a reflection of her worth within the public sphere, would occupy less space than that of the men who had kept her at home in the first place, away from the public sphere. Even after her death, men would, for the most part, still make the final decisions about a woman's obituary (its content and length).

2. POPULATION DISTRIBUTION AND THE SHARING OF OBITUARY SPACE

The statistical analysis shows that obituary space is not equally shared by the sexes. Table 2.4 provides statistics on the distribution of deceased women and men in the obituary pages of all three newspapers, individually and combined. Overall, fewer women than men are represented (43 percent versus 57 percent). Likewise, within each culture group fewer deceased women are represented than deceased men. The first question that arises then is: does this distribution fall within an accepted norm and, if so, what is that norm?

Demographers suggest that the normal (biologically determined) sex ratio at birth is 104–8 male births to 100 female births, and that under normal conditions, the percent of male deaths (assuming a normal lifespan for all) should, therefore, be higher, estimated at 51–52 percent of all deaths (females representing the remaining 48–49 percent).[13] The 57 percent figure obtained from the obituaries is therefore higher, suggesting bias in favor of deceased men (table 2.4). The actual death rate among males, it might also be argued, should be higher than among females in view of such external factors as wars that would disrupt "normal" conditions. But how much higher? Also, the death rate among females can be higher in some cultures as a result of health conditions affecting female mortality (for example, childbirth). Again how much higher?

To pursue this alternative, actual death rates would have to be obtained for each of the years studied in each culture group. The figures would then have to be averaged for each group and comparisons made with these figures. I pursued this approach in analyzing the Arabic obituaries (Eid 1994a), but found that the resulting ratios are quite divergent from the death rates reported in the literature. Mortality rates for Egypt were obtained for four of the six years studied (1938–68). The difference between the sexes was nowhere near what the obituaries demonstrated. Table 2.5 provides percentages obtained for these years and the corresponding rates from the obituaries (Eid 1994a). The percentages in the obituaries are consistently higher than the actual death rates, more so in some years than in others.

On the basis of these results, I decided not to pursue the comparison with actual death rates in relation to English and Persian obituaries. First, the

Table 2.4. Population Distribution by Sex and Culture

	Arabic	English	Persian	Total
Female	548	**679**	_393_	1620
	41%	47%	38%	(43%)
Male	789	_760_	631	2180
	59%	53%	62%	(57%)
Total	1337	1439	1024	3800
	(35%)	(38%)	(27%)	(100%)

$\chi^2 = 21.2$ $p < .0001$

Table 2.5. Percentages of Deaths by Sex: Actual versus Obituaries (Egypt)

	1938		1948		1958		1968	
	Actual	Obits.	Actual	Obits.	Actual	Obits.	Actual	Obits.
Female	46.8	37.8	46.68	46	47.46	40.5	50.2	42
Male	54.2	62.2	53.32	54	52.54	59.5	49.8	58
% Diff.	8.3	24.4	6.64	8	5.08	9	−0.4	16

ratio in the obituaries is quite divergent from the actual death rates. Second, whereas the death rates consistently move to close the gap between female and male deaths, the obituaries give no such indication. They have a life of their own, independent of actual deaths. The demography of the obituaries further suggests that their population may not be representative of the whole spectrum of the social and geographical stratification of the world outside them (see chapter 5). Economic considerations are sufficient reason to argue here that families who populate the obituaries do not represent all socioeconomic groups. Thus deaths reported in the obituary pages would not necessarily correspond to the overall death rate.

Thus, in determining distributional bias, or lack thereof, in the obituaries, I rely on the analysis of expected values and compare the population distribution by sex of the deceased in relation to another variable. The following discussion is focused first on the combined effect of Sex and Culture on population distribution, then the combined effect of Sex, Culture, and Time.

2.1 The Interaction Effect of Sex and Culture on Population Distribution

Differences in population distribution resulting from the analysis of the data by Sex and Culture (table 2.4) are statistically significant ($p < .0001$). The analysis of expected values shows significant discrepancies between the actual numbers obtained from the analysis and those expected to have been obtained, had the distribution been unbiased among these groups. The analysis identifies three groups in particular as having significantly different actual and expected numbers: women and men in the English obituaries, and women in Persian obituaries. Of these three only the female group in the English obituaries is overrepresented, with an expected value of 613 for that group, 826 for the English male group, and 436 for the Persian female group. Although the distribution of the other sex-by-culture groups may not correspond to the expected values, they are not divergent enough to achieve the required significance level.

Taking numerical representation as a measure of visibility in the obituary pages, we conclude that deceased women occupy less of the total obituary space than do deceased men and by implication are less visible within that domain. Figures 2.5–2.7 provide three alternative views of the distribution of the sexes and their occupation of obituary space. Iranian women as a group

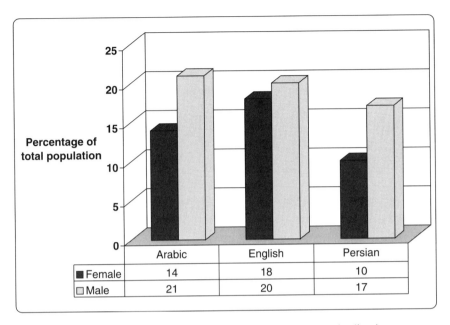

	Arabic	English	Persian
■ Female	14	18	10
☐ Male	21	20	17

Fig. 2.5. Obituary Space as Reflection of Population Distribution

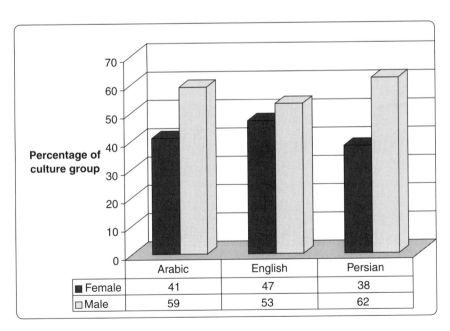

	Arabic	English	Persian
■ Female	41	47	38
☐ Male	59	53	62

Fig. 2.6. Sex Differentiation within Culture Groups

occupy the least obituary space and are thus the least visible within the overall available obituary space (figure 2.5). Most visible are Egyptian and American men. American women follow in visibility (with 18 percent of obituary space), followed by Iranian men, then Egyptian women. Sex differentiation within culture groups (figure 2.6) is most divergent in Persian obituaries, with a female-to-male representation of 38 to 62 percent. English obituaries are the least divergent (47 to 53 percent), and Arabic obituaries fall in between (41 to 59 percent). Despite this ranking, female representation in each case is less than 50 percent, demonstrating varying degrees of distributional bias in favor of deceased men.

Finally, when the distribution is viewed as a function of the space occupied by each sex group (figure 2.7), American women occupy most of the female space and Iranian women the least. The ranking within male obituary space differs only slightly. Thus distribution by sex group ranks American women and men highest with respect to their respective sex group, and Persian women and men last. Because this in a sense is a ranking of cultural contribution, or effect from culture, this ranking may reflect the overall distribution of the population by culture in the obituaries. English

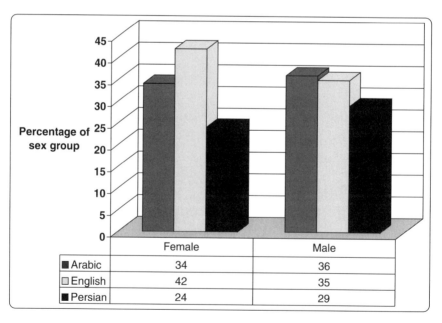

	Female	Male
■ Arabic	34	36
□ English	42	35
■ Persian	24	29

Fig. 2.7. Culture Differentiation in Distribution by Sex

obituaries make up 38 percent of all obituaries under study, Arabic 35 percent, and Persian 27 percent. Within each culture group, then, women are underrepresented in the obituary pages of their respective newspapers. They are underrepresented as a group as well as in comparison to men within the overall population of the obituary pages. Table 2.6 provides linear ranking of these results as a function of different group totals.

These rankings produce two generalizations relevant to our purposes here. First, within each culture males are more highly valued, as a result of their representation and visibility, than females. Second, English females are always higher on the ranking scale in comparison to Arabic and Persian females. The ranking for males follows the order Arabic > English > Persian, except in ranking by culture group where the Persian male is ranked highest, reflecting his greater position within his culture group as opposed to that of the Persian female.

The divergence in the distribution of the sexes in the Persian obituaries, it might be argued, is not necessarily due to bias in favor of men, but is the result of political events such as the Iran-Iraq war during the 1980s and the earlier movement to end the monarchy and establish the Islamic Republic. Since more men are likely to participate in such activities, the number of deceased men during these periods would increase and by implication so would the total number of men's obituaries. A number of counterarguments can be presented here. First, in collecting the Persian data, there was an abundance of obituaries for *shuhada* (martyrs of war) in some issues of the newspaper. A separate section, however, was devoted to the martyrs in the obituary pages of *Ettela' at.* To eliminate this kind of statistical bias, obituaries of "martyrs" were excluded from the original count. Second, if the bias were due to the influence

Table 2.6. Rankings by Total Population, Culture Groups, Sex Groups

Total Population	Culture Groups	Sex Groups
Arabic-Male	Persian-Male	**English-Female**
English-Male	English-Male	Arabic-Male
English-Female	Arabic-Male	English-Male
Persian-Male	English-Female	Arabic-Female
Arabic-Female	Arabic-Female	**Persian-Male**
Persian-Female	Persian-Female	Persian-Female

of war, then we would expect to find the statistics for these periods (1978 and 1988) to be vastly different from those of other years. But as subsequent discussion of individual years shows, they are not. Third, if the divergence in the figures were indeed due to the effect of war and other political events in Iran, then why are the figures not as divergent in the English and Arabic obituaries as well? Both the United States and Egypt were involved in major wars during this fifty-year period: Vietnam and Korea (United States), World War II, Egypt's wars with Israel, and its troop involvement in Yemen are only some examples.

Attempts to explain the divergent distribution among deceased women and men in the obituary pages as being the result of external cultural events that justify a higher ratio of death among men, though possible, are not adequate explanations. Perhaps they would have been, if indeed the ratios in the obituary pages are a reflection of actual death rates (which they are not) and if the obituaries are indeed a reflection of society as a whole. An alternative explanation is proposed later in this chapter, based on the sharing of public space among women and men. I argue that as a genre, the obituary pages can create their own "reality," which is often not (and need not always be) a reflection of other existing sociocultural "realities."[14] But, like other genres, obituaries inevitably reflect to some degree attitudes prevalent within the cultural contexts in which they are authorized by their writers and their readership. Thus what has been viewed as bias in the distribution of women's and men's obituaries is now interpreted as a reflection of the underlying attitude or perception that women are less "relevant" when it comes to public space. It follows that as this attitude changes within a community, women's occupation of obituary space would change accordingly (hence the relevance of Time to this discussion).

Before turning to change over time, recall the obituary role-orientation discussion in relation to obituary size and the prediction that sex differentiation would be least valuable for English and Arabic obituary types, albeit for different reasons. The analysis of population distribution shows that sex differentiation is least marked in the English obituaries. But it also shows that the distribution of the sexes is significantly divergent from the expected values analysis, based on the distribution of the whole. Women in English obituaries are overrepresented whereas men are underrepresented. Furthermore, the distribution in Arabic obituaries is not significantly divergent from the expected values although women are underrepresented (table 2.4).

The English obituaries have been classified as -Status, +Deceased, the Arabic as +Status, -Deceased, and the Persian as +Status, +Deceased.[15] Because Persian is both, the underrepresentation of its female population is in some ways expected. The English situation is also expected since obituaries are not status oriented in American culture. But how do the Arabic results fit? Since Arabic obituaries are family (not deceased) oriented and have a strong status role, the female population is underrepresented but not significantly so.

2.2 The Effect of Time on Population Distribution

The statistical analysis performed to test the interaction of Time and Sex did not achieve a statistical significance, suggesting that Time alone does not have a significant effect on the representation of the sexes in the obituary pages. In none of the six time groups is sex differentiation divergent enough (from the expected values) so as to be of statistical significance. Thus the distribution of sex groups during these six years remains stable. Although the two groups as a whole may be quite distant from each other, the distance between them is maintained with no significant effect from time.

2.3 The Combined Effect of Time and Culture

To assess the combined effect of Time and Culture on population distribution, the data (3,800 obituaries) are broken down by Time and Culture. The analysis achieves a high level of statistical significance (χ^2 = 224.7 and p < .0001), showing a strong interaction effect. Figure 2.8 displays these results. The distribution across the three cultures is quite divergent in the first three years. In 1938, for example, 60 percent of the deceased come from the English obituaries, 37 percent from Arabic and the remaining 3 percent from Persian. By 1968 the distribution across the three cultures appears to have stabilized.

This result can be partly explained by the research design itself, but also partly by what I have called the "newspaper effect." The relative contribution of each culture (number of obituaries, which translates into number of deceased) was randomly set at approximately 240 obituaries from each newspaper per year. Recall that target could not be reached in some cases (for Persian, 1938–58 and for Arabic, 1938), which explains the discrepant distribution during the first three years and relative stability that follows. Only in 1938 are Arabic obituaries underrepresented with 148 obituaries obtained from the thirty-day

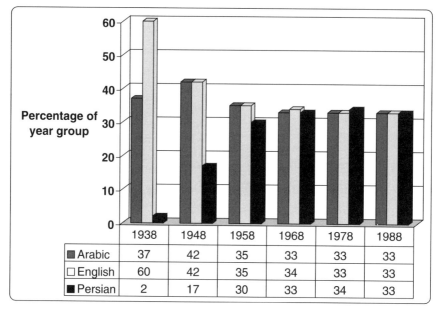

Note: Percentages do not always add up to 100% due to rounding.

Fig. 2.8. Population Distribution by Culture over Time

period. Persian obituaries continue to be underrepresented through 1958. Only in 1968 was the number of obituaries collected large enough to allow for the selection of the targeted number of 240.

These results, then, relate to earlier discussions of newspaper development and its effect on obituary size and change therein. The analysis here shows that it affects population distribution as well with disproportionate contributions from some cultures during the early periods. This, however, should not affect the relationship between the sexes within each culture group and over time.

2.4 The Interaction of Sex, Culture, and Time

We have seen so far that the two-way interaction of Sex and Time has no significant effect on population distribution but the interaction of Culture and Time does. As a result, sex-differentiated change over time could not be established for the overall population.

To assess the interaction effect of the three variables, two analyses were performed. One tests for sex differentiation in population distribution within culture groups over time (table 2.7) and the other tests for culture differentiation within sex groups over time (table 2.8). Analyzing population distribution separately within each culture group, we ask if the representation of women and men relative to each other changes over time within these groups. Analyzing population distribution within sex groups separately, we ask if the representation differs for culture groups over time.

The first analysis performed, by controlling for each culture group and testing for sex differentiation over time, did not reach a level of statistical significance for any of the three culture groups, as table 2.7 shows. The differences in the distribution of the sexes within each year and culture group is not sufficiently different from the expected values for any of these combinations: twelve sex-by-time groups within each culture.

The second analysis, performed by controlling for sex groups and testing for culture effects over time, proved to be significant for each sex group—confirming further the strong effect of Culture on population distribution by Sex, independently and combined with Time. The results of the analysis, reported in table 2.8 as percentages of each year group, tell different stories about change as it affects women's and men's obituaries and as it is affected by

Table 2.7. Distribution of the Sexes by Culture over Time

	Arabic			English			Persian		
	Female	Male	Total	Female	Male	Total	Female	Male	Total
1938	56	92	148	120	119	239	3	6	9
	38%	62%	100%	50%	50%	100%	33%	67%	100%
1948	109	130	239	109	131	240	41	54	95
	46%	54%	100%	45%	55%	100%	43%	57%	100%
1958	96	141	237	108	132	240	82	120	202
	41%	59%	100%	45%	55%	100%	41%	59%	100%
1968	100	136	236	114	126	240	88	150	238
	42%	58%	100%	47.5%	52.5%	100%	37%	63%	100%
1978	92	146	238	126	114	240	91	150	241
	39%	61%	100%	52.5%	47.5%	100%	38%	62%	100%
1988	95	144	239	102	138	240	88	151	239
	40%	60%	100%	42.5%	57.5%	100%	37%	63%	100%
Total	548	789	1337	679	760	1439	392	632	1024
	41%	59%	100%	47%	53%	100%	38%	62%	100%

the culture groups from which they come (and the newspapers in which their obituaries were published).

Among the female population, significant overrepresentation occurs in 1938 in the English obituaries, 1948 in the Arabic, and 1988 in the Persian. Among the male population, only the deceased from English and Persian obituaries show any significant variation: in the first two years, overrepresentation in the English obituaries and underrepresentation in the Persian obituaries. The last three decades (1968–88) show significant overrepresentation in the Persian obituaries. The distribution in the other two groups does not reach any statistical significance except for the 1978 underrepresentation in English.

Overall, then, the Arabic population in both sex groups shows little significant difference from the expected values analysis for the respective group (except for 1948 females). The English population differs a little more (1938 females and 1938–48, 1978 males), and the Persian population the most (1938–48 females and males, 1988 females, 1968–88 males).

Table 2.8. The Effect of Culture on Population Distribution by Sex over Time

	1938	1948	1958	1968	1978	1988	χ^2
FEMALE							98.2*
Arabic	56	**109**	96	100	92	95	
	31%	42%	34%	33%	30%	33%	
English	**120**	109	108	114	126	102	
	67%	42%	38%	38%	41%	36%	
Persian	_3_	_41_	82	88	91	**88**	
	2%	16%	29%	29%	29%	31%	
Total	179	259	286	302	309	285	
MALE							133.3*
Arabic	92	130	141	136	146	144	
	42%	41%	36%	33%	36%	33%	
English	**119**	**131**	132	126	_114_	138	
	55%	42%	34%	31%	28%	32%	
Persian	_6_	_54_	120	**150**	**150**	**151**	
	3%	17%	31%	36%	37%	35%	
Total	217	315	393	412	410	433	

*p < .0001

Figures 2.9 and 2.10 show the distribution over time of the female and male populations, respectively. Percentages in these figures are of culture groups, rather than the year groups reported in table 2.8. Over this fifty-year period, the only group to post a decrease is the English female group, with an overall loss of 3 percent (from 18 percent in 1938 to 15 percent in 1988). The other groups report varying degrees of increased representation. The groups posting the greatest overall increase are Persian females (up 22 percent) and males (up 23 percent). The Arabic female group has increased by about 7 percent and the male by 6 percent overall, while the English male population posted a 2 percent increase. Thus none of the male groups and only one female group decreased their representation in the obituary pages over this period. Accordingly, change in numerical representation within each sex group is differentiated by culture, thus supporting the combined-effect analysis by Sex, Culture, and Time on the population distribution of the deceased.

Figures 2.11 and 2.12 provide a different view of the data in figures 2.9 and 2.10, respectively. They provide a clearer comparative perspective on the direction of change and the impact of culture on change in each sex group. Among the female group, for example, the shape of the trajectory representing English obituaries is distinct from the two other trajectories in that it starts the highest and ends the lowest. The movement (hence the distribution over the years) is relatively stable, unlike the movement demonstrated by the trajectories for the other two groups with sharp increases in the first decade for the Arabic trajectory and the first and second for the Persian trajectory. Among the male group, the trajectories are quite different. The trajectory representing the English obituaries is relatively stable until 1968, whereas the Arabic and Persian trajectories demonstrate sharp increases until 1958 for Arabic and 1968 for Persian. A comparison of the two figures for each culture group shows how sex differentiated the change may be. The trajectories for the Persian groups, for example, are similar in form, projecting a sharp increase in the early years followed by relative stability for both groups but a slight curve down among the women group in 1988. The trajectories representing the Arabic and English groups take different shapes for deceased women and men.

2.5 Conclusion: Population Distribution and Obituary Space

Little change has taken place in the numerical representation of sexes relative to each other. Overall, the percentage of women represented in the

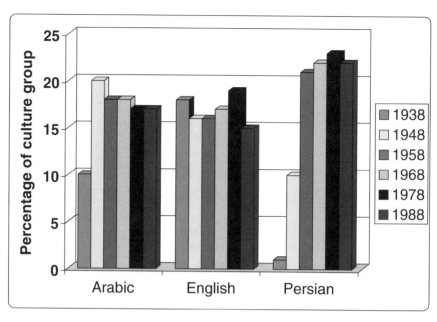

Fig. 2.9. Female Population Distribution by Culture over Time

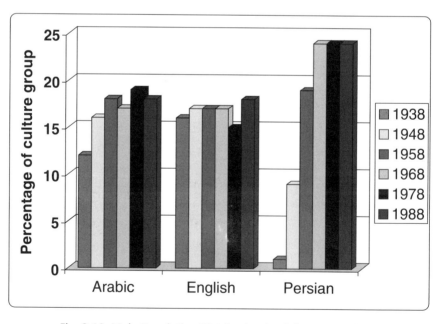

Fig. 2.10. Male Population Distribution by Culture over Time

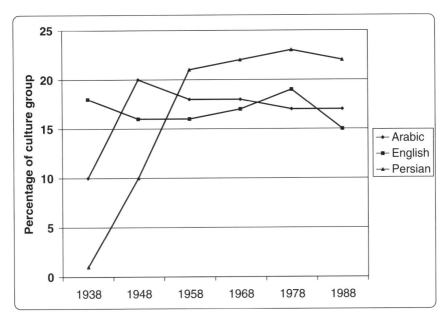

Fig. 2.11. Change over Time by Culture (Women)

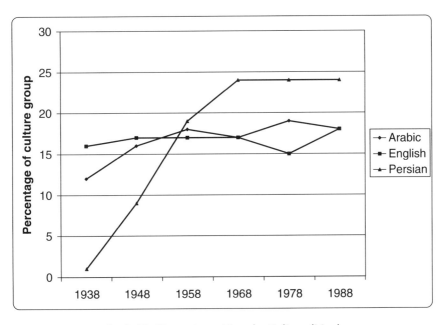

Fig. 2.12. Change over Time by Culture (Men)

obituary pages is consistently lower than that of men, and this percentage has not dramatically changed over the fifty-year period. Men in all three cultures have occupied more obituary space during each time period and in each culture, with two exceptions—in English obituaries, female representation reached 50 percent in 1938 and about 53 percent in 1978. Otherwise, a fairly large gap has been maintained in the distribution of the deceased by sex over the years.

The obituary space occupied by the sexes has not been equitably shared in the newspapers representing the three cultures. In each case a certain amount of space is allowed for each sex, disproportionately in favor of men, and that space has not dramatically changed over the years. The results are somewhat surprising and contrary to expectation. If indeed the obituary pages reflect the sociocultural attitudes of time and place, they should also reflect changes therein. Women in all three cultural contexts have indeed gained visibility and improved their status over this fifty-year period, but the obituaries do not reflect these changes. The obituary pages continue to show deceased men occupying a disproportionate amount of obituary space.

In the next and final section of this chapter, we examine these results in relation to other sociocultural issues related to public space outside the obituary pages in an attempt to assess the relationship between obituary and other public space. The discussion also provides some historical and cultural perspectives within which to understand gender roles, as well as relationships between women and men within culture groups and across them. Equally important is women's perception of their situation and their voices in redefining and changing perceptions of gender roles, to the extent that they have been changed. These voices are clearly not those of the deceased. But they provide a context within which to understand the time and place in which the deceased had been living. Equally important are voices of opposition to women's changing their situation, voices of the predominant discourse in which proponents of the status quo have been engaged—for it is most likely that they, or people like them, would have been responsible for writing the family obituaries and constructing identities of the deceased.

3. WOMEN, MEN, AND PUBLIC SPACE

Perhaps one of the more important debates of the twentieth century has been over the issue of women and men in public space. Women's voices in all three cultures reflect a sense of isolation accompanied by anger and rejection of their situation, an awareness of the injustice done to them as a result of male-dominated, sex-segregated social structures, and a realization that their relegation to the private domain of home and family is responsible for their exclusion from public space, thereby silencing their voices within that space and depriving them of their rights as citizens and as humans (to varying degrees across cultures). Above all we hear a voice determined to bring about change, supported at times by some men debating the status of women but mostly opposed by the voice of the predominant male authority. Thus the literature of the period reflects voices of both opposition and support for the "emancipation of women" and their treatment as citizens and as humans equal to their male counterparts, voices that become increasingly louder throughout the twentieth century in all three cultures.

At the end of the nineteenth century, women in Egypt and Iran of the middle but particularly the upper classes[16] had been literally confined to the home in a sex-segregated harem-like environment, veiled and silenced in public. Their sisters in the United States, also of the middle and upper classes, were better-off, although they also suffered from being relegated to the private sphere.[17] Sex segregation was not as prevalent and did not encompass all spheres and walks of life as it did in Egypt and Iran at the time. Perhaps it is partly for this reason that American women have fared better in the population distribution of the obituaries. Neither Egyptian nor Iranian deceased women were ever significantly overrepresented in relation to men or in relation to American women.

Writing in the context of Iran, Milani (1992:5) describes it as a "veiled society," where "walls surround houses" and "houses become compartmentalized with their *Daruni* 'inner' and *Biruni* 'outer' areas. Feelings become disjointed in *Zaheri* 'external' and *Bateni* 'internal' spheres." She extends the cultural significance of the veil beyond its obvious role in concealing a woman and its "moral, sexual, political, economic, and aesthetic considerations concerning her" to "notions of masculinity, privacy, and taboo." Veiling is interpreted as concealing what is considered "private." In that sense, Milani argues, veiling is no longer just a woman's problem since it serves to polarize and delineate boundaries, consigning "power," "control," "visibility," and "mobility" to one social category at the expense of the other. "The indoors, the domestic, the 'private,' the 'personal,' the world of women is trivialized. And the out-of-doors, the 'public,' the world of masculine politics and money is affirmed, elevated" (5).

The term "veiled society" as extended by Milani can be applied to turn-of-the-century Iran as well as Egypt, but not so much the United States, despite attempts to keep women within the private sphere. In 1938, not only were American women already participating in aspects of public life not available to women in Egypt and Iran at the time, but they have had different historical and cultural experiences as well that allowed them more access to public space.

3.1 1938 United States

The early period of American history encompassing colonization and the Revolutionary War could not in some sense afford sex segregation. Women's contribution in the settlement stage and in the war that followed were not confined to the private sphere since the boundaries between the private and the public had not as yet been delineated, let alone assigned social, economic, or cultural values. Many historians attribute the development in the United States of such notions as private and public spheres to the emergence in the nineteenth century of a middle class, who "lived in towns and cities" as opposed to farms "and derived their wealth from commerce" (Hymowitz and Weissman 1978:64). Hymowitz and Weissman (1978:64–75) suggest that on colonial farms, where the labor of both sexes was equally necessary, men and women were partners. "Family" was not distinguished from "work." Although family membership had always been women's most important affiliation, it was also an affiliation shared with men. The situation changed, however, with the more settled state and the economic changes that accompanied it: "Among the new middle class, home and family came to be seen as separate from the world of work and money. . . . In their homes, middle-class women continued to perform their traditional work—to cook and clean, make clothing. . . . What they did, however, was no longer considered the 'real work,' because, unlike men, they earned no money thereby" (64). As a result this was the first time in America, according to Hymowitz and Weissman, that "a class of women emerged who were seen as being 'supported' by their husbands. No longer partners, they become dependents" (65). This was compounded by industrialization, which, after the Civil War, contributed to the further devaluation of women's work. The factory gradually replaced the home as the major producer of goods. As a result, women who lived in towns and cities became more and more dependent on their husbands' income to buy factory goods. It was within this context then that stereotyped images of women and men and their (gendered) roles were created and eventually passed on to the nineteenth century: "In the 1700s it was possible to think of a woman as strong, brave, daring, hardy, adventurous. By the mid-1800s these qualities were thought to apply only to men. . . . Women who were obviously strong or brave were seen as deviant and maladjusted to their 'natural sphere'" (66). It is within this context and in reaction to such changes that the first wave of feminism developed and continued throughout the nineteenth century, demanding equal rights for women and focusing on their economic and political rights, in particular their rights to occupation and to vote.

From this perspective, the experiences of American women of the middle and upper classes are quite different from those of their counterparts in either Egypt or Iran. Having enjoyed more civil rights as a result of being part of a system of government proclaiming "democracy" and "egalitarianism," having participated in at least two wars and a number of political activities including the abolitionist movement and the movement for women's rights in the nineteenth century, and having fought for almost seventy years to finally secure women's right to vote as part of the Twentieth Amendment to the Constitution in 1920, American women in 1938 had already had experience and success in political organization and public work. Theirs was not a "veiled society" but it was not a perfect society, either. The fifty-year period under study here continued to present challenges to American women in the areas of equal opportunities in occupation, pay, higher education, and reproductive rights, among others.

3.2 1938 Egypt

In Egypt, the first part of the twentieth century prior to 1938 had witnessed tremendous social and political change. It had also witnessed tremendous gains by women (socioeconomic, political, and cultural) together with an improved access to public space and an increased public awareness and debate over what has come to be known as "the woman question" or "the liberation of women." Egypt had been colonized by the British since 1882. At the turn of the century, a strong nationalist movement for independence was under way and with it a debate over the nation's modernization and empowerment. The country was engaged in a process of self-definition with slogans such as "Egypt for the Egyptians" gaining popularity. If Egypt were to be for the Egyptians, what would "Egyptianhood" mean and what would this transformational process entail? Badran (1995), in her analysis of the feminist movement in Egypt and its relationship to Islam and nation, argues that this debate enabled feminist women to frame the "woman question" within similar terms.

> While their country experienced increasing Western economic and political intrusions, Egyptian men articulated two major discourses of revitalization and empowerment: Islamic modernism and secular nationalism. Islamic modernism constituted a call to Muslims to reexamine Islam in terms of interpretations, opening up Islam as a vital force in women's and men's daily lives plunged into uncertainties by massive economic and technological change. The discourse of secular nationalism, articulated in the wake of colonial occupation, involved collective self-review as part of a project of national reinvigoration to win independence. Feminist women legitimized their own discourse of revitalization and empowerment in the discourse of Islamic modernism and secular nationalism. (4)

The nationalist movement allowed women to emerge physically into public space. In 1919, for example, and in response to the arrest and banishment to Malta of three prominent leaders of the Egyptian political party al-Wafd, Egyptian men, but more important women as well, took to the streets to protest the treatment of their leaders and demand independence. This event, which has come to be known as the 1919 Revolution, is a landmark in Egyptian women's history since it was the first time women of the upper and middle classes had appeared in public as a group, (face) veiled as they were.

In 1922 Egypt gained partial independence from Britain. An Egyptian constitution was drawn up and adopted in 1923, which denied Egyptian women the right to vote. Disappointment and anger are reflected in women's writings of the time over this issue, reminiscent of those expressed by American women writers after the Civil War and the constitutional amendment that followed giving black American men the right to vote but denying it to American women. After independence and when the right to vote was denied them, a group of three women (Huda Shaarawi, Seiza Nabarawi, and Nabawiya Musa) established the Egyptian Feminist Union (al-'itihad al-nisai al-misri), marking the first time the term feministe was applied within the movement for women's rights in Egypt (Badran 1995). This same year saw Huda Shaarawi unveil her face in public for the first time.

Prior to 1938, then, Egyptian women had unveiled their voices and their faces and had won some of their battles. Women activists had been traveling and participating in various public activities both within Egypt and abroad. Schools, both private and public, had been established for the education of women. The Egyptian University had opened its doors in 1908 with a section for women, although it was closed for a couple of years (1912–13) due to objections from male students. Education was available at all levels to women; some even studied abroad. As a result many more women writers emerged, publishing in both journalistic and literary fields. Women had also joined the workforce, primarily as teachers and nurses. They had developed public organizations in support of the nationalist struggle as well as those focused on women's and feminist issues. Nevertheless, they were not acknowledged as full citizens nor as full partners in the institution of marriage. Demands for the right to vote continued until after the 1952 revolution, which ended the monarchy and established the Republic of Egypt. A new constitution was adopted in 1956, which finally granted women the right to vote. But the fight for an improved Personal Status Law[18] also started before 1938, continues.

The ban on women's presence in public space had been removed; it would thus be reasonable to assume that their presence in the obituaries would increase. Women's representation within the obituaries of 1948 reached 46 percent, an increase of 8 percent over their representation in 1938. It dropped after that to the 40 percent range and has remained within that range. If there has been an increased visibility for women in the world outside the obituaries, it is not reflected in their representation in the obituaries.

3.3 1938 Iran

By 1938, Iran had reached a stage similar to that of Egypt, although it had gone through different nationalist and feminist experiences. Iran in the early 1900s is described as being in political and economic chaos due to "corruption, repression, and wasteful spending of public money" (Sanasarian 1982:15) and to concessions made to Western countries during the reign of Naser al-Din Shah (1848–96), giving Russia and Britain monopolies over the construction of highways and roads as well as fishing, shipping, and mineral rights. The intelligentsia and the clergy had tried to work with the Qajar court to bring about reforms in Iran but had failed.

The Constitutional Revolution of 1905–9 emerges as a major event of the early part of the century, together with the nationalist movement that followed. Women's participation in the revolution and its aftermath gave them (particularly middle- and upper-class women) an opportunity to emerge from behind the walls of their segregated homes to gain some access to and a voice in the male-dominated public domain. The movement for women's rights in Iran can be dated, according to Sanasarian, as far back as 1910 when the first women's periodical was founded (1982:29).[19] Thus the focus on women's right to education (reading and writing) emerges here as it did earlier in Egypt as one of the primary demands made by women and the men who supported them.

In the early 1900s, according to Sanasarian, Iranian society did not allow women to learn to write: "During the Qajar Dynasty, some women were allowed by their families to learn to read but were strictly prohibited from writing. It was believed that if women were allowed to write they would send love letters to men and disgrace their families" (1982:30). Iranian feminists pursued the establishment of girls' schools to promote their education, but their efforts were opposed by the clergy, who accused the schools of being "centers of prostitution and corruption" (39). Within this cultural context and taboo associated with words written by women, the publication of women's magazines and newspapers could be described as a "revolutionary act."[20]

In her analysis of the women's movement in Iran, Sanasarian describes a general discontentment with the condition of women, recognized and expressed by a number of women and men in different parts of the country. The majority of women's societies stressed women's rights as their major goal, rights to education, training, and work. Some, however, put the nationalist agenda, the independence of Iran from foreign domination, as their major goal. Regardless of their orientation (feminist or nationalist), these societies and organizations all recognized the inferior position of women. They differed, as many historians have explained, only on the cause and the remedy. Their publications became the public voice through which they were able to gain access to the public domain.

Another major event prior to 1938 was the end of the Qajar Dynasty and the accession to the throne of Reza Shah, whose reign was marked by a decline in the strength of the women's movement despite the introduction of some reforms early on during his reign (Sanasarian 1982:61ff). Reforms were centered in three areas: changes in marriage and divorce laws, expansion of educational opportunities for women, and prohibition of the veil. In 1934 laws were approved for the establishment of a number of teachers' training colleges for women. The University of Tehran opened in 1936 and the first group of women entered the university along with men that same year. Public and private schools began to expand after the first public girls' school opened in 1918. The veil and the chador (long cloth covering women's body from top to toe) were outlawed in 1936. Although the women's movement had opposed the veil, earlier attempts by women to unveil had failed. The law was opposed most strongly by the Islamic clergy. But some women opposed it as well, claiming they felt naked without their chadors while others felt they found other needs such as the right to vote to be more vital than the removal of the veil.

Although Reza Shah, according to Sanasarian, may have been interested in improving the status of women, he was not interested in empowering them. He was unwilling to allow independent activities supporting women's causes to expand; his overall philosophy was that governmental action was the only legitimate way to achieve changes that he perceived right for Iran. During his reign, governmental controls increased everywhere: labor unions were banned, the Majlis (Parliament) became his tool, and the constitution was changed to give him more power. Strict censorship was applied to the media. Most liberal reform-oriented newspapers and magazines, many of which had voiced strong support for women's rights, ceased publication, and the number of newspapers and magazines was reduced to fifty. Women's publications were naturally no exception. This was followed by government manipulation of women's organizations.

Thus an unprecedented relationship was forged between the government and women's organizations whereby the latter worked under the auspices of the government. Their goal was no longer to win equal rights for women, but to make them pro-establishment organizations, their work being geared toward social and charitable activities for women. Sanasarian has described Reza Shah's interest in improving the status of women as being focused on those aspects of change that would present Iran as a country on its way to modernization, to make girls better wives and mothers through education (68–69). His approach was followed by his son Mohammad Reza Shah (1944–78). It is interesting to note that what Reza Shah did to the women's movement in Iran during this period was done later in post-1952 Egypt as the state took over responsibilities for the social and political welfare of its citizens.

The Iranian women's movement, according to this account, gained momentum between 1919 and 1932, but lost it thereafter between 1932 and 1952, when the government took control of women's groups. Again this increased visibility, gained through participation in political and feminist activities, is not immediately reflected in the obituaries. Only in 1948 and 1958 does the female-to-male representation in the obituaries reach near parity, at 43 percent and 41 percent, respectively.

3.4 Egypt, Iran, and the United States

The historical and political experiences of Egypt and Iran as nations and nation-states also set them apart from the United States. Having been part of the same region for centuries, they inevitably had shared experiences in facing invasions, for example, or accommodating cultural changes in the region such as the spread of Islam beginning in the ninth century, which has resulted in both countries becoming predominantly Islamic. This is in addition to ties, economic and otherwise, that develop by virtue of proximity. Iran had been a monarchy for centuries, ruled by the Qajars (1785–1925) and later the Pahlavis (1925–78). It adopted the republic form of government in 1978 with the advent of the Islamic Revolution. Egypt had been ruled for centuries by outsiders, including in recent history Ottomans. Modern Egypt dates back to the rule of Khedive Mohammad Ali *basha,* an Albanian soldier in the Ottoman army in Egypt who during the early years of the nineteenth century wanted to establish independence from the Ottoman authority in Istanbul. A monarchy was established early in the twentieth century while Egypt was occupied by the British, but it did not last long. In 1952 with the advent of the Egyptian Revolution headed by Mohammad Naguib and Gamal Abdel Nasser, the monarchy was overthrown and a republic established. Changes in political systems of this magnitude by necessity imply, and sometimes expedite, other changes (social, cultural, economic, and political) as a result of different philosophical positions and pragmatic needs. Both countries have undergone such changes, and their experiences have to a great extent been similar, yet different.

Three dominant discourses emerged during that period (late nineteenth and early twentieth centuries): modernization, nationalism, and traditionalism (religious, Islam). These continued to dominate in the twentieth century as well, but within slightly modified contexts and forms. The women's movement in both countries is said to have been framed within these discourses, using modernization to gain a voice and focus on the plight of women and their causes, nationalism to allow them to be seen in public and acquire a space therein, and traditionalism to make their demands more palatable, thereby acceptable to public opinion and to the authorities. In both Iran and Egypt, the state plays a major role in bringing about change since policies are often dictated and at times enforced by the state's agencies and authorities.

The similarities between Egypt and Iran cannot be ignored, nor can the differences. In both cases nationalist interests, of different types and scopes, are involved, and in both cases women's participation in these nationalist interests allowed them to break through the public veils and silence. Egypt's nationalist agenda was to gain independence and statehood; Iran's statehood was for the most part unchallenged. Both countries have been subject to "foreign control"—and both were involved in a search for, and an assertion of, national identity. In Iran the national struggle was more internal than it was in Egypt, where the presence of occupation forces since 1882 had, to a great extent, silenced internal factions.

The call for the liberation of women has also been similar. In both cases it was not a call for empowerment; instead it was embedded in the discourse of modernity. Egypt had started early in the nineteenth century to build a modern state, due to Mohammad Ali's attempts to gain independence from the Ottoman government. The education of men within the professions started then. As men became more educated, and women did not, the difference between the two became more marked. Men traveled abroad primarily to France for education, as did Iranian men. When they returned, they were struck by the difference between women in the "West" and those at home. Thus some men eventually became supportive of change in the status of women on a utilitarian basis: men realized the benefits this change would have for themselves as men and husbands, for the family, and for the national interests (which at times included an improved international image based on a perception of women's improved status). They did not support women's empowerment necessarily, but national / social benefits and appearances.

In both cases religion, specifically Islam, plays an important role. As part of the modernization discourse, some members of the religious establishment argued that Islam was not contradictory to modernization. The arguments for women's liberation in Egypt and Iran were therefore couched in a religious and nationalist discourse—providing support from the former and pointing to positive results in the latter. Opposing voices launched their own counter-arguments, based on these same discourses but framing the issues differently and offering alternative interpretations.

In Egypt and Iran, women, and the men who supported them, had to fight many battles, first to emerge from behind the walls and the veils of the nineteenth century and acquire some form of public voice with which to secure basic human and citizenship rights, including rights to education and work as well as marital and custodial rights. In the early stage of the movement for women's rights (last quarter of the nineteenth century in Egypt and perhaps a little later in Iran), the battle was over the principle of treating women of the middle and upper classes as dignified humans with rights that should at least be comparable, if not equal, to those of men. Although the causes may have been the same, or similar, in all three countries, the details and the timing have been different. As an example, a debate emerged in the late nineteenth century in all three countries about the education of women and their right to work outside the house. But in Egypt and Iran the fight was over accepting the principle of public education for girls in itself and on the basis of equal opportunities for girls and boys. That battle had been over in the United States (if it had ever begun) and the debate at the end of the nineteenth century was focused instead on higher forms of education and other occupational opportunities.

Arguments about women's seclusion and / or veiling have in all three cultures been a middle- and upper-class phenomena. Rural communities and the urban working classes could not afford sex segregation as it was practiced by the other more affluent classes. Women among these groups continued to work and to be economically productive in their own ways.

3.5 Conclusion: The Independence of Obituary Space

The brief comparison presented of where women would have been in Egypt, Iran, and the United States as the period begins and the stages they may have gone through even earlier suggests a more similar place for women in Egypt and Iran than for women in the United States. The distribution of space and visibility in the obituaries, although highly impacted by culture and sex, does not reflect this difference. The analysis of obituary size has established that women's obituaries in all three cultures are shorter than men's, but the statistical analysis could not establish significant sex differentiation in obituary size within culture groups. The relative cross-cultural difference in visibility among women is, therefore, not reflected in the size of their obituaries, taken as a measure of visibility. Nor is the increased visibility of women in each culture group reflected in a significantly increased obituary size. By this measure of visibility then, a strong case could not be established for the different place in which women in the United States were positioned during this period.

Population distribution as a measure of visibility is not as straightforward. It does reflect, and significantly so, a greater presence from American women and a lesser one from Iranian (and Egyptian) women. This relatively more prominent presence, however, is not maintained over time since no significant increase, or even fluctuation, could be established over time, here or in the representation of the sexes relative to each other in each culture group. On both counts, then, the obituary pages and the world they represent do not acknowledge an increased presence for women in any of the three cultures during this time period—a result most would agree is not a true reflection of the social realities of public space outside these pages. Furthermore, if cross-cultural differences in the relative degree of changed public visibility have been established for women from Egypt, Iran, and the United States, the obituary world does not reflect that differentiated cultural change either. It does not discriminate between women and men in terms of increased or decreased visibility over time, where visibility is measured by obituary size and numerical representation.

As a result, explanations have to be based on obituary cultures and their relationship to the corresponding cultures of the world outside. The link between the two worlds will be developed within a space-sharing model of analysis, which includes obituary role and orientation as linking principles to resolve discrepancies between cultures of the obituary world and the social realities beyond them. The model will be developed in subsequent chapters as other principles are introduced to relate the two worlds within each culture group, across cultures, and over time.

Part II

The Representation of the Deceased

Statistical Analyses and Results: An Overview

From gender equity and the sharing of obituary space we turn to gender equity in the identification of the deceased. In the following three chapters we investigate patterns in the naming of the deceased through the analysis of personal names, titles, and occupations. The identification of the deceased in the obituary pages, like that of people in the world outside them, is constructed through linguistic forms appropriately chosen according to context. Such forms would include not only the individuals' names but at times their titles and occupations as well. Not all, however, are always necessary. The choice is often dependent on the individual and on the context within which the identification is made. Context is defined broadly to include conversations vis-à-vis written texts, degrees of formality, and other sociocultural and linguistic considerations. We assume that all people would be identified by their names, by their titles within certain cultures depending on the situational context, and by occupation also according to context. But the questions we ask in the next three chapters are about the identification of the deceased in the obituary pages: to what extent does it conform to or diverge from expected norms of identification as we know them within and across cultures, and to what extent does context (obituary space) affect this identification?

To establish patterns in the identification of the deceased and determine the degree of significance they may attain, I rely on quantitative measures of distribution. These are discussed briefly in this overview within the context of the various analyses that have been applied to the data, the overall statistical results, and the way they are reported in the next three chapters.

I have relied on statistical results from the contingency table analysis as it is performed on Statview Statistics software. A number of statistical tests of significance are reported in that analysis. I have relied mostly on the chi-square test of significance to determine the effect each independent variable (Sex, Culture, and Time) may have on each of the three linguistic variables (Name, Title, and Occupation), more specifically, the probability that the distribution of the population resulting from such combinations is significantly different from normal variation. To measure the strength of the association between each pair, I have relied on Phi or Cramer V analysis depending on which is reported through the contingency table analysis. The tables of statistics (appendix B) report actual numbers and percentages, results of the chi-square test of significance (χ^2), and level of significance achieved (p-value). Where relevant, results of the analysis of actual and expected values are also reported in the discussion, as was done in chapter 2. In the tables of statistics, I have used boldface to indicate significant overrepresentation and underscore for significant underrepresentation of a group.

In view of the relatively large number of variables involved—three major linguistic variables to be analyzed by three independent variables—a number of data sets have to be reported. To avoid producing a large number of tables and to allow the reader to locate the results in one area, at least for comparative purposes, I have combined the results and reported them in single tables for all linguistic variables according to the type of combinatorial analysis involved and I have included them all in appendix B. Results from the analysis of social and professional titles are also included in the tables and in the figures presented in this overview for completeness and space considerations, but they should be viewed as subtypes of Title to be discussed in chapter 4. It is for this reason that they are listed in the tables and graphs of this section after Occupation, to remind the reader that the first three listed and presented (Name, Title, Occupation) are the three major linguistic variables and that including social and professional titles with them here is just a convenience.

A number of combinations or alternative analyses of the data are available to test for effects between each pair of variables (dependent and independent). First is the analysis of each set of linguistic data for significant independent effect from Sex, Culture, and Time. One purpose of this overview is to determine if the distribution of the linguistic data by each of the three variables is significantly different from the expected distribution at the usually accepted statistical significance level of probability (p < .05). If it is not, the possibility that the distribution is simply due to chance, or normal variation, cannot be ruled out, and whatever pattern of variation found in the data may be a pattern not very likely to repeat itself. The other purpose of this overview is to provide an overall picture of how the population identified with these linguistic variables is distributed by sex, by culture, and over time, thereby assessing the effect of each variable for the overall population of the obituaries. Figures 1–3 in the next sections show the distribution of each linguistic variable (or measures of equity).

In addition to this analysis for independent effects, the data are also analyzed for interaction effects, again to establish that the distribution is likewise not due to chance and to assess the strength of the association between the variables. Thus each linguistic variable is analyzed by the (two-way) interaction effect of Sex and Culture, Sex and Time, Culture and Time, and the three-way interaction of Sex, Culture, and Time, essentially following the same analytical approach applied to the nonlinguistic variables in chapter 2. All interaction-effect analyses will be discussed in detail in subsequent chapters. The results are reported in the tables of statistics in appendix B, where I also provide a brief introduction to the analyses and results.

Overall, 3,557 (94 percent) of the deceased population of 3,800 are identified by first name, 1,559 (41 percent) by title, 642 (17 percent) by occupation, 317 (8 percent) by professional title, and 1,264 (33 percent) by social title. Some aspects of this distribution conform to our expectations; others contradict them. Perhaps the two most unexpected results come from the analysis of name and social title. Six percent of the population (about 241 deceased) are identified without a first name. The fact that one-third of the population is identified by social title is also unusual, particularly when compared to the percentages of those identified by professional title and occupation. Part of our purpose in this part of the volume then is to find out which population(s) may be responsible for the divergent distribution—here divergent from my expectations, and not any specific statistical measure—and provide some explanation for the results as they emerge.

I. LINGUISTIC VARIABLES BY SEX

Sex appears to have its strongest impact on variation in identification by Name and Occupation. Women constitute 39 percent of the deceased population identified by name, and men 61 percent. The association of Sex with Occupation appears to be much stronger. Men represent 93 percent of those identified by occupation, women only 7 percent.[1] But the relationship between sex and identification by title is not as strong, although the percentage of 41 percent to 59 percent female-to-male representation by title is close to the percentages obtained for distribution by Name (see figure 1). The overall variance appears to be weaker between Sex and Title (χ^2 = 4.1 and p < .05) than it is between Sex and each of the two other variables. Table B.1 reports the results of the overall population distribution by Sex, Culture, and Time. (Relative strength of association between the variables can be read from the higher χ^2 and probability values reported in this and other tables.)

The analysis of expected values also shows the distribution to be biased against the female population. Had the distribution not been biased, that is, if sex of the deceased had no effect on their mention by name, fewer women and more men would have been mentioned without a name. Specifically, as many as 139 men and as few as 103 women would have been mentioned without a name, as compared to the actual numbers obtained: only 2 men and 241 women. As a result of this bias in the distribution, women's visibility in the obituary pages is greatly reduced because their identification without a (first) name almost always implies their identification through a male. And since it is the man's name that is mentioned, the obituary pages would have an abundance of men's names allowing them to occupy more, and women's names less, obituary space. If space and visibility have a mutual effect on each other, as suggested in chapter 2, then the overall effect of identifying women without

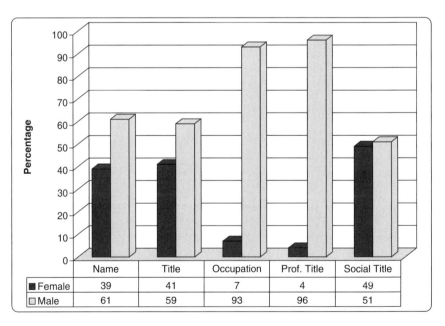

Fig. 1. Distribution of Linguistic Variables by Sex

a name is the rendering of women less visible in this particular medium and thereby reinforcing a stronger male presence in this public space. It is partly for this reason that I have called this method of identification "name avoidance," arguing that its overall effect is to exclude women by omitting their names from the obituary pages (Eid 1994a, 1994b).

Bias against female mention by occupation is also strongly supported by the data. Had the distribution been unbiased, 273 women and 368 men would have been mentioned by occupation, but the actual results show only 43 women and as many as 599 men mentioned by occupation. Bias in the distribution of titles by sex of the deceased is not as strong. The numbers are less divergent—664 expected females but 634 actual; and 894 expected males but 925 actual. The difference between the sexes is still statistically significant, although sex differentiation is not as strong here as it is in identification by name and occupation.

These results raise a number of interesting questions. Why, for example, should there be such a discrepancy between the sexes, and what can explain this differentiated effect from Sex on the variation in Name, Title, and Occupation?

The strong effect from Sex on Occupation is understandable within the context of gendered societies. Sex roles, accepted norms of behavior for each sex, and the divergent roles women and men have had in the workforce are all responsible for the strong association of men with occupation across cultures. It is perhaps universally true that women's participation in the (public) workplace (employment) has always lagged behind that of men and that women's role as mothers and caregivers within the family has taken precedence over their participation in the workplace.[2] As a result, one would expect deceased women to be identified by their occupations less so than men. By the same token but contrary to the results obtained, we expect them to be identified less by their titles as well. The results, however, show that the discrepancy between the sexes is less marked in identification by title than by occupation.

Perhaps the most unexpected result is the strong association between Name and Sex, particularly in light of the strong sense of association that usually exists between individuals and their names, specifically first names, their basic self-identity in both the private and public spheres (see chapter 3). The fact that all deceased mentioned with no name, except two, are women makes Name a very strong factor in constructing gender in the obituaries and in affecting female visibility in that medium. The probability that a deceased person without a name would be a woman in the obituary pages is almost

100 percent, making it perhaps the strongest indicator of (female) gender. It also provides a first step toward an explanation of the unexpected distribution result mentioned earlier, that 6 percent of the total population would be identified without a name. The analysis by sex of the deceased points to an explanation based on gender differentiation since almost all 6 percent are women. In subsequent chapters we pursue this line of thought to determine the extent to which culture plays a role in this explanation. The analysis by Culture below provides a first step toward this goal by demonstrating that one culture does not participate in this variation.

2. LINGUISTIC VARIABLES BY CULTURE

The effect of Culture, like that of Sex, is indeed very strong in relation to all three sets of linguistic data. The relation of variance, however, appears to be strongest in this case with Title, less so with Occupation and Name. Figure 2 shows the distribution of the linguistic variables by culture groups to illustrate the relative impact of individual cultures. English obituaries contribute the most to the deceased population mentioned by name, Persian obituaries the least. This may be due to the relatively smaller deceased population of the Persian obituaries, for reasons explained in the previous chapter. The actual numbers reported in table B.1 support this explanation, particularly when the 990 deceased identified by name in Persian obituaries represent 97 percent of its total population (1,024).

The deceased in the English obituaries are differentiated from those of the other two cultures in their distribution by Name and by Title. None of the deceased in English are mentioned without a name, but as many as 209 (16 percent) of the deceased in Arabic obituaries and 34 (3 percent) in Persian obituaries are. If the results of this distribution by culture were not biased, English obituaries, according to the analysis of expected values, should have only 589 deceased mentioned by name (not all 1,439), Arabic only 548 (versus the actual 1,128), and Persian 419 (versus the actual 990). Thus Arabic obituaries contribute the most to the population without names and must, therefore, be held most responsible for the unexpected 6 percent of the nameless deceased. Likewise, the distribution of titles distinguishes English obituaries from both Arabic and Persian obituaries. English obituaries

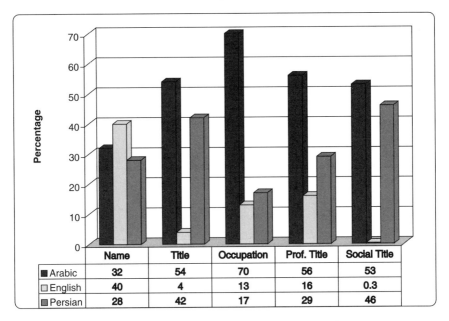

	Name	Title	Occupation	Prof. Title	Social Title
■ Arabic	32	54	70	56	53
□ English	40	4	13	16	0.3
▨ Persian	28	42	17	29	46

Fig. 2. Distribution of Linguistic Variables by Culture

represent only 4 percent of deceased identified by title. By comparison Arabic and Persian obituaries represent 54 percent and 42 percent, respectively. This clearly suggests cultural divergence in identification by title: less value is associated with titles in the English obituaries vis-à-vis Arabic and Persian obituaries. Finally, identification by occupation sets Arabic obituaries apart from English and Persian obituaries: 70 percent of the deceased mentioned by occupation come from Arabic obituaries, leaving the remaining 30 percent to be shared almost equally by English and Persian obituaries (13 percent and 17 percent, respectively).

The statistical analysis of Name, Title, and Occupation establishes a significant independent effect from Sex and Culture (based as it is on newspapers from which the obituaries have been collected). A number of conclusions can be drawn. First, the sex of the deceased plays a crucial role in identification by name. Only women are mentioned without a name in the obituary pages, they are less likely to be identified with a title, and their occupations are minimally mentioned. Second, the practice of identifying the deceased without a name is most common among Egyptian families and less so among Iranian families. American families, on the other hand, have not adopted this practice at all in identifying their deceased. Third, Egyptian families are the most likely to identify their deceased with a title and an occupation. American families are the least likely to identify their deceased with a title, but not so when it comes to occupation. Iranian families are the least likely to identify their deceased with an occupation. By comparison, then, the effect of Culture appears to be less uniform than the effect of Sex.

What would explain these divergent results and the cultural differences behind them? Specifically, why are the results from English obituaries at odds with the rest of the population in relation to the variables Name and Title, and why are the results from Arabic obituaries at odds in the case of Occupation? We look for explanations in subsequent chapters as we examine the interaction effect of Culture and Sex of the deceased on these variables.

3. LINGUISTIC VARIABLES OVER TIME

The effect of Time, as table B.1 shows, is also significant in the identification of the deceased by Name, Title, and Occupation. By comparison with Sex and Culture, the statistical results suggest that the association is weaker with Time. This may be attributed to the distribution of the data over more cells: six Time groups by two values each (Yes and No), rather than just two groups for Sex with two values and three for Culture also with two values. As a result the numerical distribution of the data by time cells (twelve for each dependent variable) yields relatively smaller numbers in each, and consequently may have affected the statistical results.

One generalization emerges, however. Overall, the contribution from each year of names, titles, and occupations increases over the fifty-year period and across individual time periods, but to varying degrees. (See figure 3, where the distribution of each linguistic variable over the six Time groups is presented.) The distribution of the deceased population identified by name over the six time periods shows a clear underrepresentation in the earlier years (10 percent in 1938, for example). The figure doubles (20 percent) in the final two years. In 1938, the identification by title is 8 percent, which by 1988 more than doubles (22 percent). Finally, identification by occupation starts at 9 percent in 1938 and ends in 1988 with 26 percent, almost three times the original figure.

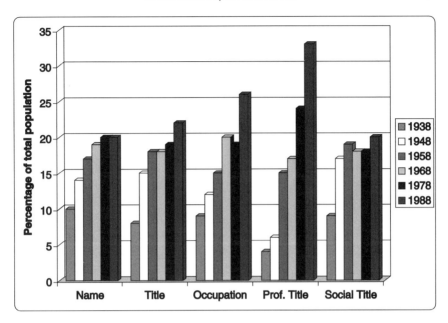

Fig. 3. Distribution of Linguistic Variables over Time

The final year, 1988, has its strongest impact on Occupation and, to a lesser extent, Title. These observations are further supported by the analysis of expected values, which points to 1988 in all three variables as significantly overrepresented and to 1978 as overrepresented in the distribution by Name.

A slightly different picture emerges when we examine percentages of deceased identified with these variables in individual years. In 1938, for example, the 359 deceased identified with name constituted 91 percent of that year's population (396). By 1988 full representation by name was still not achieved. With 98 percent representation by name (706 deceased), 2 percent are still identified without a name (out of 718 total). By the end of the period the deceased population had also changed dramatically with regard to mention by title and occupation, with almost half the population identified by title and close to a quarter of it by occupation. But do all populations change in the same, or similar, directions at the same or different times? In other words, to what extent is the change differentiated by sex and culture?

We turn for answers to the chapters of part 2. In chapter 3 we focus on identification of the deceased by Name and examine the interaction effects of Sex, Culture, and Time in our attempt to understand why deceased women more so than deceased men are identified without their first names. We ask how these women are identified when they lose their names in the obituaries, how this practice may be gendered and culture differentiated, and what overall meaning such a practice may have for the obituaries as a genre and for the societies within which the practice is observed. In chapters 4 and 5 we ask similar questions about identification by title and occupation, respectively.

Chapter 3
Naming the Deceased: Basic Identity

My name is the symbol of my identity and must not be lost.

    —Lucy Stone, c. 1855[1]

Some day we will realize that it is quite absurd for newspapers to give account of events that take place in the Women's Club and list those who attend as: Mmes. Richard Tucker, Lloyd Wright, Pablo Picasso, and Lawrence Olivier.

    —Key 1975:48

How many times a day do we identify ourselves to others by name? Probably more often than we think. We do so in introducing ourselves to others, making appointments, and signing checks, among a host of other activities we perform. How many times do we refer to other people by their names, be it in their presence or in their absence? Probably more often than we refer to ourselves. When we ask, "Who are you?" most people would respond by giving their name. Their response signifies that their name is a symbol of their identity. It is hard to conceive of a world without names. Children are given a name days after they are born; sometimes names are chosen even before birth. Even pets are given names—perhaps it is the first thing we do to animals when we make them pets. We teach them to respond to their name, that is, identify with it. When children play, the first thing they ask of each other is their name, as though without this knowledge they remain unknown and perhaps dangerous to play with. If play is a form of association among children (intimate or at least friendly), it is enhanced by knowing the other's name. The sharing of names, themselves symbolic of selfhood, represents an invitation to familiarity, which for the child implies play.[2]

Personal names are labels that represent, in some sense, a person's basic identity. Other labels such as nicknames, teknonyms, and those referring to a person's status, social and professional, represent identities acquired during a person's lifetime.[3] Some are relatively temporal and may be subsequently discarded (for example, nicknames); others are more permanent—once acquired they usually remain part of a person's identification for life, and perhaps even after death (for example, religious titles).

We begin with a discussion of personal names as symbolic of an individual's basic identity, situating the discussion within the context of naming conventions in Arabic, Persian, and English. We then turn to the analysis of the obituaries and variation in the identification of the deceased through personal names across these three cultures and over the fifty-year period. In the final section we relate results from the analysis of naming the deceased in the obituaries to patterns of naming in other sociocultural contexts outside the obituaries and to issues of visibility and gender equity pursuant to our earlier analysis of women, men, and public space. The discussion further develops our investigation into the status of the obituary pages as being reflective (vis-à-vis their being independent) of the sociocultural context of the world outside them.

I. NAME AS BASIC IDENTITY

All human societies bestow personal names on their members, thus making names an indisputable cultural universal.[4] Naming conventions are centered on a person's given (or first) name, middle name, and surname (last or family name). The literature, however, reflects tremendous cross-cultural variation therein. (See in this respect Adler 1978; Alford 1988; and Smith 1985, among others.) Alford's study of naming practices in sixty societies chosen from across the globe outlines five areas where variation was found:

> In some societies, individuals receive a single given name; while in others, individuals receive one or more given names, along with one or more patronyms, matronyms, or surnames. Names are bestowed according to a rigid timetable in some societies; while in others, weeks, months, or even years may pass before a child is given a name. In some societies personal names are very diverse and serve well to distinguish different individuals; while in other societies, a small stock of conventional personal names is

applied to a large number of individuals, and personal names cannot clearly distinguish particular individuals. In some societies, individuals receive their given names at birth and use these same names throughout their lives; while in other societies, individuals traditionally change their names at important points in their lives. And, finally, in some societies, personal names are freely used in social interaction; while in other societies, personal names are regarded as intimate and private, and they must be kept secret. (1988:2)

According to Alford, the process of initial naming serves various functions. Pragmatically, names are bestowed upon children to distinguish one individual from another. But the process is often given additional social meaning: it signifies social legitimacy and parenthood.[5]

Thus names serve to identify a child's parental lineage and assert her/his identity as a member of a social group. As a result, local, ethnic, and religious traditions may prescribe certain patterns regarding the choice of given names as, for example, a means of preserving the memory of important figures, be they family members or public figures, or as a means for asserting group (religious/ethnic) membership or affiliation.[6] To this end, names encode information necessary for the assertion of both individuality and group membership, uniqueness and continuity—information such as the individual's sex, family/clan lineage, ethnicity, and religious affiliation. Eventually this amalgam of information comes to be associated with the person's basic identity and name becomes the symbol of that identity. Consequently, name avoidance as a strategy in the identification of people can justifiably be construed as a meaningful act symbolic of the relationship between identifier (speaker or writer) and identified, and reflective of the identifier's attitudes toward the identified.

The literature on naming and identity in both anthropology and sociolinguistics stresses the relationship between names and concepts of self and personhood. A person's name is no longer viewed as just a label, a signpost, or a pointer. It symbolizes a person's identity by providing information to members of the society as to who a certain individual is and by providing information to the named person as to who s/he is (or expected to be). The meaning of names and at times their association with ancestral figures, be they religious, historical, political, or just family, may impact not only an individual's expectations of her/himself but also community expectations. In this way a relationship between name and self is established. Thus we concur with Smith that "For most of us, a name is more than just a tag or a label. It is a symbol which stands for the unique combination of characteristics and attributes that defines us as individual. It is the closest thing that we have to a shorthand for the self-concept" (1985:38). A name must therefore be so entwined with a person's sense of identity that to lose one's name, or part of it, would represent a loss of some aspect of the self, as Lucy Stone announced more than a century ago. In fact, in societies where name changes are conventionalized, the process often corresponds to an emerging or transformed identity, to use Alford's terms. Teknonymy, or the naming of the parents by their child's name (conventionalized in thirty-one of the sixty societies in Alford's sample) would, for obvious reasons, take place only after a child is born, thus marking a new, or emerging, identity for the parents. Likewise, in the United States and other European societies, a woman's giving up her family name in favor of her husband's surname coincides with their marriage, thus making the process symbolic of a change in identity.

Differences in naming practices occur among our three culture groups in at least two of the five areas outlined by Alford: one is the single versus multiple first names, the other is in the area of name change.

In Egypt and the United States, an individual is typically given one first name; only in Iran is a tradition of multiple first names reported. "Since Iranians are usually given two first names—one for use by the family, one for those outside it—the custom has been to make one of these Muslim and the other not. The choice is really whether a child will be Ahmad or Fâteme to the family and Rostam or Mândânâ to the world, or vice versa" (Stilo and Clinton 1988). In the United States a middle name is also given and usually corresponds to the sex of the child. It is often used to connect the child to some other person by choosing that person's name as middle name. This notion of bestowing a middle name is absent in Egypt. A child is given a first name to which is attached the father's name, first and last.[7] Thus what appears to be a middle name in Arabic and Persian is actually the father's first name. This practice has been standardized in Egypt, and I believe Iran, making names tripartite: the individual's given name, the father's given name, and the father's last name (which, according to the *Dictionary of Arab Names,* p. 6, may be that of the grandfather, the family, clan, or tribe).[8]

In all three societies, an individual has the choice of changing her/his name by going through the appropriate legal procedures. In Egypt (and to a lesser extent Iran), teknonymy is practiced among certain socioeconomic groups. In Egypt it is more prevalent among rural communities, the urban poor, and the more traditional or *baladi* neighborhoods such as those portrayed in Naguib Mahfouz's *Trilogy*, particularly *Midaq Alley*, or the Bulaq community studied in Evelyn Early (1993). In the latter case, excerpts published from the author's interviews with members of that community often identify women and men through their children's names—for example, *Um Nadia* (mother of Nadia) (10) and *Abu Mohammad* (father of Mohammad) (19).[9] In all three cultures, individuals are usually known by their given (first) names throughout their lives, and in all three there is not a tradition of changing one's first name.[10] It is only in the United States that women have until recently been required to undergo a name change upon marriage by adopting the husband's surname. Neither Egypt nor Iran have had such a tradition, although women may be socially known by their husband's names. In Egypt and Iran a woman retains her family (father's) name throughout her life, just as a man would.

There is one convention, however, to which all others involving name-giving are subordinate: the name is chosen to reflect the child's sex. Thus gender identity can be said to be constructed, at least partly, through the naming of a child.

First names are sex differentiated in all three cultures, although some names are applicable to both sexes. In Arabic, names are sex differentiated not only through connotations associated with names (for example, *Hind* as a woman's name) but through morphological gender as well. Women's names usually carry the feminine marker, graphically represented by a *taa' marbuuta* and phonetically by a suffix *-a(t)*. Because Arabic names are often regular words in the language (adjectives or nouns), the grammatical marking of gender becomes an obvious way of identifying the sex of the named. As an example, *kariim*, which means "generous," is a man's name; its counterpart, *kariim-a*, is a woman's name, and both are adjectives used in the language as well. Although in Iran names have two major sources (Arabic and Persian), sex differentiation is maintained in both. Arabic names for the most part follow the principle outlined for Arabic, with a difference in vowel quality usually represented as a mid-front vowel, *e(h)*, for Arabic names in Persian—for example, Shohreh for Arabic Shohra. For Persian names, the presence of certain morphemes—for example, *dukht* (daughter) in the name Parvindukht or Nashatdukht—indicates a reference to a woman and words like *khan* (man) and *gholee* (son) to a man as, for example, in the names Abbaskhan and Subhangholee.[11] Furthermore, names with the word for God in them (*allah* or a version thereof) are applicable only to men as, for example, *asadullah* (God's lion) and *ruuhullah* (God's spirit, life, or soul). This is true in Arabic as well, where in addition any name with *abd* in it—for example, Abdulrahman (colloquialized in Egypt as Abdelrahman)—is exclusively male. Finally, in English the vast majority of given names, as reported by Smith (1985:39) and others, carry clear feminine or masculine connotations. But naturally not all names are sex differentiated. Names like Dale and Lee are acceptable for both males and females but are also rare. Familiar and apparently ambiguous names, like Jo, Chris, and Pat, are usually abbreviations for longer unambiguous forms—such as Joseph or Joanne, Christine or Christopher, and Patricia or Patrick. Such undifferentiated names, it has been observed (Smith 1985 and references therein), tend to be less popular and lose their appeal over time by virtue of societal and family norms for sex differentiation. In the corpus of Arabic names collected for *The Dictionary of Arab Names* (1991), about 13.6 percent of the names were found to refer to both females and males.[12]

In all three cultures, then, at least one name, specifically the first, is given. Variation occurs, however, with respect to middle names and to name changes. Personal names in all three cultures encode identities of gender, lineage, ethnic or religious affiliations, and possibly marital status. In the United States women have the option of taking their husband's surname, retaining their own surname, or combining both. Women's marital status, and the identity derived therefrom, is still for the most part encoded in their names. Their husbands' names, however, remain unaffected by their marital status.

The availability of such options to women notwithstanding, feminist literature on language and gender has over the past three or four decades documented cases where women under certain conditions "lose" their names—first, last, and sometimes both—and continue to be identified by their husbands'. Nilsen, for example, in discussing sexism in the language of marriage, attributes women's "loss" of name to marriage.

> I looked through a standard desk-sized dictionary for ways we treat men and women differently, and was surprised to find what appears to be an attitude on the part of editors that it is almost indecent to let a woman's name march unaccompanied across the pages of a dictionary. A woman's name must somehow be escorted by a male's name, regardless of whether he in

his own right was as famous as the woman. For example, Charlotte Brontë was identified as Mrs. Arthur B. Nicolls, Amelia Earhart was identified as Mrs. Charles McArthur, Zena Gale was identified as Mrs. William Llywelyn Breese, and Jenny Lind was identified as Mme. Otto Goldschmidt. (1977:138)

Despite their stature, the women above are identified through ("escorted by") their less-known husbands. Key, among others, attributes the practice of a woman's change of name upon marriage to a sense of ownership on the part of the man usually associated with marriage. She compares it to slavery: "[O]n the day of the wedding she becomes 'Mrs.' Like the slaves of old, she takes the name of the man who 'owns' her" (1975:49). This system of naming is by no means universal. Key explains that in Mexico, for example, coming across such a title as "Mrs. George Smith" would be unheard of, for "to call a woman by a man's name" was thought to be ludicrous.

Against this background I turn in the next section to the practice of naming women and men in the obituary pages. I ask: How do the less famous women of the obituaries fare, those who have performed "unhistoric acts" during their lifetime, to recall George Eliot's earlier words from *Middlemarch*? To what extent do the naming conventions of their place and time affect their representation in the obituaries? Or do their deaths allow them to transcend such limitations?

These questions, together with the implied comparison between the obituaries and other forums, are legitimate. In fact they are empirical questions, for there is no a priori reason why the representation of women and men should be uniform across all walks of life (or even death). The evidence shows discrepancies between the naming of women in the obituaries and those cultural conventions, legal or otherwise, governing such practices in other forums or social interactions as those mentioned above. If the obituaries were governed completely (only) by the cultural conventions governing naming practices and forms of address as practiced in daily social interactions, the number of women represented by their husband's names would be expected to be highest in the English and lowest in Egyptian and Iranian obituaries as a reflection of these cultural conventions. The results presented in this chapter, however, do not confirm this expectation. They suggest instead that the obituary pages may have developed conventions of their own, which only at times reflect predominant sociocultural conventions.

2. BUT WHO IS SHE?

The obliteration of a person's identity occurs when all aspects of a person's name disappear and that person is identified in relation to someone else, making "invisible" any independent personal identity for that individual. When a person is identified without a name, say as the father or mother of John Doe, importance is associated with the named (John Doe), and whoever else is being identified is mentioned only in relation to John Doe. The gender basis of this type of identification is the focus of this section. We start with the statistical analysis, examining the impact of the three variables Sex, Culture, and Time on naming the deceased.

We have already established that Sex, Culture, and Time have significant and independent effects on variation in Name (see table B.1). Sex had the strongest effects on variation in Name. Almost equally strong was the effect of Culture. A significant degree of bias has been established against deceased women's identification by (first) name, with women constituting almost 100 percent of deceased mentioned without a name in the obituaries. Divergent results were also obtained from the cross-cultural analysis where the deceased in the English obituaries were all mentioned by name, hence no sex-based variation could be established therein. A more detailed analysis of the data on Name is pursued here, where the data is broken down by various combinations of the three variables Sex, Culture, and Time.

2.1 Interaction of Sex and Culture

The results in table B.2 reflect the population mentioned by name in each culture group independently: the 1,128 deceased in Arabic, the 1,439 in English, and the 990 in Persian. In Arabic obituaries, 30 percent of the deceased identified with a name are women and 70 percent are men; in Persian obituaries 36 percent are women and 64 percent are men; and in English 47 percent are women and 53 percent are men. The percentages for English obituaries actually correspond to population distribution by sex since all 1,439 deceased are mentioned by name. When the analysis was performed controlling for Culture and testing for sex differentiation, the statistical analysis failed to produce any results for English obituaries. But it proved to be significant for both Arabic and Persian obituaries (χ^2 = 356.7 and 46.1, respectively, p < .0001 in each case).

There are two possible explanations for this difference, one cross-culturally based and the other obituary based. The first alternative would claim that this particular variable, identification with or without a name, is significant in some cultures (Egypt and Iran) but not others (the United States), thus American women and men are *always* identified by their first names. It is easy to refute this position in view of arguments and documentation presented in the literature on language and gender, some of which have been quoted earlier in this chapter (Nilsen 1977; Key 1975, among others). American women are often identified without their first name not only in written documents but also in daily interactions. School children, for example, typically know their teachers as Miss/Mrs., or Mr., plus their last name. Although on the surface no apparent gender distinction in this naming practice may be detected, on a deeper level more visibility is actually assigned to men's names since women's last names are in fact men's names. The loss of the first name for female teachers, or any woman identified with a last name only, allows more space and visibility to men's names. Furthermore, whereas men's identity remains stable as Mr. plus a last name, women's identity is variable and changes with their marital status. Anthropologists and sociolinguists have for a long time noted this sex-based differentiation in naming women in various communities: "Whilst men have surnames, or at least stable names with which they are endowed throughout their lives, this is not so in modern societies as far as the women are concerned. In most modern countries, a woman has to take her husband's name at marriage by law [?]. This is being resented by many women in recent times because they see in it an expression of their sexual role" (Adler 1978:131). An alternative explanation would attribute this result to obituary-based differences, including practices adopted by the newspapers. Deceased women and men, under this alternative, are always mentioned by first names in English because of newspaper policies. Although the *New York Times* has no explicit policy on the content or language of the obituaries in general, the absence of variation in this particular case is in fact the result of the newspaper's layout of the obituary pages and not necessarily a reflection of the way women and men are named in the United States. The *New York Times,* like many other U.S. newspapers including the *Chicago Tribune* and the *St. Louis Post-Dispatch* (but not the *Salt Lake Tribune*), lists the deceased alphabetically by last name—a common practice in English for name lists and other directories (for example, phone books). This eliminates variation in identification by first name.[13]

Variation in naming deceased women still occurs in English obituaries, but it takes a different form and may be numerically less significant. Because of the prevalent tradition that women adopt their husband's surname upon marriage, deceased women are sometimes identified with their maiden name in addition to their married name through the use of née. Of the 679 deceased women in the English obituaries, 83 were identified in this fashion. Thus the vast majority of American families writing obituaries for their deceased female family members chose *not* to identify their maiden name; only 12 percent did. The remaining 88 percent decided not to identify the deceased with her own family (maiden) name—perhaps following accepted norms and practices by which the deceased has been identified during her lifetime. Needless to say, none of the 760 deceased men showed variation of this type in the way they were identified.[14] As a result of these findings, the bulk of the subsequent discussion of names is focused on Arabic and Persian obituaries.

Within the context of Arabic and Persian obituaries, women's representation without name means that neither the first nor the last name is mentioned; it means invisibility and obliteration of (basic) individual identity. These women are identified through a male relative, whose name, title, and occupation may all be mentioned. The distribution by sex of the population identified by name is comparable in Arabic and Persian obituaries: 30 percent women to 70 percent men in Arabic obituaries; 36 percent women to 64 percent men in Persian obituaries (table B.2). Iranian women, however, fare much better than their Egyptian sisters when the results are viewed from the perspective of sex groups within each culture. Among the (393) deceased Iranian women, 92 percent are identified by their own first name whereas among deceased Egyptian women (548), only 62 percent are identified as such. Deceased Egyptian and Iranian men, however, are nearly always identified with their name.[15] The analysis of expected values predicts that as many as 462 women and as few as 666 men would have been mentioned by name in Arabic obituaries had the distribution been not biased (versus the actual 339 and 789, respectively) and in Persian obituaries, 630 women and 611 men (versus the actual 360 and 379, respectively).

But how are women without names identified? And what would explain this difference between two closely related, predominantly Islamic cultures in the value assigned to the public naming of women?

To answer the first question, we examine how women without names are identified: the family relationships and linguistic terms used to identify them. Through this analysis we gain insight into how and why women become invisible in the obituaries; in doing so, we answer the second question as well. Tables 3.1 and 3.2 give statistics on the types of relationships used to identify deceased women in Arabic and Persian obituaries, respectively. Four major relationships are identified: marital, parental, filial, and sibling. These refer to how the identified (the deceased) and the identifier (relative or family member) are related: spouse, parent, child, or sibling.

Turning first to Arabic obituaries, two groups of women are represented in table 3.1: those identified without a name and those identified as having a "shared spotlight." Both appear to be identified through a male family member, but there is a major difference between the two types.

A marital relationship (a form of "wife of") is by far most commonly used in identifying women without names (75 percent). A parental relationship ("mother of") comes next; 15 percent of deceased women were identified through their children. The remaining 10 percent were identified by their fathers ("daughter of") and their brothers ("sister of"). Male figures are substitutes for female identification: the women are merged with the men, their personhood and basic identity obliterated. The identified are the women but the identifiers are the men.

In addition to these 209 women without names, about 37 deceased women were mentioned by name but appeared to share the center, or focus, of the obituary with a man. Their names were mentioned first, centered and at times in boldface, but were followed by a man's name, also centered and

Table 3.1. Relationships in the Identification of Women through Men in Arabic Obituaries

	Without names		Terms used	Shared spotlight		Terms used
marital	157	(75%)	ḥaram 148, zawjat 5, qarinat 2, armalat 2	34	(92%)	ḥaram 32, zawjat 1, armalat 1
parental	32	(15%)	walidat	1	(3%)	walidat
filial	16	(8%)	karimat	2	(5%)	karimat
sibling	4	(2%)	shaqiqat	0		
Total	209	(100%)		37	(100%)	

in boldface. These obituaries look as though they belong to two deceased, not one. (See, as an example, obituary 9 in chapter 1.) Women who shared the spotlight did so with their husbands 92 percent of the time. When the statistics for both groups of women are combined (perhaps under the rubric of "women identified through men"), the statistics show that 246 of the 548 deceased Egyptian women (45 percent) would have been identified through another male, either completely (women without names, 85 percent) or partially (women with shared spotlight, 15 percent). Under this analysis 78 percent (or 191 of the 246 women identified through a man) are indeed identified through their husbands. The majority of the remaining 55, about 13 percent, are identified through their fathers, 7 percent through their sons, and 2 percent through their brothers.

In a way the analysis here provides support for the argument that marriage is the cause of women's relative invisibility, their loss of public identity. In this context we recall Robin Lakoff's words: "The sexual definition of women, however, is but one fact of a much larger problem. In every aspect of life, a woman is identified in terms of the men she relates to. The opposite is not usually true of men: they act in the world as autonomous individuals, but women are only 'John's wife' or 'Harry's girlfriend'" (1975:31). Although, strictly speaking, Lakoff's comments were intended for the United States, the results here suggest possible applicability across cultures and genres to a place as far away as Egypt and a genre as unusual as the obituaries. The Egyptian obituaries, I would add, treat women worse than children. In his book on naming and addressing across cultures, Alford quotes Lucile Hoerr Charles: "Naming gives one existence; makes him [her] part of the world of men," adding: "As Charles suggests, naming a child makes him a part of the social world. Just as naming objects and places in the natural world makes them socially significant by providing a common label, naming a child is a part of the process of bringing the child into the social order. A named child has, in a sense, social identity. To know a child's name, in a sense, is to know who that child is. And when the child is old enough to know his own name, he, in a sense, knows who he is" (1988:29). If that is so for children, loss of name for women in the Egyptian obituaries means loss of social identity, if Charles is right, and loss of basic identity.

The results from the Persian obituaries (table 3.2) provide a different picture in terms of both relative size and hierarchy of relationships used. The number of women without names is much smaller: 32 compared to the 209

Table 3.2: Women without Names in Persian Obituaries

	Without names	Terms used
parental	16 (50%)	*madar* 11, *valideh* 5
marital	11 (34%)	*muta'aliqeh* 5, *hamsar* 1, *banu* 1, *khanum* 2, *ayal* 2
sibling	3 (9%)	*hamshireh* 3
filial	2 (6%)	*sabiyyeh* 2
Total	32 (99%)	

in Arabic. Exactly half are identified as mothers, 34 percent as wives, and the remaining 15 percent as sisters (9 percent) and daughters (6 percent). Identification through a parental relationship is here more important than identification through a marital relationship, which is different from the Egyptian obituaries where a marital relationship takes precedence.

The terms used to relate the wife to the husband are also interesting. Four terms were used in each case, as tables 3.1 and 3.2 show. In the Persian obituaries the term most often used is *muta'aliqeh* followed by *ayal*, both derived from Arabic, and *khanum*, which together with the remaining two, *hamsar* and *banu*, are Persian. The term *hamsar* actually means "spouse" and is used in reference to either a male or a female. The terms *muta'aliqeh* and *ayal* are not used with a woman's first name. In this respect their usage resembles that of *haram* in the Egyptian obituaries, as will be explained below. The meanings listed in the *New Persian English Dictionary* (Haïm 1969) for *muta'aliqeh* and other related words include "dependency," "attachment," and in one case, *muta'aliqan* (servitude); for *ayal* they include "wife (and children)," "family," and "household."[16] There is, however, a difference between *khanum* and *banu* vis-à-vis all the other terms in table 3.2: they can also be used as titles to introduce a woman's name. Furthermore, *khanum* may be used with names of unmarried women as well. In the three cases where a woman was identified without a name, the husband's name (first and last) was used instead—*banu Khusro Shahi* (OB#24, 1978)—and in two cases his family name was used—*khanum Rasiyan* (OB#281, 1978) and *khanum Sayyed Madani* (OB#9, 1948). As we will see in the next chapter, their usage as social titles is much more common. The remaining terms, *muta'aliqeh* and *ayal*, are relational words: they relate the identified to another family member; when the identified person's name is not mentioned, the identifier replaces the identified.

Of the three terms meaning "wife" in the Arabic obituaries (table 3.1), *ḥaram* is by far the most common, followed by *zawjat,* then *qarinat.* The words are derived from different sources (or roots) and thus have slightly different connotations and usage. *Qarinat* comes from a root meaning "to relate, attach, compare," implying an attachment of the woman to the man. The masculine version of this word (*qarin*) is not used in the context of marriage—its most salient meaning is "comrade, colleague," that is, someone who can be linked or related to another on a more or less equal basis. *Zawjat* derives from a root meaning "pair," thus implying a pairing of husband and wife. *Ḥaram* comes from a root that means "prohibition, forbidden, sacred, and holy." It is interesting to observe that the *Hans Wehr Dictionary of Modern Written Arabic* lists the meaning "wife" between "sacred possession" and "sanctum, sanctuary."

The popularity of *ḥaram* is also partly due to its association with usage among the upper classes, which is probably where it originated.[17] It is the least restricted in usage, used both in formal and informal daily interactions as well as in written discourses of all types. *Qarinat* is much more restricted; it is rarely if ever used in conversational discourse, only written forms such as wedding invitations and newspapers. Like *qarinat, zawjat* is also restricted to written discourse, partly because in spoken Arabic of Egypt, *mirat,* derived from the root for the word *marʾa* (woman), is used to mean "wife." From the sociolinguistic perspective, it is interesting to note how many words Arabic (in Egypt) has to refer to "wife" and the different connotations they have. There are fewer words for "husband," as expected: *zawj* for written discourse with its corresponding *gooz* in Egyptian Arabic spoken discourse, and the very uncommon *baʿl,* originally meaning "lord, husband."[18]

The fourth term in table 3.1, *armalat* (widow of), also applies to women. Although the masculine form *armal* is in principle possible, it does not occur in the data and I doubt its use outside the obituaries. This may be partly due to the inappropriateness of relating a husband to his deceased wife. In this respect the word behaves very much like its English counterpart, *widower.* Although both (*armal* and *widower*) may be used to identify a man's marital status, they are not used to relate the husband to his deceased wife. Robin Lakoff has noted a difference in acceptability between *John is a widower* and *John is Mary's widower,* the latter verging on ungrammaticality in her judgment (1975:34). The corresponding Arabic expressions behave similarly, although the first, *Mohammed armal,* is much worse than its English counterpart, and the second, *Mohammed armal Nadia,* is impossible on that reading.[19]

If women without names are identified mostly by their husbands in Arabic and by their children in Persian, and if those who share the spotlight (Arabic only) share it with their husbands, how do women mentioned with their own names fare? What about men? Are the relationships considered most important in identifying deceased women and men the same?

To answer these questions, in analyzing the data, I coded for the first relative mentioned on the assumption that this would represent the relationship considered most important by families writing the obituaries. But what constitutes "first relative mentioned" for the above 246 Egyptian women and 32 Iranians identified through a man? For the women without names (209 Egyptians and 32 Iranians), the men used in their identification were not considered "first relative mentioned" on the basis that the mention of a man to name the woman is not a case of a first relationship mentioned, but rather it is the deceased mentioned—her husband's (or other identifier's) name/identity becomes hers in some sense. Counting deceased women with shared spotlight (37 Egyptians) is slightly more complicated. These could legitimately be counted with women mentioned by name (since their names were in fact mentioned), but they could also be counted with the 209 women mentioned without name on the basis of the shared spotlight argument.

In analyzing the data for the purpose of identifying a hierarchy of relationships, I adopted the second alternative. A man is still part of the identification of a woman and appears to be an "escort" for her. It seemed as though the families felt that a woman, even if deceased, should not stand on her own. Although these women may be mentioned by name, title, and occupation just like a man, they still need the company of a husband. Furthermore, the number of such obituaries increases over the years. They appear first in 1958 represented by only two obituaries. The number doubles in 1968 to four, doubles again in 1978 to nine, and finally to twenty-two in 1988. Although the number is small, the pattern is interesting, perhaps suggesting that as women's public visibility increases and as they gain independence from home and family (indicated in the obituaries by an increase in women's mention by name), it becomes difficult for patriarchy to accept the change and relinquish control. (Patriarchy is here represented by the family writing the obituary, which is most likely headed by a man.) Obituaries with shared spotlight, however, represent patriarchy's resistance to allowing deceased women stand on their own by reintroducing male presence through such textual visibility-creating devices as centering and boldface.

By excluding the 246 deceased women for whom a first relative mentioned was at best ambiguous, the comparison between women and men in terms of identification through a relationship becomes clearer. Table 3.3 provides these statistics for Arabic obituaries; it also includes statistics on women identified through men (combining no name and shared spotlight in table 3.1).

The results are revealing from the perspective of gender differences and the perception of gender roles. A marital relationship continues to be by far the most important relationship for the identification of deceased Egyptian women. About 61 percent are identified first as wives but only 17 percent as mothers. On the other hand, the majority of men (56 percent) are identified as fathers, not as husbands. Next in importance for men is their identification as sons (16 percent) and brothers (14 percent). Their identification as husbands comes last; only 11 percent of deceased men had their wives identified before children, parents, or siblings. For deceased men, their identification as fathers takes precedence over all other relationships; for women, identification with a marital relationship takes precedence. The remaining relationships follow the same order of precedence for both women and men: parental > filial > sibling.

On the basis of these results, Egyptian men are viewed first and foremost as fathers, then sons, then brothers, and finally as husbands. Egyptian women, on the other hand, are viewed first and foremost as wives. Their public identity as wives is also stronger than men's identity as fathers.

Table 3.3. Relationships in Identifying Deceased Women and Men in Arabic Obituaries

Relationship	Women with names	Women through men	Men
marital	**184 (61%)**	**191 (78%)**	_88_ _(11%)_
parental	52 (17%)	33 (13%)	**444 (56%)**
filial	43 (14%)	18 (7%)	127 (16%)
sibling	_22_ _(7%)_	_4_ _(2%)_	110 (14%)
Total	302/548 (55%)	246/548 (45%)	769/789 (97%)

This result is interesting from the perspective of our analysis of gender construction in the obituaries and its relation to the social construction of gender. In popular Egyptian culture, perhaps supported by popular Islamic culture as well, women are identified as mothers first and foremost. Among the "truths" passed on from one generation to another is a saying attributed to the Prophet Muhammad in which he is supposed to have responded to a question regarding the ranking of the parents. The Prophet is supposed to have said: "Your mother. Your mother. Your mother. Then your father." The implication is obvious: motherhood as a role is to be more highly valued than fatherhood partly as an appreciation of mothers' work in bearing and raising children. Another popular proverb states: "Paradise lies under the feet of mothers," implying that respect and reverence for one's mother (and motherhood in general) is one way to Paradise.[20] In view of this cultural elevation of motherhood and women's role as mothers, it is surprising—and in a way disappointing—to find that in the Egyptian obituaries it is not motherhood that is celebrated and ranked highest for women but their role as wives. This is yet another way by which patriarchy reproduces itself and asserts its authority, allowing men to reclaim women as their property and deny them in their death the role they have come to appreciate and identify with most in their lifetime.

In more than one way, the obituaries have so far been found to diverge from expected cultural "norms." A number of contributory factors may be identified here and pursued in our final explanation: the cultural significance of the obituaries and their status orientation (status typically associated with family as represented in its male members), patriarchy and the question of who writes the obituaries (typically male family members), and the cultural tradition of identifying women through men but not vice versa.[21]

How do deceased women and men in English and Persian obituaries fare in terms of the hierarchy of relations used to identify them?

By far, the most common first relationship mentioned in the English obituaries is marital, with spouses mentioned first in 1,024 (71 percent) obituaries. It is followed by parental, with 157 (11 percent), filial 84 (6 percent), and sibling 79 (5 percent).[22] Among deceased women, 65 percent were identified as wives and widows, 16 percent as mothers, 7 percent as daughters, and 6 percent as sisters (table 3.4). The same ranking is found for men's obituaries, although the percentages are slightly different, with 77 percent identified as husbands and widowers, 6 percent as fathers, 5 percent as sons, and 5 percent as brothers. The main difference between the sexes lies in the parental relationship, where the percentage of women identified as mothers is more than double that of men identified as fathers.

The results from the Persian obituaries proved to be unexpectedly interesting. Family relationships were mentioned in only 431 of the 1,024 obituaries (42 percent); the remaining 593 (58 percent) provide name lists representing families and individual relatives, without always specifying the nature of the relationship. This practice is unique to the Persian obituaries. Both Arabic and English obituaries always identify the relationship to the deceased of the individuals mentioned in their obituaries.[23] What is most interesting, however, is the strong gender-based differentiation found along this line. Of the 431 obituaries with family relationships specified, 254 (59 percent) are obituaries of women and only 177 (41 percent) of men. This difference reinforces the idea that women's identity in the public domain is dependent on family, whereas men's is independent of it, at least relatively more so. A deceased man's obituary in the Persian obituaries is less likely to mention relationships, and when relationships are mentioned, they are likely to identify other prominent men, such as Muslim religious scholars with titles such as *hujatul-Islam* or *ayatullah* who may be relatives of the deceased.

The classification in table 3.5 shows that deceased women and men in Persian obituaries are identified most often as parents.[24] But the distribution as percentage of the 219 women and 160 men identified with a major relationship distinguishes between the sexes. Under this analysis, the percentage of deceased women identified as mothers is much higher than that of deceased men identified as fathers (42 to 31 percent). For women, identification as wife

Table 3.4. Identification by First (Major) Relationship in English Obituaries

Relationship	Women		Men	
marital	**441**	**(65%)**	**583**	**(77%)**
parental	111	(16%)	46	(6%)
filial	45	(7%)	39	(5%)
sibling	42	(6%)	37	(5%)
Total	639/679	(95%)	705/760	(93%)

comes next (37 percent), then as daughters (13 percent); for men it is as sons (29 percent), then as husbands (25 percent). Finally, the sibling relationship is ranked lowest.[25]

This analysis of first relationships mentioned in the identification of the deceased makes Persian and Arabic obituaries similar in some respects but different in others. The similarities between them also set them apart from English obituaries. Table 3.6 provides the ranking of relationships (the four major ones only) for all three cultures. English obituaries show no sex differentiation in relationship hierarchy: the ranking is the same for women and men. In Arabic and Persian obituaries, however, some relationships are ranked differently for women and for men. In Persian obituaries, the highest- and lowest-ranked relationships are the same for both sexes: parental and sibling, respectively. In the ranking of marital and filial relationships, however, for deceased Iranian women, identification as wife is more highly valued than identification as daughter. For deceased Iranian men, being a son is more highly valued than being a husband. The discrepancy between the sexes, however, is the strongest in the Egyptian obituaries, where a marital relationship is ranked highest for deceased women and lowest for deceased men. Otherwise, the ranking parental > filial > sibling is maintained for both sexes.

This difference between Arabic and Persian obituaries in the ranking of the marital relationship may be explained on the basis of obituary format. Recall that in Persian obituaries (but not Arabic), an additional format is available, one in which families and individual relatives of the deceased (who often are the announcers of the event) are listed typically in a subsection following the main text. An interesting sex-based effect emerged from the

Table 3.5. Identification by First (Major) Relationship in Persian Obituaries

Relationship	Women	(% of all)	% of 219	Men	(% of all)	% of 160
marital	81	(21%)	(37%)	40	(6%)	(25%)
parental	**91**	**(23%)**	(42%)	**50**	**(8%)**	(31%)
filial	28	(7%)	(13%)	46	(7%)	(29%)
sibling	19	(5%)	(9%)	24	(4%)	(15%)
Total	219/393	(56%)		160/631	(25%)	

Table 3.6. Hierarchy of Relationships in the Identification of the Deceased

ARABIC		ENGLISH		PERSIAN	
Women	**Men**	**Women**	**Men**	**Women**	**Men**
marital	parental	marital	marital	parental	parental
parental	filial	parental	parental	**marital**	*filial*
filial	*sibling*	filial	filial	*filial*	**marital**
sibling	**marital**	sibling	sibling	sibling	sibling

analysis of marital relationships identified with the term *hamsar* (spouse) that appears to be associated with obituary style. A closer analysis of the way *hamsar* has been used with deceased women and men shows a difference perhaps due to options allowed by different obituary styles. The term can relate one spouse to the other through the grammatical construction known as the *idafa* or possessive construction equivalent to the English "spouse of." But like other kinship terms, it can also be used to describe status or relationship, particularly so in the context of a list of names (here survivors)—a situation similar to the English "survived by."

When a wife appears in her husband's obituary, she usually appears at the top of the list of survivors below the text, as did 32 (82 percent) wives identified by the term *hamsar*. But sometimes she appears in that location without her name, identified only as *hamsar* (spouse), as did 8 others (18 percent). A husband, on the other hand, has three options available to him when he appears in a deceased woman's obituary as *hamsar*. His name can appear at the top of the name list below the text with the term *hamsar,* as did 16 husbands (25 percent). He may also be identified in the same location but without a name (just as *hamsar*), which only 2 (9 percent) of the husbands did. The third option available to him is linking his deceased wife's name to his via the possessive construction. This is certainly the preferred strategy for Iranian men, as 46 (72 percent) of them chose to identify their deceased wives in this way.

Again we see how preferred status and visibility are associated with men in their relationship to their deceased wives. First, more women are identified without a name as spouses of deceased men, and second, they do not link their husbands' names to theirs in the obituary pages. This excludes their mention from the text section of the obituary, the identificational and more prominent part of the obituary.

2.2 Identification by Last Name

Returning to other aspects of women's identification by name, we note variation occurs in surname or last name as well. The Egyptian deceased show no variation in last names, with the exception of a couple of deceased women in 1948 who had a second last name in parentheses. Likewise, the English obituaries showed little variation. A few women, particularly in the later years, used hyphenated last names. In the Persian obituaries, however, variation in last names was more striking.

Whereas only three Persian men are identified without their last name, 40 women (or 10 percent) are mentioned without a last name. Among the remaining 353 women, 54 (15 percent) are mentioned with two last names. In 10 of the obituaries, parentheses are placed around one of the names. Based on the names of the families signing the obituaries, the two names are identified as being the woman's maiden name and her married name. In some obituaries, such as that of Shamsulmoluk Saburi (Ordibheshti) (OB#296; 1978), the married name comes first. The names and relationships identified in this particular obituary suggest that the name in parentheses is most likely her maiden name and that *Saburi* is that of her husband's family. This is so because she is identified as *hamsar* and dear *madar* (mother) of the following: Taqi Saburi, Zahra, Mansureh, Gholamali, Reza, and Mohammad Saburi, whose names appear separately at the end of the obituary. Since they all have the same last name, we assume the first is that of the husband, with his first and last names mentioned, followed by the children. The name Ordibheshti appears only once in the obituary, in parentheses as shown above.

Other deceased women have their two names in a different order. In another obituary (OB#282; 1988), for example, the deceased is identified as *banu Esmatozaman Sayyad-Safai (Vahdani),* wife of the late Mohammad Ibrahim Vahdani. Among the families signing the obituary are the names of both Sayyad Safai and Vahdani. This makes it clear that both are family names and that Vahdani is that of her husband. Unlike Shamsulmoluk, Esmatozaman has her maiden name given first, followed in parentheses by her husband's family name.

The difference between the sexes in identification by last name then lies primarily in the absence of variation among the obituaries of men: only three are mentioned with no last name. By comparison women's obituaries show more variation. Only 43 percent of deceased women are mentioned with one last name, while 10 percent are mentioned with no last name. The remaining 47 percent are mentioned with two last names. In most of these cases it was not clear which is the maiden and which the married name. For those identified with certainty, 16 are identified by their married name first, 28 by their maiden name first, and 10 used parentheses around one of the names. The association between sex of the deceased and mention by last name is also statistically significant ($p < .0001$).

2.3 Toward an Explanation: The Principle of Mutual Benefit

We have focused on the interaction effect that Sex and Culture may have on variation in naming the deceased. Naming women has been found to almost always be variable. Variation occurs in identification by first name, last name, or both to varying degrees and depending on culture group. In one case (English), variation occurred only in last name (identification through *née*), in another (Arabic), only in first name, and in the third (Persian), in both.

Differences have also emerged between naming in the obituaries, taken as a genre (or a newspaper form), and the sociocultural contexts within which they are written. In the English obituaries, all deceased are identified by name, but in the world outside them variation does occur in women's, and men's, identification by name in at least two ways. One is the use of *Mrs.* to identify women totally or partially through their husband, and the other is the use of a husband's surname, with or without the wife's maiden name. For men, first name is not always used either, particularly in formal situations. Discrepancies were also noted between the identification of Egyptian and, to a lesser extent, Iranian women in the obituaries versus the world outside. In Egypt and Iran there is not a tradition, legal or otherwise, for women to take their husband's name. Yet all women without names in the obituary pages are from these two cultures. The discrepancy noted in the English obituaries (absence of women without names) was attributed to the newspaper's policy of listing the deceased by last name first. Such an explanation cannot be offered for the Arabic and Persian obituaries. Here cultural pressures against female public visibility predominant during most of the time period covered may be responsible for the difference. If they are, we expect the analysis of names over time to reflect women's increased public visibility, an issue we address in the next section.

But in concluding this section and as a prelude to the subsequent analysis of change over time, I outline a framework within which to approach a possible explanation of the results. The plausibility of the proposal can then be tested and modified through the subsequent discussion of change.

The search for an explanation has so far been geared toward finding some reason(s) why obituaries of deceased women in some cultures mention them without names and why this is significantly different from the identification of deceased men within these same obituary cultures. Here I approach the question from a different angle and ask why not. Why should deceased women be mentioned by their names in newspaper obituaries written by their families? I argue that issues of visibility and public space determine the role obituaries have in the funeralization process and the construction of deceased identity therein. But visibility and public space are themselves impacted by sociocultural factors outside the obituaries. This duality, based on a relationship of mutual benefit—between the obituaries and the world outside them—is crucial to our understanding of cultural differences and change over time.

The relationship between the obituaries and the world outside is mediated by the funeralization process whose purpose is partly to satisfy the needs of the bereaved to grieve over their loss and to put their deceased to rest in whatever way they find appropriate.[26] A Principle of Mutual Benefit, or just Mutuality Principle, can tentatively be proposed to capture this relationship. It is based on the idea that the obituaries, written by the families of the deceased, must be perceived to have an important role in the funeralization process. Otherwise, why would families spend time and money writing the obituaries and have them published in respectable newspapers?

The Principle of Mutual Benefit

As part of the funeralization process, obituaries are created to communicate information designed to produce certain results in the world outside them. Success in this role determines the extent to which they conform to or diverge from conventions, or accepted norms, within that world. They change, to accommodate the world outside or diverge from it, when the change better serves their needs.

Their primary role, or raison d'être, is the communication of information (announcements). But communication is always for a certain purpose (increased participation in the funeralization process). This purpose, or goal, can be accomplished in different ways depending on how it is defined. Increased participation is enhanced by visibility and by projecting an image of importance or stature to encourage the attendance of potential participants. Increased participation, we recall, is beneficial to both the survivors and, in some cultures, the departed soul of the deceased and, as I suggest below, to the participants as well. If so, then every word that goes into these obituaries must be chosen so as to serve this primary purpose. Otherwise, why would the families go through the financial expense?

The Principle of Mutual Benefit, some would say, takes a cost-oriented, utilitarian approach toward the obituaries and their role. Nevertheless, it provides a relatively straightforward answer to the question, why mention deceased women by name? Names are mentioned, irrespective of gender considerations, when they serve the primary purpose of increased visibility and participation in the funeralization process. Although the way to achieve this goal is culture dependent, it usually involves perceptions of value on the part of potential participants that may be associated with the deceased, their family, and the event as a whole. These perceptions may be based on the personal (private domain) and derive from friendships or family relationships with the deceased and other family members, but they may also be based on the professional (public domain) and derive from a sense of duty or obligation. Perceptions and motivations are obviously more complex. A sense of duty can motivate participation in a family funeral just as friendship and sympathy can motivate participation in funeralization events involving professional relationships.

The Principle of Mutual Benefit together with the role and orientation of the obituary, as defined by obituary culture, form the basis of a model within which we can understand the results and determine future directions that obituary pages may take.

If women's value in the public domain is not as high as men's, their names on their own would not adequately serve the purpose of increased visibility and participation in the funeralization process. The most status-oriented obituaries are the Egyptian obituaries, and they are the least concerned with identifying women with their names. So long as women belong to the private domain, their public identity is derived primarily from their families and their husbands. Deceased men, on the other hand, gain visibility not through the wife's name but through the other male members of her family. The relatively higher percentage of deceased women identified by name in the Persian obituaries further confirms their proposed classification as between English and Arabic obituaries in obituary orientation. These are relatively more personal, with a majority identifying deceased women and men alike first as mothers and fathers. The least status- and most deceased-oriented obituaries are the English ones, in which all deceased are identified by name.[27] Consider also that the situation in English obituaries is the expected, given that names are symbols of an individual's basic identity. On that basis they need not be explained. It is the deviance in Arabic and Persian obituaries that needs an explanation.

The obituaries, according to the Principle of Mutual Benefit, would conform to or diverge from cultural conventions and accepted norms depending on how well these conventions serve their primary role. We saw in chapter 2 that they diverge from certain norms such as those represented in death rates, for example. The world of the obituaries is better served if populated by men, and so it is. In this chapter we see the world of the English obituaries diverging from what could have been a culturally accepted norm to refer to a woman by her husband's name. But they do not. Instead they name all deceased by their first and last names, which also better serves this particular type of deceased-oriented obituary.

To what extent then can name avoidance among deceased women in the Arabic and Persian obituaries be a reflection of accepted norms or cultural conventions? The answer is difficult to assess in the absence of studies on the identification of women in other public contexts. I venture to say that it happens, perhaps more among certain groups than others, depending on such variables as family background and other class/group affiliations (religious, geographic, and socioeconomic). These cultural variables are based on Egyptian obituaries, which are most biased against women's identification by name. To pursue this line of thought, we briefly examine background information available on families identifying their deceased without names.

In the Persian obituaries all 32 women identified without a name come from Muslim families, which in itself is not a strong indication since the vast majority (95 percent) of Persian obituaries are Muslim.[28] Two men are also identified without a name, one Muslim and one Zoroastrian; in both cases the children wrote the obituaries (they are addressed to "our father"). In the

Egyptian obituaries, however, there is a stronger representation of Christian families. The overall Muslim to Christian representation is 820 (61 percent) to 515 (39 percent), respectively. Of the 548 deceased women, 310 (57 percent) are Muslim and 237 (43 percent) are Christian. Their distribution by name is significant. Whereas 191 (81 percent) of deceased Christian women are identified by name, only 147 (47 percent) of the Muslim women are, a statistically significant distribution (p < .0001).

On the basis of these results, one cannot escape family background, reflected here in the form of religious affiliation, as a factor in determining the cultural value, or lack thereof, associated with identification of deceased women by name.

Another aspect of family background is geographical location, reflected in family origin or residence. Insofar as certain parts of a country are known to be culturally more or less conservative not only in their overall outlook but also in their attitudes toward women's visibility in public space, geographic location or family origin may also be a contributory factor in naming deceased women. In Egypt, the southern part of the country is known to be more conservative than the north. Seventy-four deceased women without names come from Cairo (38 percent), but a healthy 63 (32 percent) come from areas in southern Egypt.[29] Another 43 (22 percent) come from the northern provinces and 17 (9 percent) from Alexandria. When this population is further analyzed by religious affiliation and location, two groups emerge with a distribution significantly different from that predicted by the analysis of expected values: Muslims from Cairo and Christians from southern Egypt. Both groups are significantly overrepresented. The first group (66) represents 43 percent of the 154 Muslim women without names but with an identifiable location. The second group (26) represents 60 percent of the corresponding Christian population of 43.

I raise one final point before turning our attention to the effect of time. What meaning, social or otherwise, can be assigned to this strategy of name avoidance? The meaning varies depending on the orientation of the interpreter. Some, perhaps those influenced by the predominant and more traditional (male) voice of authority, consider it a form of respect for a woman not to have her first name mentioned in public. Others, perhaps those influenced by an emerging discourse embodied in feminist voices, proclaim it an attempt to exclude women by putting them on "pedestals" and offering them protection from the hardships of public life. These may be two sides of the same coin, a reflection of cross-cultural variation in naming practices.

The quote from Alford's 1988 study earlier in this chapter identifies five areas where variation was observed in his sample of sixty societies. According to Alford, in some societies "personal names are regarded as intimate and private, and they must be kept secret." Likewise, anthropologists have reported various cultural traditions surrounding personal names that often have to do with myths and magic. (See Adler 1978 and review of the literature therein.) A person's real name is not made public in some societies so as not to expose it to strangers who may use it in a magical manner. For this reason children in some cultures may be given two names. In ancient Egypt, for example, "every Egyptian received two names, which were known respectively as the true name and the good name, or the great name and the little name; and while the good or little name was made public, the true or great name appears to have been carefully concealed" (Adler 1978:99).[30]

One major difference, however, between societies with such traditions of dual names and those within which these obituaries are written is that in the latter the practice applies only to women's names, suggesting that it is more appropriately related to the gendering of public space and attempts to maintain female lack of visibility within that space. Why else would fear of the supernatural be applicable to women alone, unless, of course, it is to protect them from such forces by keeping them in the safety of the unknown.

3. THE EFFECT OF TIME

The analysis of deceased identification by name discussed in the overview has shown an increase in representation over this fifty-year period. In 1938, 91 percent of the deceased (396) were identified by name; in 1988, 98 percent were, a 7 percent increase but still shy of 100 percent. Although the first three years were underrepresented, the percentages of deceased with names in 1978 and 1988 were significantly high by comparison to the expected values analysis.

3.1 Interaction of Sex of the Deceased
and Time on Variation by Name

Since identification of the deceased without a name is almost exclusively a female phenomenon in the obituaries, the analysis of the data by Sex and Time was not significant for the male population. No change is indicated, or expected, since only two of the 2,180 deceased men are mentioned without a name. Both appear in 1958 Persian obituaries, and in both the obituary comes from the children announcing the death of "our [their] father."

Change over time, however, is significant among the obituaries of women (χ^2 = 72.3 and p < .0001). The number of women mentioned by name has almost doubled over the fifty-year period, starting with 142 of 197 deceased women (72 percent) in 1938 and ending with 273 of 285 women (96 percent) in 1988. With the exception of a 5 percent drop in 1948, the percentage increases every time period as of 1948 with varying degrees of increase, ranging between 4 and 7 percent. Furthermore, the distribution is significantly divergent from the expected values in every time group except 1968, where the number obtained (258) is not different from the expected value (257). Otherwise, the first three years are significantly underrepresented and the last two overrepresented by comparison to the analysis of expected values. Annual percentages are found in figure 3.1 below, where they are contrasted with annual percentages from individual cultures, specifically, Arabic and Persian.

3.2 Interaction of Sex, Culture, and Time on Variation by Name

The analysis of variation in Name over Time by controlling for Culture produced no statistical results for English obituaries, since all deceased are identified by name. But the association between Name and Time in the Arabic and Persian groups is strong (χ^2 = 62.3 and 41.5, respectively, p < .0001). Thus change over time in the naming of the deceased is significant for these two groups. Because men in both culture groups are all represented by name, the analysis by Culture undermines the actual variation, reflected most clearly by analyzing the female population in the two culture groups.[31] This analysis reveals important differences between the Arabic and Persian female populations.

The two populations start in 1938 with about the same percentage of deceased women identified by name (38 percent in Arabic and 33 percent in Persian), but they end in slightly different positions. Whereas in Persian obituaries deceased women's identification by name reaches the 100 percent level in 1988, in Arabic obituaries it is only 87 percent. Thus more deceased continue to be identified without a name in Arabic until the last year of the study, and the representation of women by name in Persian obituaries ends 13 percent higher than the Arabic obituaries (see figure 3.1). Iranian women's

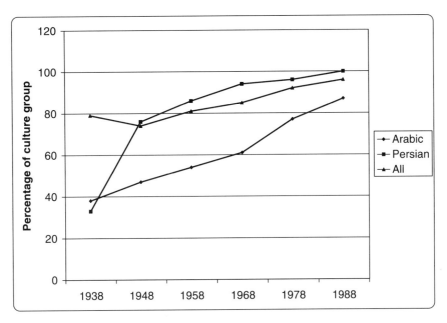

Fig. 3.1. Women's Identification by Name

obituaries show a 67 percent increase over this period in identification by name compared to a 49 percent increase in the Egyptian obituaries. What could have expedited the process in Iran but delayed it in Egypt? Even in 1998, Egyptian women did not achieve 100 percent representation by name (see chapter 6).

The largest increase (over 40 percent) for any decade occurs between 1938 and 1948 in the Persian obituaries. The pace slows in the next two decades but still posts 11 and 7 percent increases, respectively. It continues to slow after 1968, perhaps because little distance is left to achieve full representation. The pace of progress in the Arabic obituaries is different. Increased representation by name is steady during the first four decades (1938–68) but not in excess of 10 percent in any time period. The most dramatic increase occurs between 1968 and 1978, when the percentage of women identified by name improves by 16 percent. The 10 percent gain that follows during the last decade (1978–88) falls short of achieving full representation by name in 1988.

The major questions that arise from these data have to do with the reason for this change and the direction it has taken. Why does women's representation by name change so drastically over this period? What can explain the direction it has consistently taken—always progressing although the pace is varied? The absence of any regression in either culture group is sufficient to support a strong initial bias against female representation by name in the obituaries. For if the situation were not biased, what would explain the unidirectional change and the speed with which it has progressed? As we show in later chapters, none of the other variables have changed in this same way. Perhaps progress has taken the form it has because it was so unfair to women, particularly the deceased, to strip them of their basic identity. For some, this author included, the progress is not fast enough. In 1988, 13 percent of deceased Egyptian women are still without names.

3.3 Toward Understanding the Change

From the perspective of change in women's identification by name, the most surprising result is the difference between the Egyptian and Iranian obituaries. Both start with a relatively low percentage of women identified by name, perhaps reflecting attitudes toward female (in)visibility at the time, as explained in chapter 2. What is surprising, however, is the way the two populations progressed and the different places in which they end in 1988. This is particularly surprising since there is no specific cultural difference that immediately suggests itself as a possible explanation.

Egypt and Iran are both predominantly Islamic countries, although both have relatively large non-Muslim populations. The majority of families represented from these cultures in the obituaries are Muslim, and we have already seen that this population is responsible for 100 percent of deceased women without names in the Persian obituaries. In the Arabic obituaries, Muslim families, much more so than Christian families, are responsible for the high percentage of deceased women identified without names. Thus religious affiliation, if appropriately defined, may explain the phenomenon itself but not the difference in the change noted between these two groups.[32]

Furthermore, women in Egypt and Iran have been influenced by similar, but not identical, cultural trends. Historians of the twentieth century studying women in relation to political and social movements in these countries (Badran 1995; Paidar 1995; Sanasarian 1982, among many others) have, as explained in chapter 2, approached the relationship from the perspective of three major discourses dominating the century: modernization, nationalism (revolution in Iran), and Islamicization (or traditionalism). Both populations have experienced a similar process of transformation which, it might be expected, should translate into similar experiences of change in the obituaries as well. But it does not, at least insofar as naming the deceased is concerned.

Despite the similarities, women's experiences in Egypt and Iran are also distinct. The differences, however, would argue for a more "liberal" attitude toward women's visibility (identification by name) within the Egyptian context. Consider, for example, the following. The physical veiling of women (particularly in the upper classes) ended in Egypt by the late 1920s. Although a different form of "veiling" has been reintroduced since the 1980s, primarily head cover and long dresses, it has remained a choice for Egyptian women, not a state requirement. In Iran, laws have been passed at times to require women to veil and wear the chador in public, but they have been repealed at other times. Thus (un)veiling becomes a state requirement, not an individual's choice, which is not to say that Iranian women have not exercised their right to resist such a requirement or that some have chosen to adopt it because they felt exposed without the veil (Sanasarian 1982).

In 1988 Iran, however, when veiling is enforced and women's visibility in public space is reduced (relative to men's), all Iranian deceased women are identified by name. But in 1988 Egypt, where veiling is optional and where the state maintains its opposition to extremist religious groups, only 87 percent of deceased women are identified by name. As a result, it is difficult here to establish a direct relationship between the world outside the obituaries and that within them independent of some principle that relates the two. Such a link may be provided through the Principle of Mutual Benefit.

These observations argue for a return to the obituary world itself to better understand what the identification of women without a name means in each culture group through an analysis of the distribution over time of the actual terms and relationships used to identify deceased women without names. Through this analysis we determine what changed for this population and thereby understand the reasons behind that change.

Recall that only 32 Iranian women have been identified without a name—50 percent identified as mothers and 34 percent as wives. In Arabic obituaries, 209 deceased women appear without a name—75 percent identified as wives and 15 percent as mothers. As argued earlier, this suggests different meanings for this strategy. Whereas in Egypt it signifies an attempt to link the deceased woman to her husband, in Iran it does not. The majority of deceased Iranian women are identified in their relation to the writers of the obituaries (the children of the deceased). This explanation is supported by the distribution over time, as tables 3.7 and 3.8 show.

The distribution in the Persian obituaries is not statistically significant. Furthermore, the only term that consistently appears throughout 1938–78 is *madar,* as would have been expected. Except for two women identified in 1978 as *banu* and *khanum* together with their husband's name, identification of deceased women through their husbands essentially ends by 1958. Only mother and sister appear in 1968, and in 1978 only mother and daughter.

By contrast, in the Arabic obituaries the distribution over time of the seven terms used in identifying deceased women without names is statistically significant. Only two of the seven terms, however, survive through the final year: *ḥaram* (wife) and *walidat* (mother). But, as table 3.8 shows, identification

Table 3.7. Naming Women without Names over Time (Persian Obituaries)

	1938	1948	1958	1968	1978	1988	Total
madar (mother)	2	2	4	2	1	—	11
valideh (mother)	—	2	2	1	—	—	5
muteʾaliqeh (wife)	—	3	2	—	—	—	5
ayal (wife)	—	1	1	—	—	—	2
hamsar (wife)	—	1	—	—	—	—	1
hamshireh (sister)	—	—	1	2	—	—	3
sabiyyeh (daughter)	—	—	1	—	1	—	2
khanum (lady, Mrs.)	—	1	—	—	1	—	2
banu (lady, Mrs.)	—	—	—	—	1	—	1
Total	2	10	11	5	4	0	32

as "mother" effectively ended during the last two decades (1978–88). The distribution of these terms over the years suggests that women continue to be identified without a name because of the linkage to their husbands. In the earlier years women are identified as sisters and daughters as well as wives and mothers, but since 1968 the only two remaining relationships are those of wives and mothers. Furthermore, when these results are calculated by sorting marital versus nonmarital relationship terms into two groups, a consistent pattern of change emerges favoring identification by marital relationships over the years (figure 3.2). By 1958 all marital relationship terms have also been reduced to one—*haram*. Thus, increased identification by name in Arabic obituaries may be partly due to a reduction in terms referring to wife in the obituaries.

Understanding the change that has taken place in the identification of deceased women by name allows us to draw several conclusions. First, there is a strong bias against female visibility during the initial stage (or years). Second, we must be aware of the rapidly changing world outside the obituaries and its

Table 3.8. Naming Women without Names over Time (Arabic Obituaries)

	1938	1948	1958	1968	1978	1988
armalat (widow)	2 (6%)	—	—	—	—	—
haram (wife)	14 (40%)	36 (62%)	33 (75%)	33 (85%)	21 (100%)	11 (92%)
zawjat (wife)	2 (6%)	3 (5%)				
qarinat (wife)	2 (6%)	—	—	—	—	—
walidat (mother)	9 (26%)	10 (17%)	6 (14%)	6 (15%)	—	1 (8%)
karimat (daughter)	4 (11%)	7 (12%)	5 (11%)	—	—	—
shaqiqat (sister)	2 (6%)	2 (3%)	—	—	—	—
Total	35 (100%)	58 (100%)	44 (100%)	39 (100%)	21 (100%)	12 (100%)

p < .01
Note: Percentages do not always add up to 100% due to rounding.

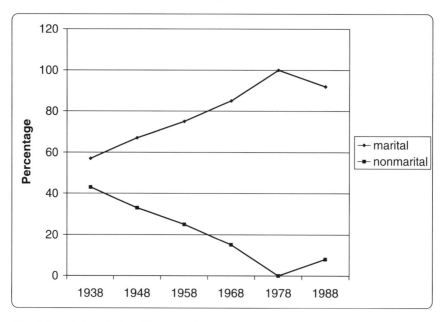

Fig. 3.2. Relational Identification of Egyptian Women without Names over Time

impact on attitudes, perceptions, and ways of life predominant among writers of the obituaries. Finally, we must recognize the role obituaries play in the lives of those who write them, why obituaries are written, and what they mean to their writers.

4. NAMING AND THE GENDERING OF OBITUARY SPACE

If names represent an individual's basic identity, the world represented in newspapers' obituary space is strongly gendered and biased against women. Only women are deprived of their names, their basic identity, in the obituary pages, and when they are, they become totally submerged into identities of male relatives. No matter what the explanation is for this, the injustice and inequity cannot be justified, particularly since it is applied to the dead. Nothing worse can be done to the memory of the deceased than to strip her of her basic identity and to reduce her to nothing more than a relationship with a male member of her family.

This practice is perhaps unique to the obituaries, for no human being can survive in this world without a name. Because this practice is such a distinctive feature of the obituaries, it would have to be ranked as the most prominent aspect in the construction of gender identity in the obituaries and in its deconstruction over time. Indeed this may turn out to be the most plausible explanation for the unidirectionality of the change, as discussed above, and the speed with which it has progressed.

Only some obituary cultures construct their gendered worlds by stripping their deceased women of their basic identities. The *New York Times* does not, which is not to say that it is not gendered. The most gendered world of all three obituary cultures is that created in *Al-Ahram,* not because of any policies that newspaper adopts but simply because of its clientele (the writers of the obituaries themselves)—their perceptions and their needs, the values they uphold, and the networks within which they operate. These all impact their decisions during the writing process. Since many of these factors are not available for analysis, the assessment that follows in the remaining part of this section relies on more available information about prevalent attitudes, events, and changes that may have impacted the writers' decisions in identifying deceased women without their basic identity (names), creating a strongly gendered obituary space in contradiction to accepted forms of individual identification. For, as Hertzler has said (quoted in Adler 1978:94), "a nameless thing is something vague, incomplete, uncanny." Although the writers of the obituaries did not intend to create "nameless" women, stripping deceased women of their identity does make them "nameless things." There is some consolation, however.

The picture changes across obituary cultures and over the years in positive ways. For example, in *Ettela' at* (Iran), women and men were all identified with their names in 1988 and equity was established. This aspect of gender has finally been deconstructed and can, it is hoped, be put to rest in this particular obituary culture. The process is successfully being negotiated in the obituary culture of *Al-Ahram* (Egypt), where equity has not been reached but the picture has improved dramatically over the years.

Positive change in social and political conditions for women help improve women's acceptability and by implication visibility in public space. Such change in turn brings about change in attitudes and outlook, which is ultimately filtered down to the world of the obituaries through the obituary writers.

The link between the obituaries and the world outside is established through their role in the funeralization process, the Principle of Mutual Benefit. Therefore, for the obituaries to change in a unidirectional fashion as they have, a perception must have developed among the writers of the obituaries that it is appropriate to identify deceased women by their names, just as deceased men are identified. This realization and the change it brings has been easier to accommodate in the Persian obituaries, not because of a weaker cultural barrier necessarily, but because of their format and their orientation. Since the initial number of obituaries in 1938 is very small (nine total), the Persian obituaries effectively start in 1948; and they do so with a 76 percent female representation by name, way ahead of the Arabic obituaries' 48 percent representation for that same year.

But the link between the obituaries and the world outside may also come through two channels: one is the form obituaries take in these two cultures. Starting with the obituaries themselves, there are differences in form which may be responsible for differences in the representation of women. The Persian obituaries tend to come from the relatives (survivors) of the deceased and are typically "signed" by them—signed in the sense that names of those presenting the obituary are included after the announcement of death and information about the burial. In this type of obituary, the tendency is to mention the name of the individual. Egyptian obituaries do not do this. In the earlier years some did, and they were mostly obituaries written by Christian families. This perhaps may have been the original format in which obituaries were imported to Arabic and possibly Persian newspapers. In Egypt another format evolved and became more customary, in which survivors do not "sign" but the deceased is identified in relation to them instead. Thus the Egyptian format is more formal, less personal.

The more personal style of the Persian obituaries makes them more amenable to identifying the deceased by name. Obituaries are often invitations from the survivors to others to attend the ceremonies in honor of the deceased. Survivors are mostly identified by their names in "signing" the obituaries, and appropriately so since they are, in a sense, extending an invitation to attend. As a result, the practice of identification by name in the obituaries is more acceptable and therefore easier to change when it involves the deceased. Thus obituary culture as represented in *Ettela'at* is more amenable to change since it already includes women by name in the list of survivors that follow the text.[33]

The second way obituary culture is impacted by conditions in the world outside it concerns the status of women—allowing (disallowing) them access to public space and visibility therein. Although changed conditions in the "world" may not necessarily translate into change in obituary culture, since they may take longer to infiltrate it, they do change the overall framework within which writers of the obituaries and their deceased would have operated. In doing so, they impact the obituary world in accordance with the Principle of Mutual Benefit.

Chapter 4
Acquired Identities: Titles

Tell me once more what title thou dost bear.
—Shakespeare, *The Merchant of Venice*

In the twentieth century, in an "enlightened" nation [USA] where all females are "equally" educated, a professional woman is still a rarity or an oddity.
—Key 1975:45

I. TITLES AND OCCUPATIONS AS ACQUIRED IDENTITIES

People often refer to themselves and others using nouns that describe an occupation or the performance of an activity, such as author, actor, professor, plumber, or blacksmith. The relationship between such descriptors and one's identity is strong, so much so that the name of a person's occupation often evolves into a family name. When a person and his/her family or clan come to be known by the name of their profession, occupation, or trade, the boundaries between personal and occupational identity disappear, allowing for the merger of the two identities into one. Thus individual identity as reflected in personal, but specifically family, names is often derived from occupation, profession, or trade. Examples have already been provided in chapter 3 as part of our discussion of naming practices in these three cultures, and the literature provides more from other languages as well.[1] Thus occupation affects the identification of people by providing a source from which names, viewed here as representations of individual identities, may be drawn. But such names, unlike those given to children at birth, constitute what may be called "acquired identities." They are negotiated, so to speak, between the individual who performs the activity and others who ascribe the label. Thus they are acquired by an individual through performance but given by others who participate in this behavior.

Occupation affects the identification of people in yet another way. It provides a source from which to derive additional descriptors or labels that are attached to an individual's basic identity as represented in their personal names. These descriptors or labels are called titles, and I have divided them into two types: professional and social. The relationship between professional titles and occupation is relatively transparent: they are labels or descriptors directly derived from an individual's occupation or profession, often reflecting the individual's rank or status within that profession. But the relationship between social titles and occupation is not as clear.

Social titles, by definition, represent aspects of one's identity that are not necessarily job dependent. Some social titles are inherited, others bestowed. On the whole they are considered to be honorific, and are related to an individual's social "status" as defined within specific cultural contexts. For example, in the Middle East, specifically Egypt and Iran, the performance of religious obligations such as the pilgrimage to Mecca for Muslims and to Jerusalem for Christians ascribes a degree of status or respect to a person. As a symbol for this attained status, members of the community address and refer to the person using appropriate forms of the term *hajj* or *muqaddis.* In doing so, members of the community can be said to have conferred upon the individual a social title in recognition of the individual's performance—a case of negotiated identity perhaps. The performance of religious obligations of this sort is generally not socially recognized in the United States, although it may be individually recognized. As a result the activity does not carry a social meaning and is not encoded in English social titles. Exceptions may exist, however, within local communities.

Social titles, then, encode information, or values, considered within a community to be worthy of recognition. This information reflects the overall cultural values of the time, and is often defined on a strictly local-community basis. Values encoded in social titles may have an economic base, thus reflecting the individual's worth, which in many societies translates into power. In societies where social organization is based on a feudal system, as was the case in Egypt during the first part of the century, land ownership becomes a measure of status. But land ownership can in such a case be considered a form of occupation as well, particularly when it is also associated with power and authority. (See Ansari's 1986 discussion of the rural elite in Egypt.) Some of the Arabic social titles, particularly those of Turkish origin such as *basha, beh,* and *effendi,* would belong to this group.

Social titles reflect yet another aspect of social status that is very much gender based—marital status. In all three languages and cultures in this study, social titles reflect the marital status of women, not men. We have already discussed in conjunction with the identification of women without names the Arabic terms *ḥaram, aqilat,* and *qarinat,* and the Persian *banu, ayal,* and *muta'aliqeh,* all meaning "wife of." The opportunity did not arise, however, to discuss the equivalent English titles indicating marital status—*Mrs., Miss,* and *Ms.*—since none of the deceased in the English obituaries were mentioned without a name. These have been widely discussed in the literature on language and gender and within the context of nonsexist language reforms since they reflect women's marital status, whereas *Mr.,* the equivalent title applied to men, does not.

In tracing the history of women's marital titles, Miller and Swift (1977) attribute the difference between women's and men's titles to women's participation in the workplace as a result of the Industrial Revolution in eighteenth-century England (and hence to occupation). They argue that prior to that time, *Mrs.* was used as an abbreviation for *mistress* just as *Mr.* was an abbreviation for *master.* The bearer of such a title had servants working for her or him. When women were excluded from the workplace, their status as married or unmarried was known within their communities. With women's intrusion into the workplace, their availability as potential marriage partners became impossible for men to determine. Eventually a semantic shift took place in the meaning of *Mrs.,* restricting its application to married women.

Miller and Swift's proposal is based on timing the shift in the meaning of *Mrs.* with the Industrial Revolution in England, which they present only as a possible explanation since the correlation may be coincidental. The proposal is interesting from the perspective of Arabic as used in Egypt. If women's emergence from the private to the public sphere challenges the patriarchy and creates confusion among its male members as to who (which woman) belongs to whom (which man), it seems reasonable that a system would evolve to resolve the issue. A linguistic form would emerge to identify female-male associations, or which woman belongs to which man. In English, a semantic shift in the meaning of *Mrs.* allowed this to happen. Perhaps in Arabic words such as *ḥaram* emerged to reflect this relationship, after having borrowed the French word *madame* to fill a gap in the Arabic title system. The term *sayyida* must be used with a woman's first name, as in *al-sayyida* Mona Radi (but not *al-sayyida* Radi). Identification with a husband can be added on to her individual identity, as in *al-sayyida* Mona (Radi) *ḥaram* Mohammad Ismail, or it can replace hers, as in *ḥaram* (*al-sayyid*) Mohammad Ismail. The borrowing of *madame,* if earlier, would have allowed a husband's name to replace his wife's, for example, *madame* Mohammad Ismail, whereupon an equivalent Arabic term such as *ḥaram* would have been introduced.[2] Perhaps similar proposals can be made for Persian marital titles, particularly *muta'aliqeh,* which is responsible for almost all identifications without name in Persian obituaries.

If this is true, the definition of social titles would have to be revised. Social titles encode values deemed important to the dominant (here male) voice of a community.

Identification by title and by name in addressing and referring to people varies from one community to another. Key explains that "those who study human behavior have observed that titles of address, use of proper names, and greetings reveal something of the structure of the community in question" (1975:45). These forms of identification reflect the roles people perform in their daily interactions and the relationships they wish to establish as speakers and hearers. Thus "status relationships are signaled in very concrete ways by the use of titles and first and last names. . . . Usage of these tags differs within organizations and according to geography. The use of first names is not common in Europe and Latin American countries. It would be unheard of between strangers. In California, however, it is not unusual to hear a speaker address a stranger by the first name" (45). Unlike in the United States, in Egypt and Iran, talking to strangers, to people perceived by the speaker as being of higher status, or to people of the opposite sex without using a title or other terms of address (Parkinson 1985) is in general not acceptable. It would indicate a level of informality that is socially uncomfortable. Variation exists depending on factors such as socioeconomic background and degree of familiarity, among others. Titles and various terms of address are typically attached to or used with a first name or first and last name, but almost never with last name only (at least in Egypt). The equivalent of Mr. Doe or Mrs. Doe does not translate into Arabic; only Mr. John Doe/Mr. John and Mrs. Jane Doe/Mrs. Jane are acceptable, suggesting that use of first name alone is too familiar and last name alone is not part of the (native) address system.[3] Title plus last name is a combination more often used by those trained abroad (in the West) who tend to adopt this pattern of identification when lecturing and sometimes writing in Arabic. During a conference held in Cairo in 1998 to commemorate the memory of Malak Hifni Nasef and her impact on the Egyptian feminist movement, one of the presenters (also a professor at an American university) was criticized for adopting this method of identification particularly in reference to women. When women are identified only by their last names, the criticism went, they are identified by a man's name and they "lose" their own name.

Titles have also been described as "less complete changes of status" that are "commonly marked by the partial qualifications of the name through the addition of a title, as if to say 'this man is now a member of the Senate, so let us accord him his due and address him as Senator'" (Adler 1978:139). The similarity between titles and names in the identification of people has not gone unnoticed in the literature. Adler points out that "there are some names, like titles, that have to be earned." He adds that, according to Strauss, "Some Indian tribes, for instance, recognized a warrior's major achievement in battle by sanctioning an entire change of name. Americans use similar devices in applying nicknames to express earned status, and by them, can denote a change in status" (139).

Insofar as titles and reference by occupations may serve as naming devices, their use, or lack thereof, by speakers/writers reflects attitudes they may have toward their subjects as well as attitudes prevalent within the social context of discourse. Respect, as many writers have pointed out, is one such attitude created and conveyed through identification by titles and occupations. Sex differences have often been discussed in conjunction with titles and occupations particularly because of the attitudes conveyed through identification or address with and without them.

To the extent that not all people have (or acquire/are given) titles and/or occupations but all people have (are given) names, identification by titles and occupations is expected to differ from identification by name, which is symbolic of one's basic identity. This is so not only in the obituary pages, but also in other forms of sociocultural discourse. Titles and occupations reflect acquired identities negotiated between the individual and his/her community at different points in an individual's life. As such they represent options available for the identification of people in accordance with context and the purpose of communication. Declining the option to use a title in relation to a person entitled to it may serve to communicate various meanings: for example, a put-down, disrespect, exclusion, or simply ignorance.

Within the context of the obituaries, identification with titles and occupations, if it is sex- and culture differentiated, would most likely be reflective of social realities, norms, and attitudes, perhaps more so than identification with names. Since titles and occupations represent identities acquired by some individuals at different times and as a result of different circumstances, their use in the identification of people in the obituaries and beyond is expected to be less frequent than that of names. Bearing in mind that the obituary pages may reflect a world of their own, somewhat independent of the social realities beyond them, titles are still expected to be used more often than occupations since they reflect a broader range of "identities" or roles (social and professional) people play during the course of their lives. This is true despite the many arguments that acknowledge the effect of occupation on people's beliefs and values, thus affecting their identity and social differentiation.[4]

This prediction is in fact borne out by the data. Of the 3,800 deceased, 3,557 (94 percent) are mentioned by name, 1,559 (41 percent) by title, and only 642 (17 percent) by occupation. How much of this may be due to the sex of the deceased? How much to cultural differences? How much to obituary conventions? We showed in chapter 3 through our discussion of identification by name a strong effect from both Sex and Culture, and from obituary-page editorial conventions. In this chapter similar questions are asked in relation to Titles. We examine first the effect of Sex and Culture, then Sex, Culture, and Time.

2. TITLES BY SEX AND CULTURE

The analysis of the overall population (table B.1) shows that Sex and Culture have strong and independent effects on variation in title use. The overall variance appears to be stronger between Culture and Title (phi = .59) than between Sex and Title (phi = .03), suggesting that identification with title is more strongly associated with Culture than with Sex. Recall, for example, that 634 (41 percent) of the 1,559 deceased mentioned with a title are women and 925 (59 percent) are men, which translates into 39 percent of the female population (1,620) and 42 percent of the male (2,180) population of the obituaries under study here. The distribution is even more divergent when viewed from the cross-cultural perspective: Arabic obituaries contribute 843 (54 percent) of the deceased titled population; Persian obituaries 659 (42 percent); and English obituaries only 57 (4 percent). Cultural differences become even more pronounced when these figures are computed as percentages of each culture group separately. The Arabic and Persian obituary populations turn out to be almost identical in terms of the percentage of deceased identified with a title—63 percent and 64 percent, respectively— with the English obituaries turning in by far the lowest percentage—less than .5 percent.

In what follows we pursue the analysis in more detail, focusing first on the combined effects of Sex, Culture, and Time on identification by Title, and then on an analysis of titles by type based on the roles they reflect as professional and social titles.

2.1 Interaction Effect of Culture and Sex on Titles

The association between sex of the deceased and identification with title is very strong in all three cultures. (See significance levels and χ^2 results reported in table B.1.) But the distribution of the sexes among the titled population is not equitable in any of the three cultures to varying degrees (see table B.2). In the Arabic obituaries, women represent 38 percent of the population mentioned with title and men 62 percent, whereas in the Persian obituaries they represent 47 percent and 53 percent, respectively. In English obituaries, however, women represent only 11 percent of the titled population and men 89 percent. Figure 4.1 demonstrates these results, with English obituaries showing the strongest sex differentiation and Persian obituaries the least. Women remain underrepresented in their identification by title in all three cultures.

A different picture emerges, however, when the data are analyzed by sex groups within each culture. A substantial majority of deceased women in both Iran and Egypt are identified by title: a strong 79 percent in Iran and a smaller but still strong 58 percent in Egypt. Among the male populations, Egyptian men constitute the largest titled group (67 percent); Iranian men follow closely (55 percent). American women and men come last. But when the sexes are compared to each other within each culture, the gender gap appears strongest within the American group, where only 6 of the 679 deceased women (about 1 percent) are mentioned by title compared to 51 (7 percent) of the 760 deceased men. Iranian women turn out to be the female group most represented by title, as figure 4.2 shows, followed by Egyptian then American women (whose representation does not even show on the graph).

What role could cultural considerations have in explaining the sex-differential factor in the results? A strong cultural effect has already been

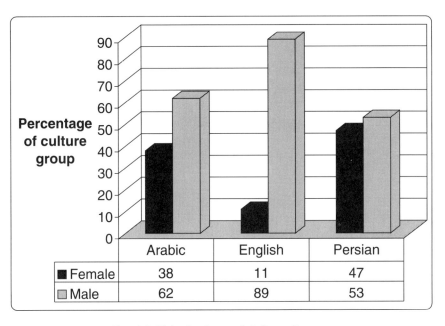

	Arabic	English	Persian
■ Female	38	11	47
▨ Male	62	89	53

Fig. 4.1. Titles by Sex and Culture Groups

established. From the comparative cultural perspective, Arabic and Persian obituaries appear to be more in tune with each other in identification by title. First, their contributions to the overall titled population of the obituaries are comparable (54 percent and 42 percent, respectively), as opposed to the English obituaries, whose contribution amounts to a dismal 4 percent. Second, the percentages of deceased identified by title within each culture is almost identical (63 percent and 64 percent, respectively), with the English obituaries at a low 1 percent. This in itself argues for a strong association between culture and title use. On that basis, one can infer that in the United States titles do not constitute a strong cultural, or sociolinguistic, symbol of identity as they do in Egypt and Iran. If societies are classified as being relatively "titled" or "nontitled," Egypt and Iran would belong to the former and the United States to the latter. Naturally, there are societies that are more titled than Egypt or Iran. In England, for example, the monarchy plays an important role in the bestowal of titles and the retention of the title system (Pine 1969). There may also be societies that place even less emphasis on titles than the United States does.

But how can this classification (titled vs. nontitled societies) reconcile

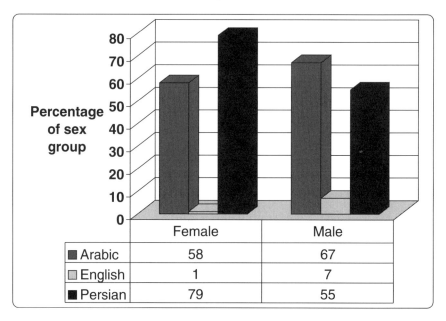

	Female	Male
■ Arabic	58	67
▢ English	1	7
■ Persian	79	55

Fig. 4.2. Comparison of Culture Groups by Sex

the sex-differential factor? If the United States is classified as a nontitled society, why would sex differences be most divergent there and less so in the titled societies of Iran and Egypt? To answer this question, we ask what role or significance titles may have in social interactions and perceptions of identity.

In his book *The Story of Titles,* Pine examines titles historically across cultures from different parts of the globe, starting with their origin in ancient Egypt and their development through the Roman Empire, the Middle Ages in western Europe, the rise of Islam, and the more current monarchies of Western Europe, among others. His research suggests that titles originated with the clergy and the monarchy as a way of defining boundaries and thereby maintaining power within and beyond those boundaries. Titles serve to establish group identity and status relationships, which then serve to include or exclude others accordingly. In some cases, as in the military for example, they also serve to establish "rights of association" whereby officers associate with officers, and rank determines, among other protocols, who initiates what and how individual officers are to address each other.

The United States, which represents a relatively more "egalitarian" and socially mobile society, is expected to have less use for titles than a society like Egypt or Iran with a more defined class structure and a more obvious socioeconomic stratification. Titles, I propose, would be less (or more) significant in accordance with the degree of social mobility (or social stratification) in a society. Furthermore, the U.S. Constitution prohibits American citizens from holding titles of nobility, which not only immediately excludes a major type of "social" title but also discourages a social stratification based on a title system. This does not, however, necessarily mean the absence of any type of title in the United States. As Pine puts it,

> Americans by their constitution may not use titles of nobility, but this has not prevented American ladies, of whom Princess Grace (Kelly) of Monaco is a charming example, from marrying titled husbands and thus acquiring a handle to their names more attractive than plain "Mrs." General Dwight Eisenhower could accept only an honorary knighthood of the Order of the British Empire but his countrymen are not deterred from membership of organizations which, within their ranks, recognize a strict gradation of title. American Masonry, for example, is much more variegated in its official styles than its British counterpart. (9)

Finally, if titles are associated with monarchies and divinity as suggested by Pine, the differences between Egypt and Iran and the United States would follow naturally. Whereas the United States has never been a monarchy, and cannot through the Constitution be one, monarchies have survived in both Egypt and Iran until recently: 1952 in Egypt when the military took over and proclaimed the Republic of Egypt, and 1978 in Iran when the movement led by Ayatollah Khomeini took over and proclaimed the Islamic Republic of Iran.

The arguments made thus far would predict that titles in the United States would carry less of a "social meaning" than they would in the more titled societies of Egypt and Iran. Although this is true for the cross-cultural distribution of titles, the argument provides no apparent reason or justification for the sex differential observed in the obituary pages and the noncorrelative effect between that and the variation in titled versus nontitled cultures.

The wide gap between the sexes suggests that factors are at work here other than just lack of cultural meaning associated with titles (or even editorial policies), for these would apply to both women and men. The use of titles in the United States is gender driven, whereas in Egypt and Iran it is culture driven. In nontitled societies, the use of titles represents the "marked case," the unexpected. It can therefore be assigned specific meanings, sex-based meanings in this case. In titled societies, on the other hand, titles are used throughout; they represent the unmarked situation, the norm. In societies of this type, the absence of titles would be associated with other kinds of meanings. Identification with title in titled societies is similar in nature, but not in degree, to identification by name: it is the expected form of identification. The absence of title, like the absence of name, would then carry those additional meanings associated with the unexpected, sometimes with the more subtle connotations of being different, typically in a negative, but at times positive or even neutral, sense.

An alternative explanation would attribute the sex differential to gender bias in favor of men and a tendency to identify them by title more so than women, as suggested in the literature on language and gender where some studies have documented differences in the ways women and men are addressed within professional contexts (McIntire 1972). This position can be justified as follows: Since titles represent acquired identities, usually associated with higher levels of accomplishments, and since men have traditionally been more accomplished in the public domain than women, men tend to acquire titles more so than women. Consequently, men are identified by titles more often than are women across cultures.

This alternative, to be tested further through the analysis of social and professional titles, incorrectly predicts that American women would be the least "accomplished" in relation to men in their culture group by comparison to the other two culture groups, and that Iranian women would be the most "accomplished." First, statistics on women in the workforce would not support this prediction. (See Neft and Levine 1997 and Seager 1997.) Second, not all titles involve accomplishments in a professional or occupational sense. The typological analysis of titles used in the obituaries, presented later in this chapter, shows that not all titles are necessarily symbols of professional accomplishments and that the meaning of titles may be constructed differently for women than for men within and across cultural domains. If so, then variation in identification by title would indeed be gender based. Our subsequent typological analysis shows that some types of titles are indeed more strongly sex based while others are more culture based.

In the next section we continue our analysis of Titles, undifferentiated as to type, by analyzing change that may have occurred in the identification of the deceased by title during this fifty-year period.

3. TITLES OVER TIME

We have established (table B.1) that the distribution of the deceased identified by title over the six time periods is indeed statistically significant (p < .0001). Only 122 titles (8 percent of all titles) appear in 1938, compared to 344 (22 percent) in 1988. These figures mean that the percentage of deceased identified with a title increases from almost 31 percent of the population (396) in 1938 to 48 percent in 1988, almost half of that year's population (718). We have argued that Culture appears to have a stronger effect on identification by title than Sex when measured in terms of overall variance between Title and each of the two variables Culture and Sex. So in assessing the effect of Time, we ask what kind of effect, both independent and combined, these two variables may have had over the fifty-year period. We begin as usual with the independent effects of Sex (table B.3) and Culture (table B.4), then their interaction effect on the distribution of titles over Time (table B.5).

The results of the analysis by Sex show significant sex differentiation only in 1938, when the ratio of female-to-male representation by title was 25 percent to 75 percent. The distribution of the sexes relative to each other in the remaining years does not reach a level of statistical significance. When the data are broken by sex groups, however, change in identification by title proved to be statistically significant for both sexes, although change appears to be greater among the female population of the obituaries (figure 4.3). Starting in 1938 with only 17 percent of deceased women identified by title, the period ends with a 45 percent representation, almost half the deceased women of that year, identified with a title. But although half the male population is also identified with a title in 1988, the change is not as dramatic. Starting higher in 1938, as high as 42 percent, this figure changes by 8 percent by 1988. Figure 4.3 shows how far apart the two populations start in 1938 and how close they are in 1988. In between, two trend reversals are observed. The first occurs in 1958 as a result of progress made among the female group, and the second between 1978 and 1988, this time as a result of progress among the male population.

While the female trajectory shows a sharp progression during the first two decades, crossing over the male trajectory in 1958 and remaining higher until around 1982, the male trajectory starts at a much higher point but remains relatively stable with a slight regression between 1958 and 1968, followed in 1978 by a sharp progression. Thus the period ends with men's identification by title recovering from its regression and slightly ahead of

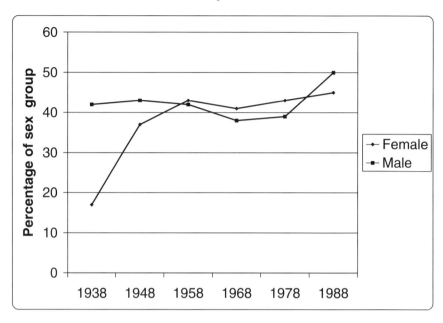

Fig. 4.3. Male and Female Identification by Title over Time

women's. The sexes are placed in an equitable position relative to each other, although the progress made by the female group is much more dramatic.

The difference between the sexes may be attributed, at least in part, to the initial gap between them. The initially underrepresented female group has to increase its pace to catch up with the other group on its path toward a more equitable representation with title. This may explain the stronger effect from Time on the female population as compared to the male. But the difference may also be attributed to sociocultural events that may have impacted the use of titles in relation to one or the other sex group within individual cultures, as will become clear through our subsequent discussion of titles by type. The timing of the weak regression in 1958 and the strong progression in 1978 among the male group points to certain sociocultural events in Egypt and Iran that could have affected the results: the 1952 Egyptian revolution and the 1978 Islamic revolution in Iran and subsequent changes in political and social structures. In Egypt some changes were directly aimed at changing the titled nature of the society, and in Iran they resulted in an increased visibility to an all-male "clergy" and other officials of the new Islamic regime. (See section 4 for more discussion.)

From the cross-cultural perspective, the analysis of Title by Culture over the six time periods proved to be statistically significant within each culture group (table B.4) and across cultures. The direction and degree of change differs across cultures, however. Only in Arabic obituaries does the percentage of the population represented by title decrease over the years, starting in 1938 with 74 percent of the deceased mentioned with title and ending in 1988 with only 56 percent (see figure 4.4). One major regression occurs between 1948 and 1958, another weaker one between 1978 and 1988. English and Persian obituaries, on the other hand, show an increase in identification by title, but they differ in frequency and degree of change. The percentage of deceased identified by title in English obituaries is much lower in each time period than it is in either Persian or Arabic obituaries. English obituaries start in 1938 with 3 percent representation by title and end with 12 percent, whereas Persian obituaries start with 56 percent and end with 76 percent, the highest percentage of all three. The figures for use of titles in English obituaries are also consistently far below those for both Persian and Arabic obituaries in every time period; some periods (1948) show no use of titles at all. Again this reinforces the idea that the United States is not a titled society whereas Egypt and Iran are much more so. Figure 4.4 clearly demonstrates this remarkable difference.

Despite the apparent indifference to identification by title in English obituaries, a level higher than 10 percent is finally reached in 1988. Arabic obituaries start out with the highest figures, but their overall pattern is one of regression with a major drop in 1958 followed by a period of stability. The period ends with another drop in 1988, taking identification by title in Arabic obituaries to its lowest point and exactly where the Persian obituaries had started in 1938. The most positive movement in identification by title, however, comes from the Persian obituaries. A strong progression occurs through the first thirty years, peaking in 1958 and then followed by an almost equally strong regression in 1968. Identification by title remains stable through 1978, after which a tremendous upward movement in 1988 posts the sharpest increase among the three cultures, exceeding even the initial level at which the Arabic obituaries had started in 1938.

The final year emerges as the most remarkable for all three. The only culture with a declining representation by title (Arabic) reaches its lowest point, and cultures reflecting an overall increase (English and Persian) demonstrate it most markedly in 1988. Representation by title in English obituaries

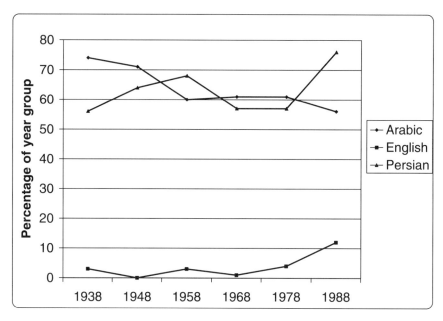

Fig. 4.4. Identification by Title across Cultures and over Time

(12 percent) reflects an increase of almost 8 percent over the 1978 figure (4 percent), and in Persian obituaries, a more impressive 20 percent increase is posted. Furthermore, the 28 deceased identified by title in 1988 represent almost half (49 percent) the titled population (57) of the English obituaries. The change in the Persian obituaries is also quite dramatic, but perhaps less so by comparison to the English obituaries. The 182 deceased identified with titles in 1988 constitute 28 percent of the Persian titled population, a figure less dramatic than the English 49 percent. But because the initial 1938 figures are better for English obituaries than they are for Persian obituaries (14 percent and 1 percent, respectively), the final 28 percent in Persian appears stronger in some sense, being twenty-eight times the initial figure.

What external events could have induced such changes? Or could the change be internal to the obituary pages? We return to this question later when the typological analysis of titles has been completed. But here it is tempting to suggest that the second trend reversal (upward) in Persian obituaries may have been influenced by changes brought about by the establishment of the Islamic Republic subsequent to the overthrow of the monarchy in 1978. Likewise, it is tempting to suggest that the decrease in identification by title in the Arabic obituaries is also a reflection of changes introduced by similar circumstances in Egypt: the overthrow of the monarchy and subsequent establishment of the Republic of Egypt in 1952. As for the English obituaries, the 1978–88 change can be explained by a combination of obituary-page effects and sociocultural changes affecting the importance of titles in certain cultural contexts.

3.1 Interaction Effect of Sex, Culture, and Time on Titled Population

Thus far the analysis of titles by Sex has shown that the female population is more responsible for the overall increase in identification by title than is the male population (figure 4.3). The analysis by Culture has shown that English and Persian obituaries show an increase in identification by title, whereas Arabic obituaries show a decrease. Now we ask how identification by title may have been impacted by the interaction of all three variables—Sex, Culture, and Time. Because four variables are now involved, more alternative analyses of the data are available, depending on which two of the four variables are controlled for. Although these alternatives have all been examined in our assessment of the interaction effects, we here discuss one statistical analysis that proved to be significant for both sex groups (table B.5). This analysis tests for cross-cultural effects on the distribution of titles for each sex group independently (see figures 4.5 and 4.6).

Figure 4.5, for example, shows that in 1938 no women are identified by title in the Persian obituaries. The 30 titled women in Arabic obituaries represent 97 percent of the titled women (31); the one titled woman in the English obituaries represents 3 percent of that population. By comparison, in 1988 the 74 titled women from Persian obituaries represent 57 percent of that year's 215 titled females. Figure 4.6 presents similar analysis of the male population. Both figures also present a view of the distribution of titles as space: how female and male title space is shared each year by cultures and how, as a result, Time may have affected the cultural occupation of that space as a reflection of the changing space-sharing of the sexes within the obituaries.

Tremendous cross-cultural effects emerge from these figures. The overall tendency for some cultures (Persian) is to increase their occupation of title space, others (Arabic) to decrease it, and others (English) to show little or no interest in occupying that space. Cultures also differ in the way they increase or decrease their share of obituary space over the years depending

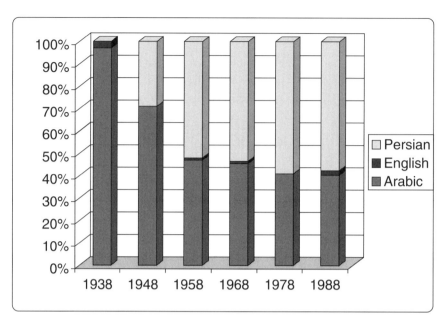

Fig. 4.5. Distribution of Titles by Culture Group (Women)

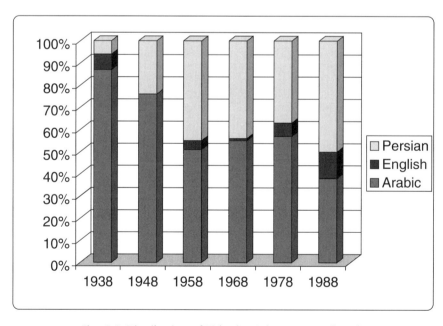

Fig. 4.6. Distribution of Titles by Culture Group (Men)

on sex groups. Among the female group, for example, the space given up by Arabic increases the Persian share since English is not interacting in this population. Among the male group, however, the interaction from English is a little stronger, particularly in 1988 and less so in 1978. From the perspective of time periods when such changes are strongest, the year 1958 is interesting for both sex populations as is the 1978–88 decade among the males. Prior to 1958, the two populations move in opposite directions: a dramatic regression among the Arabic population (both sexes) and an almost equally dramatic progression among the Persian population. After that, the occupation of title space remains fairly stable for both sex groups until the final year when a shift appears among the males. Both Persian and English increase their share while Arabic loses more of its space.[5]

Both populations changed over this fifty-year period in their occupation of obituary space due to culture effects over time. On that basis, we can now attribute the increase in identification by title in 1988 primarily to culture effects and secondarily to sex. For example, the results from the English obituaries in 1988, although due to a cultural effect, are also due to a sex effect since only the male group showed dramatic change. Likewise, the increase in the Persian obituaries' percentages, a culture effect, can also be viewed as a secondary sex effect since the figures in 1938 were for the male group only.

Finally, sex of the deceased can still influence change over time indirectly through culture effects in yet another way: when sex differences happen to be significant in one but not other cultures. Identification by title in Persian obituaries is one such case. When the data were analyzed for sex differences over time independently in each culture group, statistical significance was obtained only for Persian obituaries due to the underrepresentation of females in 1938. Figure 4.7 demonstrates how the movement within that space proceeds from an initial all-male titled population in 1938 to a more evenly divided title space in 1948. The share of title space remains unchanged until 1978, when the female share increases and for the first time exceeds the male share, only to decrease in 1988. Thus, the fifty-year period begins and ends with male domination of title space, starting with 100 percent and ending with 59 percent. In between, the space is more or less equitably distributed between the sexes.

Iranian women's representation by title begins in 1948 at 46 percent, slightly lower than Iranian men's 54 percent. This, after all, is a title-oriented society, where titles would be applied to both sexes assuming norms of usage

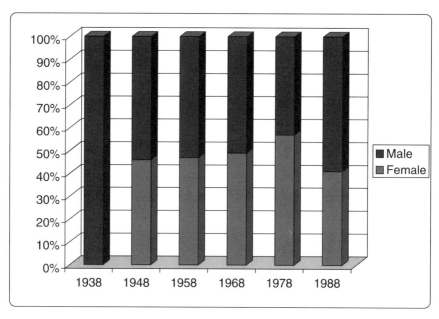

Fig. 4.7. Title Space in Persian Obituaries by Sex over Time

free of bias or other influences, which is how we can characterize the 1948–68 period. But in 1978 female occupation of title space increases and surpasses that of men, reaching its all-time high of 57 percent. This trend is reversed, however, in 1988 when male occupation of title space reduces the female share to only 41 percent, ending the period with the widest gap between the sexes.

The effect of Culture is clearly stronger than Sex in determining the shares of title space over time. But Sex has its own independent effect, although its effect is weaker in any analysis combined with Culture.

3.2 Toward Understanding the Change

Although both Culture and Sex have strong effects on change in the identification of the deceased by title, this is more a culture- than sex-based variation. Cultural factors from the world outside the obituaries strongly affect the change. The difference between Arabic and Persian obituaries illustrates this point. Egypt, like Iran, is a title-oriented society, but it is also a society that has experienced a reduction in the value assigned to titles over the fifty-year period, which can explain the difference in the direction of change between the two obituary cultures. However, it does not explain the sex-differentiated nature of the change in its interaction with culture, in particular why the change is sex differentiated in Persian obituaries but not Arabic obituaries.

Within the context of the obituaries it appears that when titles are introduced, they are first applied to men, perhaps because of their value as status indicators and identity builders on both social and professional levels. This is particularly true of the English obituaries. In nontitled societies like the United States, the application of titles to women begins after they have been established for men. On the other hand, in a title-oriented society like Egypt (and Iran), the process is slightly different. Because the cultural norm in this case favors the use of titles, their applicability to women would be in conformity, not opposition, to this norm. Such a change can spread faster since it would face little resistance from voices of authority, typically supportive of such accepted norms and of the status quo. (But once accepted, it would then be resistant to change.) In both types of societies, however, as reflected in their obituary cultures, a pattern is established first among the male population, which then spreads to the female population. As a result, change in perception and representation tends to be slower in relation to women than men.

Support for this idea comes from outside the obituaries, if indeed men are in control of public space and decisions about the distribution of that space. Earlier discussions of women and men in public space (chapter 2) support this view. In addition, gender studies point to the domination of public space by men as one of the possible causes for what is perceived as "the oppression of women." Philip Smith, for example, writes: "Men, in their dominant public roles, are seen not only to control access to public forums and communications resources, but even to control the conventions according to which experience is defined and articulated. Men are seen to be dominant: women are perceived to be muted, and one consequence may be that they find it difficult to gain access to the conceptual tools that would enable them to articulate their experience and change their position" (1985:56). Quoting Dale Spender, he concludes with a statement that perhaps best describes the situation in the obituary pages: men are the namers, women, the named. This is especially relevant to questions raised earlier about who writes the obituaries, who makes the decisions, and who decides the overall form and content in the obituaries. If public space and decisions about it are indeed controlled by men, women's admission to and subsequent occupation of that space would be dependent on their acceptance by men therein. It would follow that women would lag behind in their occupation of public space.

Women's attempts to share public space have been successful at times, but not so much at others; women's history across cultures is full of such examples. To gain access to the public domain and have a voice in it, the women's movements in Egypt and Iran (and earlier in the United States) framed their discourse within the nationalist agenda of the time. The struggle for the right to vote took many years not only in these three societies, but worldwide as well. Battles for equal rights to education, work, and access to other public domains have been won in many cases although inequity still persists.

I have interpreted increase versus decrease in representation by title as a case of bias against women and favor toward men on the assumption that the use of titles has a sociocultural meaning associated with status and respect. Other interpretations are possible, however. One can argue, for example, that decrease over the years in identification by titles is a positive sign, a liberating force that frees individuals and groups from traditional forms of identification and allows for newly formed identities to emerge independent of past norms. It may mean that families writing obituaries for their deceased women identify them as individuals independent of the social "padding" titles offer in traditional identification of deceased men. Since the widest gap between the sexes is in 1988 Iran, how we choose to interpret the gap depends on our interpretation of what titles mean within their social context and in relation to the sexes. Further insight into the sociocultural meaning and significance of titles will emerge from our subsequent analysis of titles by type, combined with an analysis of the cultural contexts within which they are used and differences in their application to women and men within the obituaries.

The results thus far, however, confirm that two specific time periods need further investigation: 1958 and 1988. If it is true that the United States is not a title-oriented society, the picture represented in figure 4.6 suggests a change may be in progress within American obituary culture toward an increased title orientation. This change is first reflected among the male population of the obituaries, as a comparison of the English share of the obituaries in figures 4.5 and 4.6 shows. Men are the pacesetters in obituary space just as they are in other public domains. Although this is true of Arabic and Persian obituaries as well, it is not as clearly demonstrated from the title data for two reasons: the effect of obituary culture and the titled nature of these societies. Only Persian obituaries show how women intrude into title space and how, once in, they make tremendous leaps forward since the change conforms to an accepted social norm: identification by title in a formal setting within a public domain such as obituaries.

Compare the progress made by Iranian and American women in figure 4.5. Iranian titled women move from occupying no obituary space in 1938 to more than half the space available in 1958 while American women make almost no progress. Perhaps this is so because obituary culture in the United States has not yet established identification by title as a norm for the male population. It would follow that if and when it does, the female population would likewise change as writers of the obituaries come to accept first identification by title in the obituary pages as a norm then its application to women. Obviously deceased women (and men) are not the players here. Their identity is created in obituary space through other family members, many of whom may in fact be men. It is this changed perception (predominantly male) that is reflected in the obituary pages. But it is ultimately women's achievements in their lifetime that bring about this changed perception, allowing their families and other writers of the obituaries to experience the change and eventually pass it on to the obituaries.

The year 1988 is important for the Arabic and Persian obituaries as well. In Iran, where the change is sex differentiated, 1988 is the year with the widest gap between the sexes. It is also one where the sexes experience a trend reversal in terms of their patterns of change in the occupation of title space. Women's share of title space is reduced by 16 percent and men's increased 17 percent by comparison to the previous year (figure 4.7). These results, particularly the timing, suggest external effects. It is tempting, as suggested earlier, to attribute this dramatic change to the Islamic regime and possible subsequent changes, in policy or otherwise, more favorable to male authority and the strengthening of its visibility within the public domain. The obituaries, being part of that public space, would also be affected by such a change in the social perception of public authority and the sharing of public space. After women's share of title space had been established in 1948, the only dramatic change in the allotment of that space occurs in 1988 postrevolutionary Iran, favoring the titled male population and disfavoring the female. This proposition can be further confirmed through the analysis of titles by type. If the increase appears to be in the area of religious titles, for example, then this would lend further support for this hypothesis.

Finally, in the Arabic obituaries, 1958 emerges as another important year in identification by title. Although not sex differentiated, the occupation of title space dropped that year. This reduced space is maintained until 1988, when the male population experiences another reduction in its share of title space. So why this overall decrease for Arabic, and why 1958? The explanation I propose attributes this change to the post-1952 era when titles connected with the previous monarchy were abolished as part of a policy promoting equity among socioeconomic groups. The following discussion of titles by type, and later of their content, elaborates on this idea and provides further support for it.

4. SOCIAL AND PROFESSIONAL TITLES

Starting from the position that titles are linguistic symbols of identities or roles acquired during a person's lifetime and that people in general move in more than one domain during their lifetime, I have taken titles as symbolic representations of such acquired identities. Accordingly, they would reflect two types of realities or identities. One is available through involvement in a professional, job-related environment and the identities derived from it. The other reflects the social, day-to-day interactions and the identities developed therefrom.[6] Thus professional titles are symbolic of professional affiliation and the status attained therein, and social titles are symbolic of values appreciated within a community such as honor, respect, and formality, which are all related to "social status."[7] Clearly these two title types are not mutually exclusive. Some people may have both and value both, while others may value one more than the other. Others, however, may move within only one plane: their everyday social reality. All people move within that plane; only some move within both. For this reason, titles in obituary culture are expected to reflect both social and professional identities for the deceased, symbolically reflecting the types of planes within which they may have moved—or have been perceived by their families to have moved—during their lifetime. By analyzing titles within these more specific dimensions, a better connection can be made between the results obtained so far from the analysis of titles in the obituaries and their sociocultural contexts.

We can ask, as we have done before, why more men are identified by titles in the English obituaries, culturally situated as they are in a nontitled society. The answer becomes obvious when we learn, as we will below, that all titles in the English obituaries, except four, are professional titles and that the classification of societies as titled/nontitled is based primarily on the existence of social titles such as titles of nobility and social status. Since having an occupation (public domain) has traditionally been more strongly associated with men than with women, it follows that titles in a "nontitled" society would be derived mostly from the professional plane.

The overall analysis of titles by type confirms the idea that among the deceased population, identities are derived more from social than professional planes. Social titles are much more widely used in identifying the deceased: 1,264 deceased representing 33 percent of the total deceased population (3,800) are identified with a social title compared to only 327 (9 percent) identified with a professional title.[8] The statistical analysis (table B.1) confirms further the statistical significance of each of the independent variables Sex, Culture, and Time on identification with social and professional titles.

The effect of Sex appears to be stronger on professional titles than on social titles. This is suggested by the higher degree of the association of variance between Sex and Professional Title (phi = .24) versus Sex and Social Title (phi = .9) and by the percentage differences between the sexes. The distribution of social titles shows an almost equal division between the sexes: 49 percent women and 51 percent men. (See figure 1 in the overview.) Professional titles, on the other hand, are quite divergent; women constitute only 4 percent of deceased identified with a professional title and men 96 percent. Interestingly enough, the reverse effect is obtained for Culture, where the overall variance appears to be stronger with Social Title instead (phi = .55 for Social and phi = .15 for Professional). Only in English are more deceased identified with professional than with social titles, confirming the classification of the United States as a nontitled society where titles are more meaningful, or valuable within this cultural context, when symbolic of professional not social status.

When social and professional titles are analyzed in relation to each sex group, social titles are found to be more evenly distributed between the sexes, only slightly favoring women: 38 percent of deceased females (1,620) and 30 percent of deceased men (2,180) are mentioned with a social title. Less than 1 percent of the female population, however, are identified with a professional title compared to 13 percent of the male population. This discrepancy between the sexes is divergent and in some ways expected, but not to the degree attained, if obituaries are assumed to reflect the socioprofessional realities within which the deceased may have moved during their lifetime and from which they would have acquired their linguistic symbols of identity. The participation of women, particularly those from the middle and upper social strata whom we assume populate the obituaries, has typically lagged behind that of men in the professional and occupational domain. As a result they may not have developed a strong sense of identity derived from participation within that plane, hence the divergence in the figures between the sexes. Within the social plane, however, where both sexes would have been strong participants, the figures are less divergent.

Titles as linguistic symbols of acquired identities are expected to be a true representation of their role within the sociocultural realities in which they are used. A question remains, however, as to their meaning within obituary culture. To what extent does identification by title—professional and social—in the obituaries represent family perceptions of social and professional worth and to what extent does it represent factual events of the deceased's life? Would families, for example, neglect to identify the deceased by titles they had acquired during their lifetime? They could, but there is no way to establish if indeed they do. In obituary culture representation of acquired identities, be they titles or occupations, presupposes a factual basis for the identification. We cannot establish, however, whether some titles have been ignored. Unlike names and their symbolic role in the representation of basic identity, not all people acquire additional sociolinguistic symbols of identity such as titles. But the question can be approached from a quantitative perspective to determine the extent of bias in the distribution and its statistical significance, and, where possible, compare the results to our knowledge of the world outside the obituaries and what that knowledge would entail for the obituary pages.

The analysis of professional and social titles in relation to culture groups yields different results for each title type. The analysis of professional titles finds that Arabic obituaries mention 14 percent of the deceased by a professional title; Persian obituaries, 9 percent; and English obituaries, 4 percent. The analysis of social titles, however, yields a different hierarchy. Persian obituaries mention 57 percent of the deceased with a social title; Arabic obituaries, 51 percent; and English obituaries, less than 1 percent.[9] The only significant differences here are the percentages obtained from the Arabic and Persian obituaries. English obituaries continue to have the smallest percentage of identification by title, both professional and social—further supporting the nontitled nature of American society vis-à-vis Iranian and Egyptian society. In the United States, titles function primarily as indicators of professional status.

The discussion thus far has ignored the interaction of the variables. How, for example, do the sexes fare in relation to each other within each culture group and across them? We start with the interaction of Sex and Culture on social and professional titles.

A number of interesting observations emerge from examining these results (see table B.2). First, in the English obituaries, all four deceased identified with a social title are women. Only professional titles are applied to both women and men; and when they are, the effect of sex is very strong: 96 percent of deceased identified with professional titles are men and only 4 percent are women. Second, Persian obituaries are the only ones where the percentage of women mentioned with a social title is higher than that of men (53 percent to 47 percent). Finally, professional titles are more often associated with men, and social titles with women. In a culture-independent analysis, the strength of the association is consistently higher between Sex and Professional Title, except in the Persian obituaries, where the association of variance appears to be stronger with Social Titles (χ^2 = 117.5 for Social, 47.8 for Professional, and p < .0001).

Figures 4.8 and 4.9 demonstrate the distribution of professional and social titles by sex groups within each culture. They show a strong gender gap in professional titles, less so in social titles. The results from the English obituaries, however, show that only women are identified with social titles, making the gender gap, under one interpretation of this result, strong there as well.

Cross-culturally, social titles are perceived as being more important for women, and professional titles for men. This is supported by the results obtained from all three cultures. A culture-independent analysis of the figures in table B.2 as percentage of each sex-by-culture group yields different results. In Persian obituaries, 78 percent of the 393 deceased women are identified with a social title; in English obituaries, only women are identified as such; and in Arabic obituaries, 57 percent of the 548 deceased women are so identified. These results have interesting implications for cultural differences and the social perception of gender, a point to be further explored when the results from titles and occupations are compared. Here it is sufficient to point to the absence of statistical significance in the distribution of professional titles between the sexes in a cross-cultural analysis (table B.2). Significant culture differences could not be established in the distribution of professional titles

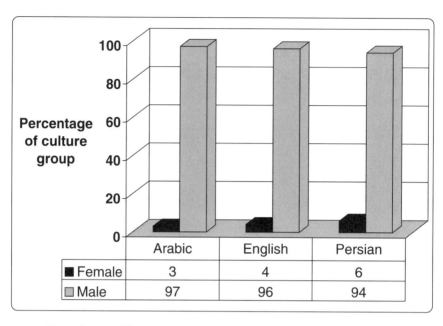

	Arabic	English	Persian
■ Female	3	4	6
▨ Male	97	96	94

Fig. 4.8. Sex Differentiation in Professional Titles by Culture Group

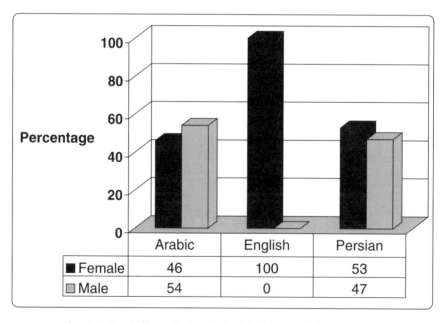

	Arabic	English	Persian
■ Female	46	100	53
▨ Male	54	0	47

Fig. 4.9. Sex Differentiation in Social Titles by Culture Group

between the sexes. Only in identifications of deceased women and men based on their social identities and resulting titles does the distribution achieve a level of statistical significance, thus pointing to cultural effects.

The results, however, are not unexpected in view of the universally accepted role of men as breadwinners (hence, their involvement in the workforce and in the public domain). Through this role they have acquired a professional and public identity, here reflected in their mention by professional titles and, as we show later, occupations. Women's universally accepted role as homemakers defines their identity, particularly their public identity, as "social" beings to be identified appropriately within that domain and in terms relating them to their socially assigned role. Analysis of the actual linguistic terms used as titles in reference to deceased women, presented later in this chapter, shows that this role is primarily intended to relate them to other males, primarily their husbands.

The sociocultural (but here universal) perception of gender roles together with cultural differences in the value associated with titles could explain some of the differences noted. Twentieth-century American culture is more "egalitarian" or equity oriented in its overall outlook, its political philosophy, and perceptions of individuals' roles within the socioeconomic structure. The period covered here has witnessed the rise of the civil rights movement and a number of equity-oriented amendments to the U.S. Constitution guaranteeing citizens' rights against discrimination in many areas (education, housing, finance, and many others). Thus one can argue that the overall mood or movement in the United States has been, and still is, toward establishing equity and providing equal opportunities for all. Whether or not this has been achieved, or ever will be, is beyond the point since people's perceptions of events around them and their reactions to such events are often influenced by the overall cultural atmosphere within which they live.

This is not so true in either Egypt or Iran, where the overall cultural atmosphere is geared toward establishing status and authority. Traditions and values from the past are to be maintained not questioned, and authority respected not challenged. Perhaps because of cultural heritage—dating as far back in time as Ancient Egypt and Persia and influenced over the years by other civilizations and their traditions (Greek, Zoroastrian, Roman, Christian, Islamic, among others)—"tradition" has come to play a strong role in the modern societies of Egypt and Iran. Reverence and respect are expected to be strictly enforced in relations with others as a result of age and status on both the personal and professional levels. In daily interactions this translates into expectations and styles of conversation dependent on various forms of address including titles and honorifics. Some children in Egypt, for example, still address their parents, their uncles and aunts, and even older siblings and (male) cousins in formal terms using *hadritak* instead of just *inta* (you), the informal version. In some circles it is still almost impolite to address members of the opposite sex without some title. Spouses in the earlier part of the twentieth century would not address each other by their first names, nor refer to each other on a first-name basis in public. They would use (social) titles, kinship terms, and various euphemisms instead (*mama, baba, basha, beh, hanim, sitt, madaam*). Conversational rules governing interactions between women and men have relaxed over the years as the barriers between the sexes have been removed with the "unveiling" of women, physically and figuratively, and their increased participation in the workplace and the public domain as a whole.[10]

Within such a context of cross-gender interactions, it is not surprising to find strong differentiation based on both sex and culture in the identification of the deceased depending on the social versus professional nature of the titles. The content analysis of titles that have been used in reference to deceased women and men will reveal content areas, or categories, of value, relevance, or saliency in the construction of professional and social identities of the deceased. The analysis is expected to reflect gender roles as they are perceived in the sociocultural contexts of the world outside the obituaries. But first we assess the effect of Time on the distribution of social and professional titles to complete that analysis and determine how each type may have impacted the overall change in representation by title.

5. SOCIAL AND PROFESSIONAL TITLES OVER TIME

The results in table B.1 show a statistically significant effect from Time on both types of titles. The overall variance, however, appears to be stronger with Professional than with Social Title. (See χ^2 results in table B.1.) Thus the effect of Time, like that of Sex and Culture, appears to be stronger on professional (phi = .14) than on social titles (phi = .06), suggesting a more dramatic change over the years for the former. Consider, for example, that the final year alone contributes 33 percent of professional titles, and the last two years combined contribute more than half (57 percent). Social titles, on the other hand, are more evenly distributed over the six time groups, sharply increasing between 1938 and 1948 but continuing thereupon with regular small percentage increases (see figure 3 of the overview). The analysis of professional and social titles in relation to the titled population demonstrates strong differences between the two. The fourteen deceased identified with a professional title in 1938, for example, represent only 11 percent of that year's titled population (122), in sharp contrast to the 89 percent obtained for social titles. By comparison, representation with a professional title increases in 1988 to almost one-third (31 percent) of the titled population for that year (344), a dramatic increase over the initial 11 percent figure. Representation with a social title drops from the initial 89 percent figure to 72 percent of the year's titled population.

Social and professional titles demonstrate divergent behavior in their change over time. A comparison of the relative frequency with which the deceased are identified with each type is presented in figure 4.10, where percentages are of the total obituary population of each individual year. In 1938, for example, 27 percent of the 396 deceased are identified with social and only 4 percent with professional titles. Social titles show a stronger presence during every year of the study and thus occupy more obituary space than professional titles throughout. Overall, professional titles post an 11 percent increase and social titles 8 percent. This comparison, however, is slightly misleading since the 15 percent representation posted for professional titles in 1988 is almost four times the original 4 percent in 1938. Change in identification by professional titles is stronger, despite the consistent difference in the relative size of the space they occupy.

To what extent is this change differentiated by sex of the deceased, by culture, and by both? Rather than discuss the details of each analysis, as was done in the previous sections, I summarize the results and ignore discussion of alternative analyses.

In a culture-independent analysis of the data, the distribution of social and professional titles by sex of the deceased is statistically significant in each culture. In a comparative cross-cultural analysis for sex differences, the distribution achieved a level of statistical significance for social titles only (table B.3). The analysis of expected values identifies 1938 and 1978 with a significant overrepresentation of males and females, respectively. Figure 4.11 shows the results of this distribution. We look for possible explanations to culture-based differentiation, which attributes the increase in 1978 to Persian obituaries and in 1938 to Arabic obituaries.

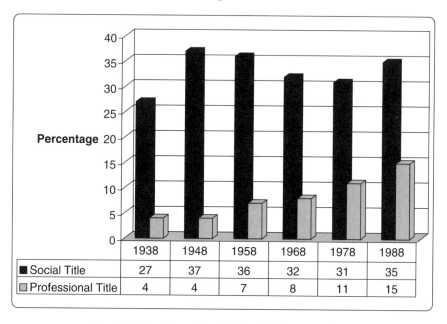

Fig. 4.10. Social and Professional Titles over Time

An equitable distribution is reached in 1988 despite the initial difference between the sexes. But it is reached in a different manner by each sex group. The female population demonstrates consistent progression until 1978, with a tremendous leap forward in 1948, another not as strong in 1958, but then regresses in 1988. The male population, starting much higher than the female, regresses consistently until 1978. It subsequently posts a strong progression, but not strong enough to be statistically significant from the expected values for that year, ending the period with the male population posting an overall loss of 20 percent in relation to women. This increased representation by one group, and decrease by the other, creates a "negotiated" social title space equitably shared by the two sexes in 1988.

The analysis of social and professional titles by Culture over Time produced different results, however. The culture-independent analyses of the distribution of these titles over the six time periods establish statistical significance for social titles in Arabic and Persian obituaries, and for professional titles in Arabic and English obituaries. The distribution in the comparative cross-cultural analysis, however, is statistically significant for both professional and social titles, suggesting differences across cultures in the way these titles

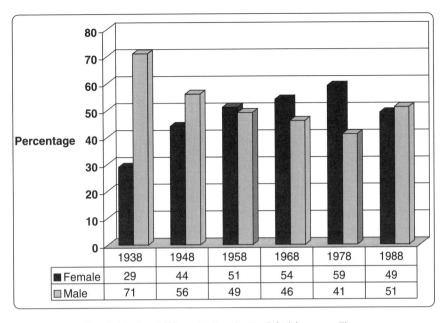

Fig. 4.11. Sex Differentiation in Social Titles over Time

change (table B.4). Figures 4.12 and 4.13 present the culture-independent analyses. The distribution of professional titles is not statistically significant in Persian obituaries, nor is the distribution of social titles in English obituaries, which is why the percentages for English obituaries are nonexistent in figure 4.12, and the results for Persian obituaries in figure 4.13 are for the most part rather flat. Both populations are included for the sake of completeness only.

In the distribution of social titles, the years 1938–48 for Arabic obituaries and 1988 for Persian obituaries are significantly overrepresented; in the distribution of professional titles, the years 1978 and 1988 for Arabic obituaries and 1988 for English obituaries show overrepresentation. That year alone (1988) contributes more than 50 percent of all English professional titles (27 out of 51). Thus the movement over time is different for each culture group depending on title type. Professional titles are steadily on the increase in Arabic obituaries; in English obituaries they post a dramatic increase only in the last year. Social titles in Arabic obituaries are consistently on the decline; in Persian obituaries they go through two trend reversals on their way up.

We thus conclude that change over time is culture differentiated for both professional and social titles, but is sex differentiated only for social titles.

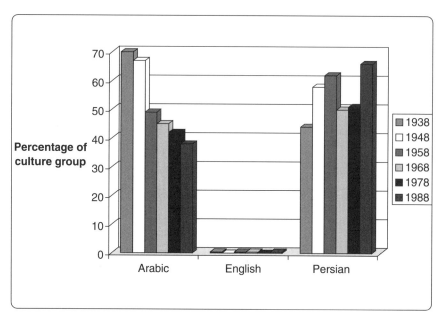

Fig. 4.12. Social Titles by Culture Group

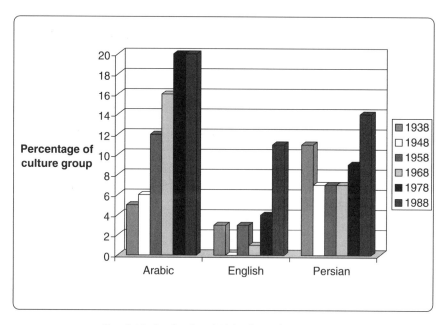

Fig. 4.13. Professional Titles by Culture Group

This is an interesting result in view of the stronger association obtained in the analysis for independent effects between Professional Title and Sex. When the data are analyzed to test for three-way interaction effects, the change is significantly impacted by the sex of the deceased in some cultures depending on title type. In a culture-independent analysis, the change in Arabic obituaries is sex differentiated for both professional and social titles, in Persian obituaries for social titles only, and in English obituaries for neither.

These results are consistent with previous analyses. Social titles in English obituaries (four occurrences) apply only to women, and professional titles (49) to men. In English obituaries, only two women are identified with professional titles; in Persian obituaries, only five. Thus distribution over time did not reach a level significantly different from the expected values. In all cases it is the difference between the sexes over time that was measured.

In Arabic obituaries, however, the distribution of professional titles is significant because of the final year (χ^2 = 14.7 and p < .05). Five women with professional titles appear in that year, making the ratio 11 percent female to 89 percent male. The analysis of expected values predicts only 1.3 percent female if the distribution were within the range of normal variation over the six years. The distribution in social titles is also significant (χ^2 = 19.5 and p < .01), the figures from 1938 being significantly divergent from the expected values. Only 30 women are identified with a social title, the expected value is 48, and as many as 73 men have social titles when only 55 are expected. Sex differences in the remaining five years do not differ from normal variation.

In some culture-by-sex groups, then, the distribution of social and professional titles over time is not different from normal variation (not statistically significant). In others (social titles in English obituaries), little or no data are available for the statistical analysis to be performed.

The results, particularly from this last analysis of sex-by-culture over time, raise the question of why such cultural differences exist and why they affect the sex groups in the way they do within these cultures. The case of social titles in English obituaries has already been discussed and attributed to the nontitled nature of American society being carried over into obituary culture and possibly supported by the *New York Times'* obituary format. Since professional titles are universally applied less often to women, their distribution over time in relation to the sexes is likely to be significantly sex differentiated, as it has been in the Arabic case, unless some aspect of obituary culture overrides. Professional titles in Persian and English obituaries then need an explanation.

In both cases the discrepancy has been attributed to the size of the (female) corpus in its distribution over time.

This conclusion, however, brings up two other issues. First, if corpus size is responsible for the absence of statistical significance in the distribution over time, then we must ask why the corpus is so small to begin with, or why women are represented less often with professional titles than are men in their culture group. Second, if women's professional and occupational realities have changed in the world outside the obituaries, why are these realities not reflected in the changing world of the obituaries?

These results appear to contradict the change hypothesis (chapter 1)— the prediction that as women's presence is increased in the public domain (the professional world in this case) and as they acquire identities independent of home and family, their representation in the obituaries will change to reflect these acquired identities. The results from the analysis of professional titles do not support this hypothesis. The timing (1988) with its increased representation of women with professional identities can be viewed as a reflection of women's realities, since employment opportunities for women have significantly improved since the 1960s. But what about Iranian women for whom the obituaries indicate no sign of improvement over the years? What about men? This result is not peculiar to women, since that year is significant for the male populations as well.

We here find ourselves arguing in one case for effects from the world outside the obituaries to explain the results, and in another for explanations from within the obituaries. The issue is further complicated by the relative unavailability of information and empirical data on how women and men are identified in various social contexts. If sex differences exist in identification by professional titles in these three cultures, then such external influences cannot be excluded, and the obituaries would have to be a reflection of the social realities beyond them.

Taking the position that the obituaries *only* reflect social realities is problematic. It leads to the conclusion that women's professional realities have not changed and that in Iran professional identification is not an important aspect of the identification of people, particularly women. An alternative, and more plausible, position would attribute the difference to obituary culture instead. The distribution of professional titles over time is not significant for the Persian population because they are not perceived by obituary writers as being sufficiently meaningful, salient, or valuable to the obituary subculture.

(This applies to the English obituaries as well, although that may have been also mediated by the nontitled nature of American society.) As a result, our original hypothesis about change, inspired as it was by the initial view of the obituaries as a reflection of society, must be modified to accommodate these and similar results. An appropriate linkage must be established between the two worlds, the obituaries and the world outside, and it is done through the Principle of Mutual Benefit (see chapter 7).

6. CONTENT ANALYSIS OF SOCIAL AND PROFESSIONAL TITLES

Professional titles, as explained earlier, reflect an identity acquired through an individual's participation in occupational activities and include such titles as *Dr., Professor,* and *Reverend.* Social titles reflect one's social status and, for the most part, are independent of professional activities. They include titles of formality/respect (*Mr.,* Persian *agha*), marital status (*Mrs., Miss*), religious status (Arabic *hajj*—"a person who has gone on a pilgrimage"), and titles of solidarity or group affiliation (brother, sister, comrade). The relationship between professional titles and occupations necessitates a degree of overlap. I have taken reference to an occupation or profession to constitute a title only when the term occurs in the same linguistic position otherwise occupied by title in relation to name. Titles typically precede the name in all three languages: Dr./Mrs. Mary Smith, *al-anisa/al-doktora Samia El-Sherif, khanum/doktor Giti Beheshti.* A name may be preceded by two (or more) titles in Arabic and Persian. English in general allows more than one title when one is an "honorific," as in *The Honorable (Her Honor) Judge Judy Smith* where *judge* would be a professional title preceded by an honorific. Combinations such as *Mrs. Dr. Judy Smith* are not possible in English, but are common in both Arabic and Persian.

A list of social and professional titles used in reference to deceased women and men is provided in tables C.1 and C.2, respectively. Although some deceased in Arabic and Persian obituaries are identified with two titles— professional and social—some are also identified with more than one social title. Multiple titles of the same category have been hyphenated and counted as one title in order to facilitate the calculations and maintain consistency with the distribution of title data.

6.1 Content Analysis of Social Titles

By far the majority of social titles applied to women refer to their status as married women (table C.1). In Arabic obituaries, 208 (67 percent) of the 312 deceased women with a social title are identified as *sayyida.* In English obituaries, *Mrs.* is the only social title used in reference to women. And in Persian obituaries, *banu* is by far the most common: 238 (77 percent) of the 308 deceased women identified with a social title are identified with *banu* only; in combination with *hajjeh,* the term is used 17 more times. The Arabic and Persian terms, although typically understood as equivalent to *Mrs.,* do not necessarily mean "married." The Arabic word, for example, can refer to older women as well. A middle-aged woman who has never married would most likely be referred to as *sayyida* (rare as this situation may be in view of cultural pressures on women to marry early). Yet it does happen, and increasingly more so. Egypt's most popular singer, Um Kalsoum, did not marry until her late forties or early fifties. Yet prior to her marriage she was known as *al-sayyida Um Kalsoum;* her early recordings, however, identify her as *al-anisa Um Kalsoum.*

The next most common category of social titles reflects women's performance of their religious duties. The Arabic *hajja* is used for Muslims in both Egypt and Iran.[11] In the Arabic obituaries 58 deceased women (19 percent) are identified as *hajja* and 13 (4 percent) with the corresponding Christian title *muqaddisa.* In Persian obituaries, second rank is more difficult to assess because of multiple titles. The ranking of single titles produces *khanum* 22 (7 percent) followed by *hajjeh* 11 (4 percent). If multiple titles are included in the calculations, the figure for *khanum* increases to 34 (11 percent) and *hajjeh* to 40 (13 percent). *Khanum* falls within the same category of marital status and respect as *banu,* but it also applies to unmarried women. If these two terms are grouped together, first and second category rankings for Arabic and Persian obituaries would be the same: identities constructed through marital/social status and respect followed by those acquired through performance of religious obligations.

Next in rank are terms that identify unmarried women: *anisa* in Arabic (18 occurrences, 6 percent) and *dushizeh* in Persian (8 occurrences, 3 percent) and/or *khanum.* Strictly speaking, *dushizeh* refers to unmarried women only, but *khanum* applies to both married and unmarried women, which may explain the greater occurrence of this term. Unfortunately, sorting out deceased women's marital status is neither feasible nor methodologically sound since it would have implied a level of reading and interpretation of the obituaries beyond the limits set to code only what is in the texts. Finally, Persian *khanum* and Arabic *hanim* are linguistically related, the latter being either directly borrowed from Persian or indirectly through Turkish. (See Badawi and Hinds 1986.) *Hanim* is also a title of respect applicable to women irrespective of marital status. It is believed to have originated among the aristocracy and upper classes, perhaps due to its linguistic source from Persian via Turkish. Combining the three instances of *hanim* with the ten of *sitt* (both meaning "lady") produces a third category of respect that is unambiguously independent of marital status.

Deceased women in all three cultures, then, are identified first and foremost with titles reflecting marital status/respect, exclusively so in some obituary cultures (English) and predominantly so in others (Arabic and Persian). An average of 70 percent of social titles applied to women refer to their marital status/respect. The category reflected by these titles must be deemed most salient, relevant, or valuable in the construction of women's (social) identity in the obituaries. The next category of value is the performance of religious duties as represented in the pilgrimage to Mecca for Muslims and Jerusalem for Christians.

By contrast, in the English obituaries, no social titles are applied to men. When this result is combined with the earlier finding of just one social title (*Mrs.*) applied to four women, the nontitled nature of this culture group is further confirmed. Obituaries from Egypt and Iran, by comparison, provide a much more diverse title base available for the construction of men's public social identities in the obituaries—a finding that further supports the view of male domination of public space and the titled versus nontitled nature of these societies.

Two major categories, however, emerge from the analysis of social titles most commonly applied to men in Arabic and Persian obituary cultures: their religious status acquired through performance of religious duties and their social (possibly socioeconomic) status (see table C.2). In the Persian obituaries the two most common terms are *agha* and *sayyid* (Mr.), which indicate social respect (and formality): *agha* is used in 86 obituaries (31 percent of men with social titles), and *sayyid* is used with 26 (9 percent). Among the religious titles, *hajj* (76 occurrences, 27 percent) is by far the most common.[12] These two titles, *agha* and *hajj,* together constitute 58 percent of all instances of social titles applied to Iranian men. The percentage naturally increases if multiple titles are added into the calculations, such as *agha-hajj.*[13] Religious titles and combinations thereof total 136 occurrences and represent 49 percent of the 277 deceased Persian men with social titles. In the Persian obituaries, then, men's social identity is constructed around two categories weighted almost equally relative to each other: social status/respect and religious status/respect.

The Arabic obituaries show similar results. Religious titles for Muslims (*hajj, sheikh*) and Christians (*muqaddis*), represent 49 percent of social titles applied to Egyptian men. Titles of respect/formality follow, the two most common being *ustadh* and *sayyid,* representing 20 percent of all instances of social titles.[14] Egyptian obituaries, however, reflect yet another category of social status based on socioeconomic and political power as well. This category is represented by three titles, *basha, beh,* and *effendi.* With 25 percent of all Egyptian men identified with one of these social titles, these titles are as significant as (perhaps even more significant than) titles of formality and respect. The 25 percent figure is somewhat unexpectedly high, in view of the story behind these titles as it has been played within the context of twentieth-century Egyptian cultural and sociopolitical history. But it also has interesting implications for information these titles may reveal about social change in Egypt and about the social status, perhaps even class background, of the deceased who populate these obituary pages.

These titles have been referred to as aristocratic titles (Ibrahim 1982: 405). As a part of the pre-1952 monarchy in Egypt, they were typically bestowed by the Palace—the rulers who occupied it and their entourage—upon individuals of certain background, which entitled them to privileges and access to positions of power not available to others. These, along with other titles associated with the monarchy, were officially abolished by the 1952 revolutionary government as one of its earliest acts to undermine inherited privileges and establish principles of fairness and equal opportunity. Some titles have survived unofficially but with a shift in meaning. For example, *beh* has lost its original meaning and reference to "second highest ranking officials" but has continued to be used as a form of respect in addressing and referring to people of equal or higher status (Badawi and Hinds 1986:27). Only *basha,* the most prestigious of the three, disappeared almost completely, perhaps because of its high rank and visibility among the elite. Many Egyptian political and economic leaders, the national heroes of the early twentieth century, are known by this title: Saad Zaghloul *basha,* president of the Wafd political party later to become prime minister in the 1930s, and Talat *basha* Harb, Egyptian banker-industrialist and founder of the first Egyptian bank, Bank Misr, to name only two.

Social titles in the obituaries, then, reflect aspects of the social reality beyond them, perhaps in nature but not in degree. The English obituaries reflect the overall low value ascribed to social titles in the United States, in the absence of social titles for men and only four instances of one title for women.[15] Does this mean that there are no social titles applicable to men in the world outside the obituaries? Does it also mean that the low level of frequency with which these titles have been applied to the deceased corresponds to their level of frequency when applied to a comparable population in the world outside the obituaries? The answer has to be negative for both.

If the world constructed in the obituary pages reflects, or is partly modeled on, a social reality beyond them, it is not necessarily a mirror of that reality or a duplicate of it. Rather the obituary pages develop conventions of their own, maintained and at times changed through participation from their readers and contributors. The subsequent analysis of professional titles will further substantiate this claim. If interpreted literally as a mirror of realities outside the obituaries, professional titles would paint a bleak and counterfactual picture for women in all three cultures and for men in the United States.

6.2 Content Analysis of Professional Titles

Professional titles for deceased women in the obituaries are limited to three types: doctors, engineers, and professors. For deceased men they are much more diverse, reflecting the wider range of professional fields open to men. Three categories emerge in the classification of men's titles: (1) professional, such as attorney, doctor, engineer, (2) religious, such as *sheikh,* reverend, *ayatullah,* and (3) military. Women's titles in the obituaries are limited to only one, the professional. (See tables C.1 and C.2.)

Titles from the professions occur most frequently in the obituaries of all three cultures. In Arabic obituaries, 75 percent of the deceased are identified with such titles; in English obituaries, 79 percent; and in Persian obituaries, 43 percent. In both Arabic and Persian obituaries, military titles occur with the next highest frequency—16 percent and 40 percent, respectively, an unexpectedly higher percentage for Persian obituaries. In the English obituaries, 24 percent of deceased men are identified with a title related to the clergy;

in Arabic and Persian obituaries, these figures stand at 15 and 17 percent, respectively. Only 6 percent of deceased men in the English obituaries are identified with a military title.

The analysis of professional titles in the obituary pages then constructs a world that is indeed gendered, perhaps more so than the world outside them. Women in the United States, for example, have acquired diverse professional identities as a result of increased availability of employment opportunities, allowing them, for example, to join the armed forces and the clergy. But the obituaries do not reflect these newly acquired identities in the form of titles families use to identify their deceased women—not yet at least. Perhaps, then, the world as constructed within the obituary pages lags behind the world outside them. The analysis of the data on occupation will provide additional support for this idea.

One unusual result, however, is the relatively small number of military titles in the Arabic obituaries, particularly as compared to Persian obituaries. One might argue that the military may have enjoyed more prestige over a longer time period in Iran than it has in Egypt. On the other hand, the world of the obituaries may be affected by other factors, such as attitude toward the military, that may influence a family's decision to identify its deceased with military affiliation. The low military profile in the Arabic obituaries can be attributed to other factors including national security. The military establishment requires the suppression of information pertinent to military ranks and locations of nonretired officers from the obituary pages without prior clearance from the appropriate military authorities. Lutfi Elkholi (*Al-Ahram,* October 5, 1997) writes in his column *ijtihadat* (Opinions): "I was not surprised when I learned that security forces and Israeli research centers consider the obituary pages of *Al-Ahram* one of the most important written sources available for information on political and social movement and on centers of influence in Egyptian society. This is probably what prompted Egyptian (security) authorities to keep under surveillance the identification in the obituaries of active officers in the armed forces."[16] This practice may, however, be more relevant to the identification of the survivors than the deceased, if indeed the deceased are more likely to be older and thus retired. Be this as it may, the enforcement of such a policy may be responsible for the smaller number of deceased with military titles and, depending on when this policy had been put into effect, perhaps a decrease in military titles in the Arabic obituaries—a point we consider in the subsequent analysis of the effects of Time. From the cross-cultural comparative perspective, it provides an explanation for the difference between Arabic and Persian obituaries in visibility and allotment of space to military titles and the lower military title profile projected among the Egyptian deceased population—the explanation being based on the obituaries as reflections of realities outside them.

By the same token, one might wonder why titles from the professions occur less frequently in Persian obituaries than they do in Arabic obituaries. One possible explanation would attribute it to the degree of prestige enjoyed by these categories relative to each other within each culture. Historians of Iran, for example, describe one scenario for the social and political change dominating the major part of the century as a struggle over power among the shah, the religious establishment, and forces of modernity. Thus the military establishment, through its power and loyalty to the shah, may have enjoyed more prestige for a prolonged period of time. Still, the weak showing of professional titles in Persian obituaries compared to that of Arabic obituaries remains unexplained, so long as the obituaries are viewed only as reflections of the realities in the world outside.

6.3 Change in Identities as Constructed through Social and Professional Titles

The content analysis of social and professional titles as applied to women and men has shown cross-cultural differences and similarities in the categories deemed relevant, salient, or valuable in the public identification of the sexes. Titles applied to men are more diverse, particularly so for professional affiliations. Whereas titles applied to women are restricted to the professions, those applied to men include those found in the military and religious establishments as well. Social titles applied to men are also more diverse in that they include titles of socioeconomic status not available to women, while social titles applied to women are much more focused on respect based on their marital status first. Both sexes, however, are given their due respect resulting from their performance of religious duties such as pilgrimage to Mecca or Jerusalem.

The analysis over time in this section is intended to show how the frequency with which certain titles are used has increased (or decreased) within and across these culture groups and the extent to which this may be an indication of a changed sociocultural perception of the sexes. Tables C.3 and

C.4 provide listings of all social and professional titles used with women (table
C.3) and men (table C.4) in each culture and time group. The bulk of the
following discussion necessarily focuses on Persian and Arabic obituaries for
several reasons: social titles are rarely used in English obituaries; professional
titles for American women appear only in 1988; and there is no significant
sex differentiation in the English obituaries over time. We begin with social,
then professional, categories for women and men in each culture.

6.4 Social Categories

The titles most commonly applied to deceased women in the Arabic
and Persian obituaries are *sayyida* in Arabic (67 percent) and *banu* in Persian
(78 percent), both typically applied to married women and to older women
regardless of their marital status. These two are the terms used most frequently
in almost every time period. However, when we look at their usage in each of
the six time periods, we can draw different conclusions.

The use of the Arabic term *sayyida* starts at 47 percent in 1938 and
ends at 49 percent in 1988, whereas the use of the Persian *banu* begins at 79
percent and ends at 53 percent. Looking at just these figures is misleading when
drawing conclusions, however, as the year-by-year analysis shows surprisingly
parallel movements in the percentages. In both cultures the identification of
women by a marital title decreases by 1988. In 1938 Egypt, marital titles
(*sayyida, anisa*) are applied to 64 percent of deceased women identified with
a social title for that year. The percentage drops in 1988 to 51 percent. In
Iran marital title usage (*banu, khanum, dushizeh*) starts at an even higher
97 percent in 1948, when deceased Iranian women are first identified with
titles. But marital title usage drops to 65 percent in 1988. (Title combinations
such as *banu-hajjeh*, listed separately in table C.3, are excluded from these
calculations.)[17]

With respect to Egyptian women, *sitt* and *hanim,* which reflect social
respect independent of marital status, are lost by 1988. The first appears
relatively strong in 1938 (applied to 33 percent of the deceased) but disappears
afterward, suggesting it was probably already on its way out when the period
begins. The second is applied to only three deceased, two in 1948 and one
1968. Their disappearance from the obituaries is not surprising since both
may have originated in the upper classes and reflect times when women were
confined to the home. Their usage in everyday interactions has also become
more limited over the years, particularly with the term *sayyida* taking over

their function as titles of respect in formal contexts. The Muslim title *hajja* (19 percent) is by far the second most frequently used title, which, together with the Christian title *muqaddisa* (4 percent), would represent the category of (nonprofessional) religious titles (signifying respect acquired through the performance of religious duties) and constitute 23 percent of all social titles applied to women. Of these three titles most frequently applied to deceased Egyptian women, only *hajja* shows a consistently strong increase in usage over the years.

Although *sayyida* is used more frequently than *hajja* in almost every time period, each term's use moves in opposite directions (see figure 4.14). In the earlier periods (pre-1958), *sayyida* demonstrates a strong increase in usage, unlike *hajja*. In 1958, however, this trend is reversed. *Sayyida* regresses sharply and continues to do so until the end of the period in 1988, thereby ending almost where it had originally started in 1938. But *hajja* shows a strong progression starting in 1958 and continuing until 1988. As a result, *hajja* ends at a point slightly lower than *sayyida,* representing 43 percent of female social titles for that year and *sayyida* 49 percent. The other religious title, *muqaddisa,* also increases, reaching a 13 percent peak in 1978, although its movement is slightly erratic.

The unexpected decline in the use of *sayyida* can be viewed as a reflection of the overall reduction in title use in Egyptian society. The change demonstrated by *hajja* is also unexpected, but for a different reason. The title carries a strong religious (and Islamic) connotation and would, therefore, be expected to increase with the increasing influence of political Islam in Egypt. The date most commonly agreed upon for this movement is the early 1970s. What is interesting then, and in a way unexpected, is the timing of the change. The progression for *hajja* starts earlier (1958–68), a decade prior to the period usually associated with the strengthening of political Islam in Egypt.[18]

A more interesting and convincing picture emerges when the results from all marital titles are combined into one category and religious titles into another, as in figure 4.15. During the first three decades (1938–58), the social perception of women as revealed through the obituaries is increasingly framed by their marital status. The fourth decade (1968) is a transitional period (marked by progression in the religious category and regression in the marital category). In the last two decades, the representation of deceased women in Egyptian obituaries reveals a balance between "secular" and "religious" identities, confirming a strong (though perhaps unexpected) change in how women are identified.

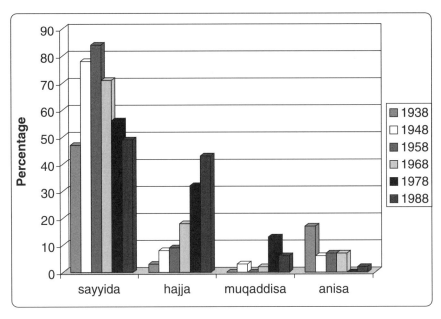

Fig. 4.14. Social Titles Applied to Egyptian Women

One might conclude, as a result, that underlying social trends manifest themselves in sociocultural forms such as the obituaries before they are strong enough to emerge as sociopolitical movements. Alternatively, one might conclude that an increased perception and representation of women as based on their religious identities, particularly in the obituaries, is independent of any sociocultural movement beyond them. People are identified with such titles, and can be perceived through such categories, if they have performed their religious duty—namely, the pilgrimage. Therefore, an increase in the representation must mean that: (a) the number of women performing this duty has increased among the population of the obituaries, and/or (b) identification by such a category has come to be perceived as salient, important, or valuable for the obituaries and the world outside them (again in accordance with the Principle of Mutual Benefit). Since changes such as those in (a) and (b) may take place independent of the strengthening of political Islam in Egypt, no necessary connection can be established between the two. Still other results support the connection, as we show in subsequent discussion.

Social titles for Egyptian men fall under three categories: religious titles, titles of formality/respect, and titles reflecting socioeconomic or social status

Fig. 4.15. Social Categories (Egyptian Women)

(as symbolized by "aristocratic" titles). Some titles have disappeared over this fifty-year period and others have increased in usage (see table C.4). *Sheikh-ʿarab* and *effendi,* for example, do not appear after 1958 and 1948, respectively. Three have increased in usage: the two religious titles, *hajj* and *muqaddis,* and one title of formality/respect, *ustadh.* The most dramatic increase is demonstrated by *ustadh*— 1 percent in 1938 to 38 percent in 1988. The two Muslim titles, *hajj* and *sheikh,* also show an interesting pattern (see figure 4.16). By 1958 they reach an almost equal level of representation, but then *hajj* sustains its progression, increasing in usage by almost 20 percent in just one decade (1958–68). Although its use decreases during the last two decades, it nonetheless ends at 35 percent representation (much higher than its original 10 percent in 1938). After 1958, *sheikh* regresses and ends in 1988 at a level lower than that of all four titles in figure 4.16 at less than 10 percent. *Muqaddis* is also interesting because its usage has increased during this period. It appears first in 1948, makes a strong progression in 1958, but then regresses in 1968. It reverses direction again, sustaining this progression throughout the final two decades and recovering all losses sustained since its peak in 1958. The nonreligious title *ustadh* is perhaps the most interesting of all, with practically no usage in 1938 and ending in 1988 with more usage than the other three titles after consistent progression.

Overall, then, the use of religious titles, both women's and men's, has increased during this period with the exception of *sheikh*.[19] By comparison, change in the "secular" titles of formality/respect is more sex differentiated.

The increase in the use of *ustadh* can be partly attributed to policies introduced in the 1950s to abolish (aristocratic) titles. As a title embodying sufficient respect and no social class stigma, *ustadh* emerges as a compromise to accommodate the cultural pressure favoring the use of titles and changes introduced by the then new regime (of 1952) disfavoring the use of titles, specifically those associated with the past monarchy, in an attempt to promote a more egalitarian society. Thus *ustadh* replaces some of the most popular titles of the first two decades—*effendi, beh, basha,* and perhaps even *khawaga.* These three alone constitute 53 percent of men's social titles in 1938, 46 percent in 1948, and then a low 8 percent in 1958, reflecting the sociocultural changes brought about by these policies and perhaps explaining the dramatic increase in the usage of *ustadh*. When statistics of other titles within this same category (*sayyid*) are combined, the results show a dramatic increase from 5 percent

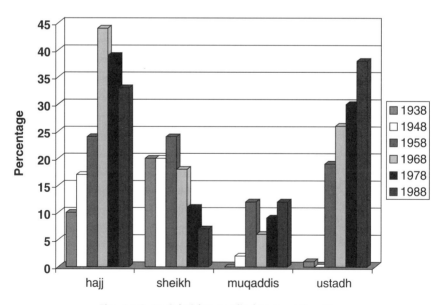

Fig. 4.16. Social Titles Applied to Egyptian Men

in 1938 to 45 percent in 1988—an increase unmatched by any other title or title group.

Religious title usage tells a different story. The combined statistics (*hajj, sheikh, muqaddis*) demonstrate a high percentage throughout, the lowest being 28 percent in 1938. The usage progresses dramatically over the subsequent decades, reaching its peak in 1968 with a 76 percent representation. But it declines during the final two decades (59 percent in 1978 and 42 percent in 1988), ending the period at almost the same place as that of titles of formality/respect, or slightly lower. Thus, although the use of religious titles has shown clear progression over this fifty-year period, it is not as impressive nor as consistent as that demonstrated by titles of formality/respect. What is most curious, however, is the post-1968 decline of religious title usage (see figure 4.17). Men's social identity, according to figure 4.17, is primarily determined by their religious status, especially in 1968. But by 1988, their social identity is equally determined by the titles of formality/respect they are given. (See figure 4.15 for a similar situation with Egyptian women.) At a time when Islamicism, or political Islam, is on the rise, the use of religious titles in Egypt is on the decline. Why?

Identification with religious titles among deceased men declines when religion becomes a political public movement, rather than a private personal matter. In the era of public secularism and private (nonpolitical) religion, identification by religious titles increases. No reprisals or political oppression could result from public demonstration of religious affiliation. But when religion becomes a political movement, as it has since the 1970s, families fear public identification with religious affiliation. This is particularly true in a place like Egypt, where political Islam is being opposed by the state, as compared to a place like Iran where it is not. Finally, differences in the usage of these titles in women's and men's obituaries further support this idea.

Recall that in Egyptian women's obituaries, the use of religious titles increased dramatically whereas that of titles of formality/respect decreased. These opposing movements began in 1958, a decade earlier than the change among the male population. This sex differentiation may be explained on the basis that women's identification with a religious title is potentially less dangerous than it would be for men. Since political Islam as a movement is generally perceived as the domain of men, women with religious titles are perceived merely as pious and not necessarily associated with political activism. As such, they pose less of a threat to the family, if any at all.

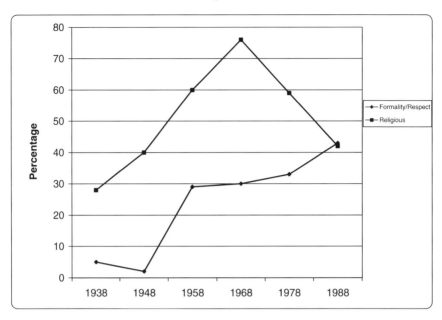

Fig. 4.17. Social Categories (Egyptian Men)

The social categories into which Egyptian women and men are placed are based primarily on the religious and social status acquired during their lifetime, however these are defined for each sex. By 1988, the data for both women and men in the Egyptian obituaries reflect similar results in terms of distribution of religious titles and those of formality/respect, though they arrived there via different, sex-differentiated paths (see figures 4.15 and 4.17). As women's identification with religious titles increased, men's identification with religious titles decreased. The opposition and movement demonstrated in this analysis is unexpected, particularly in the more gendered picture it constructs of change. It also stands in sharp contrast with the situation as projected through the Persian obituaries.

A parallel analysis of social categories projected of deceased Iranian women produces a dramatically different picture. Religious status as a category of social respect does not figure prominently in Iranian women's obituaries, while marital status (represented by the titles *banu, khanum,* and *dushizeh*) does. (See figure 4.18, which includes all three as well as the one religious title, *hajjeh.* Title combinations are excluded.)

In 1958, 92 percent of deceased Iranian women with social titles are identified with *banu;* by 1988, 53 percent. None of the other titles reaches a level of representation anywhere near that of *banu.* When the other two marital status titles (*khanum* and *dushizeh*) are added to *banu,* we end in 1988 with a 65 percent representation of deceased women with titles in the marital status category. This is sufficient to establish the predominance of this category without even including title combinations with the religious title *hajjeh* (17 for *banu* and 12 for *khanum*).

The difference in the figures for titles based on marital status and on religious status is impressive. *Hajjeh* reaches its peak representation in 1988, when it is used in eight obituaries of Iranian women (10 percent of deceased women with social titles for that year). If all instances of title combinations are added, the percentage for *hajjeh* would naturally increase, but the overall comparison between marital and religious status would remain unchanged, as title combinations for the three other titles would be added as well. To assess the change in *hajjeh* independently of its relation to the titles indicating marital status, we count all instances of this title alone and in combination. The result shows that the number of deceased women identified by *hajjeh* almost tripled during 1978–88, 9 deceased in 1978 to 25 in 1988.

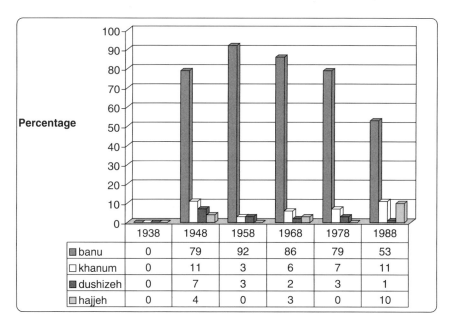

	1938	1948	1958	1968	1978	1988
banu	0	79	92	86	79	53
khanum	0	11	3	6	7	11
dushizeh	0	7	3	2	3	1
hajjeh	0	4	0	3	0	10

Fig. 4.18. Social Titles Applied to Iranian Women

Social titles applied to deceased men in the Persian obituaries also reflect two major categories: one derives from the performance of religious duties and the other from formality/respect due to personal accomplishments or background. The list (table C.4) is much longer than the Arabic list. Some religious titles reflect Shi'i traditions (*mashadi, karbalai*); others reflect different linguistic sources, as in titles of respect. *Sayyid,* for example, is Arabic but *agha* and *mirza* are Persian. Figure 4.19 presents change in the five most frequently used titles. They, and their combinations, represent 84 percent of all social titles applied to deceased Iranian men. The list includes three titles, *agha, sayyid,* and *hajj,* of which only *hajj* is religious; it also includes two title combinations, *agha-hajj* and *agha-sayyid.*

The most dramatic change over the fifty-year period comes from *hajj* and *agha-hajj;* only these two demonstrate a substantial increase. In 1988, *hajj* has the greatest usage (40 percent) of all titles used to identify deceased men for that year, almost double its initial 22 percent in 1948. Its strongest competition comes from *agha,* which appears earlier in 1938 representing 25 percent of deceased men with social titles for that year. In 1948 *agha* experiences a dramatic increase to 48 percent, the highest percentage level attained by any social title during this fifty-year period. After this point, however, *agha* declines sharply, losing 8 percent over twenty years (1948–68) and another 20 percent in just one decade (1968–78). It remains relatively stable during the final decade. Despite the gains and losses, *agha* ends slightly below its starting point. The usage of these two titles may reflect a changing social reality in Iran, keeping in mind the popularity of both titles in combinations with each other and with other titles.

In the analysis of social categories projected of Iranian men (figure 4.20), I have created a third "mixed" category to reflect occurrences in which the deceased is identified with more than one social title. Most combinations include at least one religious title and one title of respect (*sayyid-hajj*), although some consist of a combination from the same group (*hajj-sheikh* or *agha-sayyid*).[20] Not all combinations are included but figure 4.20 reflects 92 percent of social titles. Adding the "mixed" category for the Persian obituaries creates results for the religious and formality/respect categories that are vastly different from those of the Arabic obituaries (see figure 4.17). In Iranian men's obituaries, the formality/respect category dominates, especially through 1958, and then gives way to an increasing presence from the religious category. These categories in Egyptian men's obituaries do the opposite—the religious category dominates until 1968, when it gives way to more participation from

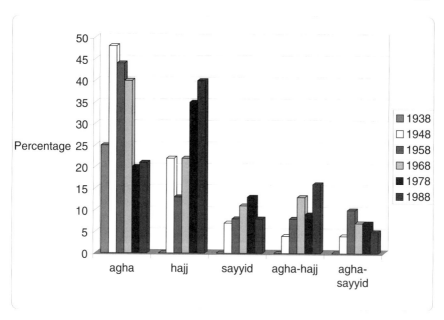

Fig. 4.19. Social Titles Applied to Iranian Men

the formality/respect category. These results are revealing, given the social and political realities outside the obituaries in both cultures. It is interesting to note further that the results from Iranian men's obituaries are in fact similar to those for Egyptian women's obituaries (see figure 4.15). Both demonstrate an increase in the religious category, unlike Egyptian men's obituaries, which demonstrate a decrease instead, and Iranian women's obituaries with little change in this category.

Despite the cross-cultural differences in the way religious titles have changed in Egyptian and Iranian obituaries, the similarities between them are nonetheless strong. In both cultures, men's public identity (social respect) is built primarily on two areas—performance of religious duties and the attainment of personal respect. Women, we recall, gain social respect in similar ways, but for women "personal" respect is attained primarily through marital status.

6.5 Change in Professional Categories

Little can be said about change in women's identification by professional titles because of the lack of data. Women's professional titles in Arabic and

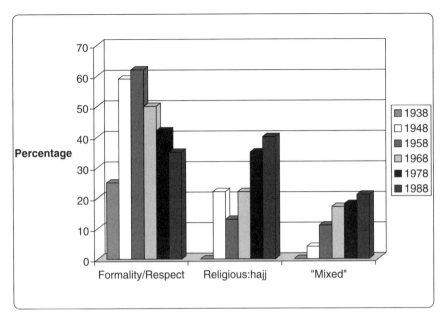

Fig. 4.20. Social Titles of Iranian Men

English obituaries appear only in 1988. Persian obituaries are the first to identify a woman with a professional title (doctor) in 1948; they identify three more in 1978.

The situation is quite different for men's obituaries. More types of titles are used, reflecting more diverse employment fields, and the data are sufficient to achieve a meaningful distribution over the fifty-year period. Three major categories have emerged for men's professional titles: the military, the professions (doctors, engineers, and the like), and the clergy or religious establishments. This information is represented by culture group in figures 4.21–4.23; details are found in table C.4.

All three cultures show strong representation from the professions category; the results from the other two categories are more varied across the cultures, as can be seen in the figures.

What appears to be an erratic movement in the distribution of professional titles in English obituaries should be situated within the framework of the social meaning of titles in the United States. The results from U.S. obituaries show that identification by title is inconsistently applied, which is not surprising since the United States is not a title-oriented society. The use of

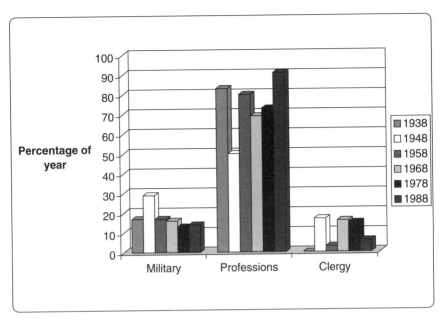

Fig. 4.21. Arabic Professional Titles for Men by Type

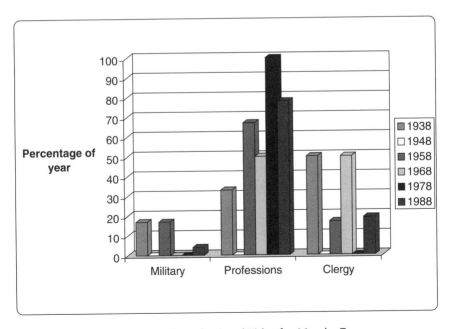

Fig. 4.22. English Professional Titles for Men by Type

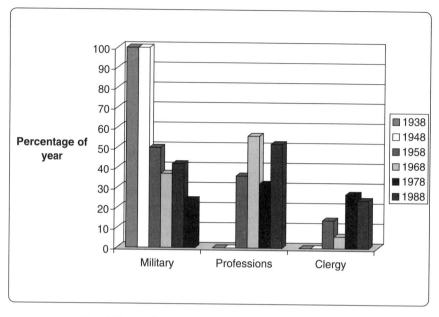

Fig. 4.23. Persian Professional Titles for Men by Type

military titles, for example, is minimal. If any group is almost always known by its titles, it is the military. Is the world projected through the obituary pages different then? Perhaps when (American) families write obituaries, they tend to perceive the deceased as individuals situated within the family (the private sphere) and not necessarily outside it (the public/professional sphere). Still, it is surprising that so few occurrences of military titles have been found, particularly by comparison to doctors. Military titles, then, are interesting for all three cultures.

Titles from the clergy category tell different stories for Egypt and Iran, receiving less prominence in the Arabic obituaries. They appear in 1948 and experience two regressions, one in 1958 and the other in 1988. The first drop may be explained on the basis of changes resulting from the political situation in post-1952 Egypt, particularly the government's crackdown on leaders of the Muslim brotherhood. The drop in 1988 may also be attributed to similar government policies, this time directed against political Islam as it is represented in the so-called (fundamentalist) Islamic groups. In the Persian obituaries titles from the clergy appear in 1958. They experience a sharp progression between 1968 and 1978 and remain stable during the final decade.

This change can be attributed to the increased power and visibility gained by the clergy with the establishment of the Islamic Republic. If so, it would be natural for this change to begin before 1978 in the world outside the obituaries and for the status and visibility gained by the clergy to be maintained thereafter. In the obituaries this is reflected in the sharp increase noted above and the stability that follows.

7. CONCLUSION

The picture of change that emerged in this chapter through the analysis of titles and the categories they represent, both social and professional, shows strong effects from gender and culture. Change affects sex groups, culture groups, and sex-by-culture groups differently depending on the category involved. Sometimes explanations based on the obituaries independently of the world outside lend themselves naturally to the results, but often events from the world outside provide a more reasonable explanation.

Underlying the analysis of titles as acquired identities is the expectation that they would indeed reflect the world outside the obituaries, for in a way they are dependent on it more so than are names. Name is a variable only in the world of the obituaries. But acquired identities are variable both within and outside the obituaries, as are the categories they represent. We can analyze these identities within the obituaries, but we have no clear assessment of how they fare in the world outside.

The explanations offered thus far have often relied on events in the world outside as possible causes for the results from the obituaries—changes in social and political structures, for example, or changes affecting the status of women. Often a necessary connection between the two worlds could not be satisfactorily established. As a result, explanations are at times based on arguments of possibility, not necessity. But insofar as the connections established between the two worlds seem sufficiently possible and plausible, they are sufficient for our present purpose until future research allows the establishment of the necessary link. The relationship between the two worlds continues to be a puzzle, which we hope to solve as we develop a better understanding of the connection between them.

Chapter 5
Acquired Identities: Occupations

Nothing irritates me more than when men claim they
do not wish us to work because they wish to spare us
the burden. We do not want condescension, we want
respect.

> —Bahithat al-Badiya, 1909, "A Lecture in the Club of
> the Umma Party"[1]

From Plato to the present, occupation has been
the most common indicator of stratification. . . .
Occupational categories are one of the major factors
which differentiate people's beliefs, values, behavior,
and even their emotional expressions.

> —Lipset and Zeterberg, in Ibrahim 1982:388

It has been claimed that in English and other European languages the great majority of terms designating occupation more readily evoke the image of a man than a woman. The following riddle serves to illustrate this point:

A man and his son were apprehended in a robbery. The father was shot during the struggle and the son, in handcuffs, was rushed to the police station. As the police pulled the struggling boy into the station, the mayor, who had been called to the scene, looked up and said, 'My God, it's my son!'. What relation was the mayor to the boy? (quoted in Smith 1985:45 and attributed to Eakins and Eakins 1978)

The mayor, of course, was the boy's mother. This kind of riddle could, as Smith (45–46) suggests, be used as a simple test of the degree to which a particular occupation or activity is more strongly associated with women or men. From our perspective, it serves to illustrate the extent to which occupation as a form of acquired public identity may be sex differentiated.

Such riddles are probably easier to construct in a language like English with little, if any, grammatical gender marking. They would be more difficult, though not impossible, to come by in languages like Arabic simply because of the grammatical gender system that permeates the language. For example, the word for "mayor" in Arabic ('umda) is marked with the feminine ending -a(t) and thus lends itself to such potential male-female ambiguity. But although the ambiguity is linguistically possible, the riddle would get a different response from an Egyptian audience. It would be viewed as a linguistic joke, a witticism perhaps, but not a realistic possibility since no woman has ever occupied the position of 'umda, someone who heads villages and towns in rural communities.[2] The word is understood to refer only to men and therefore takes masculine grammatical agreement only.[3]

The language we use to identify people reflects not only their actual achievements, positions they may have occupied, and identities acquired through such achievements but also our perceptions of the likelihood that such a person or group would have achieved or occupied such positions and of the importance we attach to such identification. Because identification by occupation and professional (more so than social) titles is clearly dependent on a person's having occupied some position in a certain occupation or profession, one is tempted to interpret this form of identification as a reflection of social realities, a demonstration of the relative status reached by women and men within a community. This approach, legitimate as it may be, ignores perceptions (perhaps even biases) the identifier may have in determining the appropriate, most suitable form of identification for the occasion. The identifier may therefore choose to ignore certain aspects of a person's identity, depending on actual context or perceived appropriateness. Such factors are important in interpreting the data on identification of the deceased by occupation and its implication for the gendered picture of the obituary pages.

In this chapter we examine the identification of the deceased by occupation in order to assess the combined effects of Sex and Culture, and later Time, on this variation. But if the analysis of occupation as a form of acquired identity is correct, as we propose it is, it predicts that identification by occupation should follow a pattern of behavior similar to that observed in other types of acquired identities. The second purpose of this chapter then is to pursue this comparative analysis between identification by occupation and by professional and social titles to further test the validity of this proposal.

I. OCCUPATIONS BY SEX AND CULTURE

Statistics on identifying the deceased by occupation proved to be significant for each of the three variables Sex, Culture, and Time (table B.1). The strong effect of Sex is demonstrated by the fact that only 7 percent of the deceased identified by occupation are women but 93 percent are men, thus reflecting the importance occupation has in constructing men's public identity relative to women's. Furthermore, strong sex differentiation is demonstrated in the professional vis-à-vis social identification of the deceased (see figure 1 in the overview). Although the percentage of women identified by occupation is almost double the percentage of those identified by professional titles (7 percent to 4 percent), the overall picture draws a clear distinction between professional versus social identity. Men are much more likely to be identified by their professional identity (occupation and professional titles) than are women. If gender equity can be said to have been achieved anywhere, it must be in the identification of deceased women in their social, not professional, roles or identities.

The association between Culture and Occupation is also strong. A full 70 percent of deceased women identified by occupation came from Arabic obituaries; 17 percent from Persian obituaries; and 13 percent from English obituaries (see figure 2 in the overview). These results are particularly interesting when compared to those of the two other categories of acquired identities—professional and social titles. The ranking Arabic > Persian > English is maintained in the results from these two categories, although the English obituaries provide no data for social titles (see chapter 4).

Two possible explanations are proposed for these results; one is culture based and the other obituary based. A culture-based explanation would see these results as a reflection of the relative cultural values, or lack thereof, attached to these categories in the social context within which the obituaries are written, thereby attributing the difference to a higher value associated with occupation in Egyptian society and a lower value associated with social titles in the United States. The results from professional identification by title would support this position. But the results from Occupation would not, since this position would predict that occupations are least valued in the United States, which is not true. We must therefore conclude, at least on that basis, that the world created in the obituary pages is not a true reflection of the world outside or a replica of it.

The obituary-based explanation would attribute the results to differences in the way obituaries are perceived across cultures. These differences are reflected in the perceptions of families writing obituaries, which evolve over time and are influenced by materials in the obituary pages themselves and by the changing role obituaries may have in the funeralization process. Under this alternative, it is not so much what cultural value is assigned to a particular variable, or category, in an abstract social context—here the role of occupation in society. What matters are the priorities and values developed within the obituary pages themselves that determine the perceived value of the category or variable in question. Thus, regardless of how much or how little value is assigned to occupation and professional or social titles in Egypt, Iran, or the United States, it is the value assigned by families writing obituaries at a particular time and place that matters. For example, in Egypt, traditions for writing obituaries that have developed over the years place value on identifying the deceased by occupation. Egyptian obituary culture is status oriented, and professional accomplishments are indicators of status. For American and Iranian families, there seems to be less value placed on identifying the deceased by occupation. On that basis, we can conclude that occupation is a more salient category in the identification of the deceased in the Arabic obituaries than in the English or Persian obituaries, independent somewhat of any value assigned to occupation in the world outside the obituaries.

We continue in our subsequent analysis to entertain these two alternative explanations in our attempt to establish, on the one hand, the independence of the obituary pages as a genre and, on the other, their reflection of sociocultural values of the world outside them. The view of obituaries as a mere reflection of society in this case makes unacceptable predictions. We continue to develop this line of thought, which in the final chapter we integrate into our conclusions and discussion of modeling the results. At this point we pursue the analysis of occupation through the subsequent analysis of combined effects of Sex and Culture, and later Time, so as to complete our analysis of the identification of the deceased.

1.1 Interaction Effect of Sex and Culture on Identification by Occupation

The analysis of the data by culture group (table B.1) shows that 451 (70 percent) of the deceased mentioned by occupation are found in the Arabic obituaries. Women constitute only 5 percent of this population and men the remaining 95 percent (table B.2). The breakdown by sex in the Persian obituaries is identical, although fewer deceased (109) are identified with an occupation; in the English obituaries, this number is even smaller (82), but the breakdown by sex shows that women represent 18 percent of this population and men 82 percent. Figure 5.1 shows how strong the discrepancy between the sexes is in each of the three cultures. Figure 5.2 shows a cross-cultural assessment of the results as percentages of sex groups.

Figure 5.2 provides a sharper picture of the differentiating effect culture has on sex groups. For the women, 54 percent of those identified by occupation are Egyptian, 35 percent American, and 12 percent Iranian. For the men, 72 percent identified by occupation are Egyptian, 17 percent are Iranian, and 11 percent are American. The ranking in the male population is consistent with earlier rankings (Arabic > Persian > English), but the ranking among the female group here is different. More deceased American women are identified by occupation than are Iranian women.[4]

In all three cultures, then, identification by an occupation is more highly valued for men than for women. The results also show a divergence among the female population from what has so far emerged as something of a norm in the ranking of the cultural impact on linguistic variables, Arabic > Persian > English. Compare these results, for example, with those from the analysis of titles. The male population conforms to this norm, but the female population does not. As the cross-cultural analysis in table B.2 shows, the percentages for deceased women identified by title in Arabic and Persian obituaries (overall and by type) are similar. (We will return to this point in chapter 7 in our discussion of modeling the results.)

2. OCCUPATIONS OVER TIME

The change in the identification of the deceased by occupation is dramatic over the fifty-year period (9 percent in 1938; 26 percent in 1988), but perhaps not as strong as the change in professional titles (4 percent in 1938; 33 percent in 1988) (table B.1). The identification of the deceased by occupation and professional titles shows a pronounced, consistent increase (see figure 3 of the overview). Most striking, however, are the results for 1988 for these two variables. Taken together, change over time in the two variables

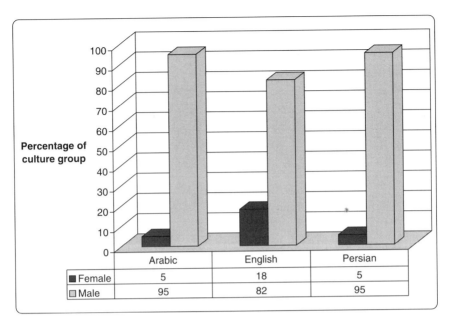

Percentage of culture group	Arabic	English	Persian
■ Female	5	18	5
□ Male	95	82	95

Fig. 5.1. The Effect of Sex on Occupation by Culture Groups

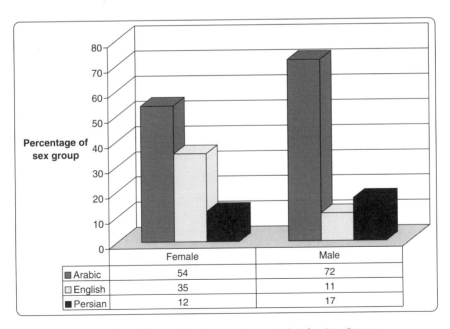

Percentage of sex group	Female	Male
■ Arabic	54	72
□ English	35	11
■ Persian	12	17

Fig. 5.2. The Effect of Culture on Occupation by Sex Groups

representing professional identity suggests a marked increase in the number of families identifying their deceased in the professional and public roles acquired during their lifetimes. This change may be interpreted as an indication that a stronger awareness has developed of the cultural value (or worth) assigned to professional activities over this period in all three societies. But it can also be interpreted as an increased awareness within the world of the obituaries and the families who create it of the value professional identification has acquired in the funeralization process, thus providing the link between the two worlds.

2.1 Interaction Effect of Sex and Time on Identification by Occupation

A breakdown of the occupation data by Sex and Time (table B.3) shows how different the representations are of the two populations throughout the period. Only one deceased woman is mentioned with an occupation in 1938, whereas 55 men are. In 1988, these numbers increase, to 19 and 146, respectively. Figure 5.3 illustrates these results, showing the much greater identification by occupation enjoyed by men over the fifty-year period (always in excess of 88 percent). The percentage of deceased women identified by occupation remains in single digits throughout the period until 1988, when it reaches 12 percent. The ratio of female-to-male representation has improved by 10 percent over the fifty years. Figure 5.4 illustrates the results when change is assessed for each sex group separately over time, revealing a more encouraging picture for women (an increase from 2 percent in 1938 to 44 percent in 1988). (The percentages are derived from table B.3.) Identification by occupation for deceased men also increases over the period (9 percent in 1938 to 24 percent in 1988), but the change is not as dramatic as that for deceased women. The analysis of expected values also identifies 1988 as the year when the actual distribution of the sexes is significantly different from the expected and in favor of the female group (table B.3).

The difference between the two trajectories points to the 1960s and beyond as the period when women's identification by occupation changes in the obituaries, posting an increase of twenty percentage points between 1968 and 1988. Changes in women's employment patterns and women's overall professional status in the world outside during this period immediately come to mind as possible explanations for this unprecedented change in the obituaries. This change may have finally had a strong impact on the identification of women in the obituary pages.

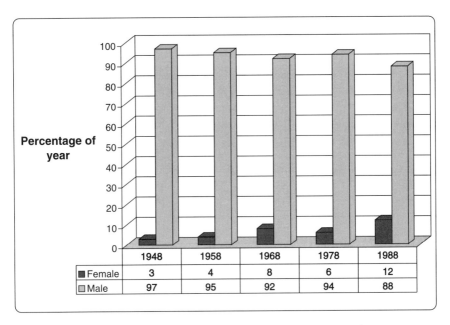

	1948	1958	1968	1978	1988
■ Female	3	4	8	6	12
□ Male	97	95	92	94	88

Fig. 5.3. Sex Differentiation in Distribution of Occupations by Year

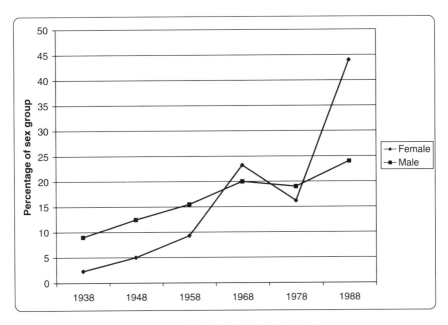

Fig. 5.4. Occupation Distribution by Sex Group

2.2 Interaction Effect of Culture and
Time on Identification by Occupation

Looking at the three culture groups over the fifty-year period, we see that Arabic obituaries consistently post the highest numbers of deceased identified by occupation (table B.4) and that Persian obituaries generally (except for 1938 and 1988) record higher numbers than English obituaries. In 1938, Arabic obituaries represent 93 percent of identifications by occupation; English, 5 percent; and Persian, 2 percent. By 1988, however, the distribution has evened out somewhat: Arabic, 58 percent; English, 31 percent; and Persian, 11 percent. Overall, then, the movement during these fifty years is toward an improvement in the distribution of occupation space across cultures. But while Arabic obituaries occupy most of this space overall (70 percent) and within each time period, English obituaries show the most dramatic change. The analysis of expected values shows English obituaries to be significantly underrepresented in the years 1948–68 but overrepresented only in 1988. Arabic obituaries, on the other hand, are overrepresented in the first two years and underrepresented only in 1988; Persian obituaries are underrepresented in the first and last years, with significant overrepresentation in 1958–68 only. Figure 5.5 shows the distribution of titles over the years as percentages of each culture group.

Three different cultural pictures emerge from the analysis of occupations over time. Only for Persian obituaries does the period end on a downward trend, having reached a peak in 1968. The Arabic obituaries show a generally steady increase in identification of the deceased by occupation. The picture in the English obituaries is perhaps the most unusual, with a slow increase in the first four decades followed by two dramatic increases in the last two decades. More than 60 percent of all identifications by occupation in the English obituaries occur in 1988.

Finally, the statistical analysis performed on each culture group independently of the others proved the distribution in the Arabic and English obituaries to be statistically significant, but not in Persian. Thus we cannot establish that Time alone has had an impact on the identification of the deceased by occupation in the Persian obituaries since the actual number of deceased identified with occupation is not significantly different from the expected values in any of the six time groups.

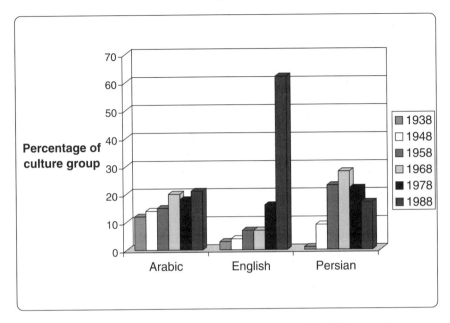

Fig. 5.5. Culture-Differentiated Change for Deceased with Occupations

The analysis by Culture, then, points to 1968 as a turning point in identification by occupation, but in different ways in different cultures. It represents a peak in the Persian and a leap forward (almost a peak) in Arabic, but whereas in Arabic the level of representation reached in 1968 is maintained, in Persian the 1968 peak is followed by a regression; in English it is followed by a tremendous progression also sustained until the end. But 1988 remains by far the most dramatic for English, and since it still represents a high point for Arabic as well, it is reasonable to conclude that the contribution from these two cultures (Arabic and English) has had a strong effect on the overall percentage increase for this final decade.

2.3 Interaction Effect of Sex, Culture, and Time on Identification by Occupation

To assess the three-way interaction of Sex, Culture, and Time, we turn to the analysis by sex groups separately, as we have done before, and compare the contribution of occupations over time from each culture (table B.5). This analysis takes as input the number of deceased women and men (analyzed separately) with occupations from each culture and year and measures the extent to which the number in each cell is divergent from the expected values. No statistical significance could be established for the distribution in the female population, suggesting the distribution of this population by Culture over the six time groups is not different from the expected values. Thus the analysis failed to establish a culturally differentiated change for the female population. Only for the male population is a level of statistical significance reached (χ^2 = 86.1 and p < .0001). The analysis of expected values points to the significant overrepresentation in English obituaries in 1988 by comparison to the other cultures, in Arabic obituaries in 1938–48, and in Persian obituaries in 1958–68. Thus the distribution of occupation over time is culturally differentiated for the male group, as can be seen in figure 5.6.

A different picture emerges from this figure of the change in identifying deceased men by occupation in each of the three cultures. The results for Egyptian men show a steady increase in such identification, with a relatively sharp increase in 1968 and a weaker one in 1988. The results for American men also show steady increase in the early period and post strong increases in 1978 and, most notably, in 1988. The obituaries of Iranian men

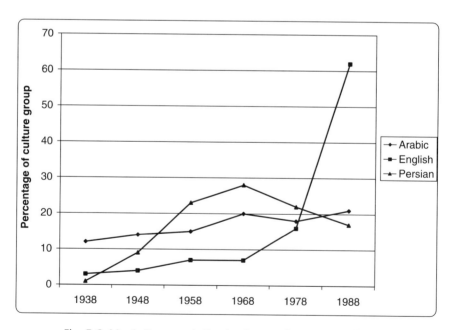

Fig. 5.6. Men's Representation by Occupation across Cultures

show increases until 1968 (the peak), after which time this trend is reversed. These differences are interesting in themselves but more important in their implication for our assessment of the obituaries as reflections of social and cultural realities. Attempts to relate these results to occupation in the world outside the obituaries—cross-cultural or culture specific—are bound to produce implausible interpretations. A more accurate interpretation would limit these conclusions to deceased men during this period; these different pictures of change that emerged from the three cultures are indications of change in obituary cultures only, perhaps reflecting change in the value of occupational identity in this public space.

Although the comparative analysis failed to differentiate among the female populations with regard to identification by occupation, culture-independent analyses of the distribution over time proved to be significant in the obituaries of Egyptian and American women (but not of Iranian women, or men for that matter). Figure 5.7 illustrates this change and can be compared with figure 5.6.

Note the similarities between the two figures as they pertain to English and Arabic obituaries. In the English obituaries of women, identification with

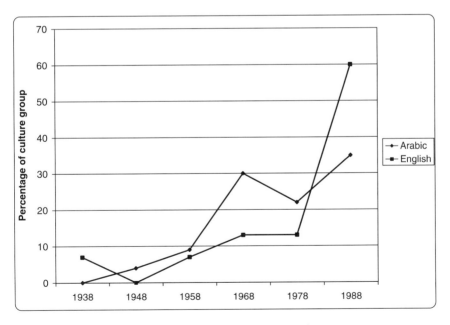

Fig. 5.7. Female Occupations over Time

occupations increases in 1958 and 1968, levels off during the 1968–78 decade, then takes an impressively sharp turn upward in 1988. This final progression, a jump from 13 percent to 60 percent, is of the same magnitude as that found among the American male group, which began its marked ascent in 1978.

In the Arabic obituaries of women, identification by occupation does not increase in any significant fashion until 1958, when a major progression occurs between 1958 and 1968, amounting to almost a 20 percent increase. A relatively sharp regression follows in 1978 (a loss of 8 percent), which is then reversed in 1988 (a 13 percent increase). The period ends in 1988 with the greatest representation (35 percent) during the fifty-year period.

The last three decades (1958–88) are the most important for both American and Egyptian women's obituaries, with respect to identification with occupation; 1988 is the most important year of these three. Seventy-seven percent of references to women with occupations in Egyptian obituaries occur during these last three decades. For American women's obituaries, 1968 is the first year the percentage of deceased women identified with occupation exceeds 10 percent; in 1988, this figure rises to 60 percent.

The year 1988 emerges from this analysis as having the strongest impact on identification of the deceased by occupation in obituaries from Egypt and the United States, particularly when we compare American men's and women's obituaries in that year, and American and Egyptian women's obituaries. We see both gender- and culture-differentiated changes, although cross-cultural effects over time could be measured only for the male population and the cross-cultural analysis of occupations over time could not differentiate between the distribution of the sexes relative to each other.

2.4 Situating the Change: Obituary Culture Or Beyond?

The different analyses of identification with occupation over time have consistently pointed to 1988 as perhaps the most important time period, reflecting the strongest increase in representation of the deceased population by occupation (see tables B.1, B.3, and B.4). We need to ask why 1988 in particular would have had such a strong effect on the representation by occupation in both Egypt and the United States but not Iran, and why in culture-independent analyses this appears strong among women's groups. Attempts to answer such questions ignoring obituary culture are problematic here as they have been for the analyses of both names and titles.

From the gender perspective, the period 1958–68 was a "liberating" time for women in the United States and Egypt, but for different reasons. In the United States, the period witnessed the rise of the second wave of feminism followed by legislation supporting women's rights to equal opportunities in areas such as employment, pay, and education. In Egypt, government reforms were introduced in support of women's education and employment as part of a redefinition of the national agenda, a process initially triggered by the change from monarchy to republic and the sociopolitical reforms that followed. Both countries had been engaged in public debates over women's rights to education and employment, their role in the public sphere, and their contribution to national development.

In the United States, for example, the feminist debate of the 1960s and 1970s was focused on equality between the sexes, on women's health and their right to exercise control over their own bodies, and on economic independence for women, among other issues. The overall focus was equality for the sexes in all areas. These issues have dominated feminist discourse in the United States since then, taking different turns as issues get settled and others emerge. Part of the feminist agenda since then has also focused on giving women a more visible public voice and public image. Numerous paths have been followed to implement the feminist agenda in achieving these goals. Relevant to our purposes here are efforts to document and celebrate women's accomplishments in all areas of the arts, sciences, education, politics, and public service, among others. These efforts gave women in the United States, by the end of this fifty-year period, an increased public visibility and a public voice they had not previously enjoyed. A strong and growing civil rights movement in the United States also provided support for the women's rights movement.

Some important events from this period include the publication in 1963 of Betty Friedan's best-seller *The Feminine Mystique*, which challenged the idealization of the traditional feminine role of wife and mother. The Civil Rights Act was passed a year later, prohibiting discrimination on the basis of race, sex, religion, or national origin. In 1972, Title IX of the Education Amendment prohibited sex discrimination in several areas including student admissions, employee hiring, and student athletics. In 1976, military academies began to admit women under a 1975 order of Congress, and in 1978 NASA accepted women for astronaut training. Opportunities opened up to women during this period, despite the failure of the Equal Rights Amendment to pass.

In Egypt the feminist movement (as described by Badran 1995 and

Sullivan 1986, among others), which had been independently supported and run during the first half of the century, had come under the auspices of the state in post-1952 Egypt. During this stage of "state feminism," women gained the right to vote in the 1956 constitution, the first to have been written after the change from monarchy to republic. The feminist debate in the late 1950s and early 1960s continued earlier debates on women's rights to education and employment, for example. But during this period the issues became part of the national agenda in the sense that they had been adopted and thereby sponsored by the state. What in the earlier years of the women's movement were arguments presented by individual and group supporters of women's rights became in this later period almost part of government policies, and as such the national political and economic agenda. The discourse on modernity, which had started in the nineteenth century but continued throughout the twentieth century, found a strong voice in government proclamations and commitment to a speedy transformation of the new republic into a modern industrialized state. To accomplish this goal, women's contribution to the economy had to be acknowledged, continuing an earlier (modernity) discourse that no nation can progress with half of its population uneducated and unemployed. Thus women's contribution to the public domain had to be solicited, encouraged, and supported financially and otherwise by the state. The overall atmosphere permeating that period was one of change geared toward the building of a different Egypt (whose official name was also changed at the time)—socially, economically, and politically. As a result, women were strongly encouraged to become active and equal participants in this national endeavor.

Together with such public pronouncements, a number of government reforms were enacted during that period designed, as state officials proclaimed at the time, to bridge the gap between the poor and the rich, reduce class barriers, and provide economic opportunities to the underprivileged sectors of society. These reforms included a series of (agrarian) Land Reform Laws in the 1950s and later in 1961 the so-called Socialist Reform Laws. The proclaimed purpose in both cases was the redistribution of income. Ibrahim, in studying social mobility in Egypt during 1952–78, refers to this period as the "Socialist Transformation Phase" in which Egypt "witnessed the height of revolutionary action in changing Egypt's socioeconomic structure" (1982:380). It was also a period of great social mobility and economic growth. For example, women constituted 8 percent of the students enrolled in universities in 1952; by 1992 they would make up 40 percent of the student body overall (Neft and Levine

1997:257). Metz (1991:144) reports that between the 1953–54 and 1965–66 academic years, women's overall enrollment more than doubled, and it almost doubled again between 1965–66 and 1975–76. Furthermore,

> The proportion of the population with some secondary education more than doubled between 1960 and 1976; the number of people with some university education nearly tripled. . . . Women made great educational gains: the percentage of women with preuniversity education grew more than 300 percent while women with University education grew more than 600 percent. . . . In the first ten years following the 1952 Revolution, spending on higher education increased 400 percent. Between academic years 1951–52 and 1978–79, student enrollment in public universities grew nearly 1400 percent. . . . The total number of female college students had doubled; by 1985–86 women accounted for 32 percent of all students. (147)

In the area of employment, 4 percent of working-age women had jobs outside the house in 1966; by the early 1990s this figure had climbed to 22 percent. In 1980, women made up 14 percent of Egypt's government workers; the number more than doubled in 1990. Finally, in 1976 Egyptian women owned only 2 percent of businesses, but by 1988 their share of business ownership was up to 17 percent (Neft and Levine 1997:258–59).

The figures presented above, although not systematically collected, are sufficient to illustrate a high degree of positive change in areas that could have had an impact on the status of women, hence their image and public identity during the period covered. Needless to say, most statistics show that men made greater advances than did women in almost all areas during this same time period. What is relevant for us, however, is not so much the status of women in relation to men in Egyptian society, but forces that may have enhanced the image of women in that society and allowed them access to the public domain, and the potential impact this may have had on the obituaries.

The factors affecting the representation of women in the obituaries most are the redistribution of income, the availability of (free) education including graduate education, and the ever-growing public sector control of the job market. The redistribution of income forced families in the upper strata of the socioeconomic scale—and who in a sense were the targets of this proposition—to realize that change was inevitable and their survival dictated that they participate in the change and accept it as part of their future and that of their families. Education and employment became a priority, extended to women as well as men. Women benefitted from the availability of free education and public sector jobs (which included almost all institutions of higher learning), where admission and hiring alike were conducted "objectively," perhaps even impersonally. These policies were developed as part of the overall national agenda set by the government to promote equal opportunities for all sectors of the society (the socioeconomic agenda for equity), but not necessarily to promote gender equity. But women benefitted from these policies since they provided relief to their families from the many financial burdens imposed on them by the education of women. In addition, other benefits to women, such as maternity leave and the availability of government-sponsored childcare facilities, allowed them a certain measure of economic independence. Statistics on women's education and employment support this view.

It is not our purpose here to evaluate such policies or assess their impact on the empowerment (or disempowerment) of the feminist movement and women's rights activists in Egypt.[5] Our primary purpose is to relate the results from the obituaries to the sociocultural context within which they were written.

If indeed education and employment among women had significantly increased in Egypt, and if the overall public (and national) awareness had been changed with respect to women's contribution to the public domain in both the United States and Egypt (admittedly through different channels), families writing obituaries would naturally be impacted by such events. The obituaries would therefore reflect not only women's changing world, their accomplishments, and their increased public visibility, but also the changed attitudes that accompany such a changing world. From this perspective, then, the obituaries do reflect overall change in the world outside but with some reservations, if not contradictions.

The analysis of change in identification by occupation could not establish sex differentiation in the obituaries. It failed to achieve statistical significance in any of the three cultures. If the obituaries are true reflections of the social realities outside them, this result would mean that the employment of women and men relative to each other has also not changed significantly during this period—at least the differences over time are not different from natural variation. This is unlikely, although a final determination must be based on a comparison of available statistics on the world outside during this same period. Moghadam (1993:197) provides statistics on women's share of employment in different countries, including the three countries under study here: Egypt, 18.7 percent in 1984; United States, 45.5 percent in 1987; and Iran, 9 percent in 1986. These statistics support the overall culture ranking in the obituaries as it pertains to women's identification with occupation and reflect the divergence among the three cultures as to the share of occupations garnered by each sex.

When employment figures are compared over time, the sex differential appears to be stronger in some years than others. In Iran, for example, women in 1966 represent 13.2 percent of the labor force, which increases to 20.2 percent in 1976 only to drop dramatically to 8.9 percent in 1986 (189). A comparison of the corresponding years in the obituaries shows the female share of occupations to be only 3 percent in 1968, nonexistent in 1978, and 11 percent in 1988, a picture different from that of the world outside. Thus the obituary world cannot be viewed simply as a true reflection or a replica of the world outside, although to ultimately prove this point these two statistics would have to be compared.

In the obituaries the identification of men as a group, but not women, changes significantly over time, suggesting that identification by occupation is not totally sex independent despite failure to establish significant sex-differentiated change (table B.5). In the English obituaries, both sex groups post an unusually high percentage increase in identification with occupation in 1988, reflective of an emerging change in obituary style and culture that encourages the inclusion of such information. The obituaries in 1988 begin to resemble résumés or vitae. The more accepted such a style becomes in the *New York Times* the more likely are the deceased to be identified with their occupations.

Obituary style based on identification by occupation has been well established in the Arabic obituaries, as evidenced by patterns developed in the identification of deceased males, the relative stability noted over the years, and the 70 percent of obituaries mentioning identification by occupation found in the Arabic obituaries. In the English obituaries, however, that obituary style had not been well established in the *New York Times*. A change toward mentioning occupations is demonstrated by the increase in their inclusion during the last two decades, particularly 1988 when occupations are significantly overrepresented in English obituaries, as compared to those in Arabic and Persian obituaries. The analysis of the 1998 data in chapter 6 shows continued increase in occupation mention for both women and men, thus supporting this view of a changing obituary culture in the English obituaries.

Overall change in representation by occupation in the obituary world, from the cultural and gender perspectives, is attributed to an increase in women's occupations, attitudes toward women's employment, and to obituary style as well. The situation in Persian obituaries, however, remains puzzling. Can it be argued, for example, that Iranian women have not made significant gains in employment over these fifty years? Or is it more likely that their representation in the obituaries by occupation, like that of men, has not changed because obituary culture in Iran has not sufficiently changed to make occupations a more valuable and salient feature of deceased identification?

3. CLASSIFICATION OF OCCUPATIONS BY TYPE

The analysis of actual occupations mentioned provides the final touches to a picture of a gender- and culture-differentiated obituary world. It also serves to create a more concrete picture of this world, situating the deceased within the socioeconomic strata to which they may have belonged during their lifetime and thereby increasing the connection between the two worlds, the obituaries and beyond. We have assumed without strong evidence so far that the deceased would have belonged to the middle and upper classes of their respective societies. This assumption has been based on the cost incurred in publishing an obituary in the newspapers. Admittedly, if a family so chooses, it can limit obituary size to the minimum size set by the newspapers, which ranges from two to four lines depending on the year and the newspaper. In this way the family can get the satisfaction of having announced the death and other funeralization ceremonies and of having fulfilled their duties toward the deceased and themselves without having incurred an insurmountable expense in the process. On that basis, we have assumed a relatively wide range of income groups from among these classes would be represented in the obituary pages. The analysis of occupations in this section supports this assumption by showing that this population is indeed limited to the middle and upper strata.

Since the Arabic obituaries feature the most identifications by occupation, I have adopted a classification of occupations based on the 1981 Egyptian government's Bureau of Statistics and Ibrahim's (1982) study of social mobility in Egypt (1952–77), modified to accommodate some occupational identities in the obituaries. Occupations in Ibrahim's version of this classification fall into essentially seven categories (392).

I. Professional and technical
II. Administrative and managerial
III. Clerical workers
IV. Sales workers
V. Craftsmen, production, processing, operators
VI. Farmers and related work
VII. Other occupations

Ibrahim suggests that the first three categories correspond roughly to the upper and upper-middle strata in Egypt, categories IV and V to the lower-middle stratum, and categories VI and VII to the lower stratum (407–9). If so, and if a similar ranking may be applicable to both the United States and Iran, then we would expect the bulk of the deceased population in the obituaries to come from the first five categories.

Category I includes professionals (doctors, engineers, teachers, clergy, artists, etc.). Category II includes those in commanding government administrative positions as well as executives and managers of public and private corporations. According to Ibrahim, these two categories represent "the upper echelons of occupational structure" in Egypt. Category III represents clerical occupations, which include white-collar workers and lower-stratum civil servants with less than a university-level education. Category IV represents sales workers (self-employed or employed by others), whose jobs would be in commercial, financial, and related fields. Category V includes skilled and semiskilled workers such as craftsmen, production and processing workers, and machine operators. Category VI represents service workers and includes unskilled workers outside both industry and farming. Category VII includes farmers, farm workers, fishermen, and forestry workers.

The obituaries in all three cultures do not reflect this wide range of occupational categories; most of the deceased mentioned with occupations come from the first four categories, especially the first two or three. Categories V–VII are almost nonexistent in the obituaries. Sometimes it is difficult to place individuals mentioned by occupation into any of the categories. For example, some deceased are identified as elected officials such as members of the Senate ('udw majlis al-shuyukh) or the House of Representatives (majlis al-nuwwab or majlis al-shaʿb in post-1952 Egypt). It is also hard to classify the aʿyan (the notables, or "rural notables" as Ansari [1986] refers to them), perhaps because they are not technically speaking part of the labor force. The *aʿyan* were formerly appointed by high government authorities as consultants because of the strong leadership roles and the status they command in their communities. Their role has changed tremendously in post-1952 Egypt and their visibility likewise diminished. In the obituaries, they appear mostly during the first three years of the study.

The classification I have adopted retains categories I and II as they are and ignores all categories beyond IV. The modified classification below can be construed as basically subdividing categories III and IV, and creating a category for the groups hard to fit into the original classification. The exclusion of categories V–VII is simply due to the realities reflected in the population of the obituaries.

> Obituary-based classification of occupations
>   I. Professional and technical
>   II. Administrative and managerial
>   III. *Aʿyan* and elected representatives
>   IV. Business (owners) and merchants
>   V. Civil service and other employees
>   VI. Clerical
>   VII. Sales

Categories I–III have already been discussed. Category IV includes business owners and merchants (who by definition also own their business), including shop owners (*sahib mahal*), factory owners (*sahib masnaʿ*), contractors (*muqawil*), and traders or merchants (*tagir*). The English translation of the Arabic terms makes it hard to distinguish this group from "businessmen (or women)," but in Arabic they are distinct. A person identified as *ragul aʿmal* (businessman) is perceived as being more of a manager/administrator who may also own the business. Category IV includes only owners, contractors, or merchants. The Arabic terms suggest a more local, traditional background for this group while the term *ragul aʿmal,* a loan translation from English, carries with it a different concept of business. Category V is a subgroup of the original category III. It reflects an identification of the deceased just as *muwadhaf* (employee), who can therefore be either in the government (public sector) or in the private sector (companies, banks, and the like). Some deceased are identified as employees, but others are identified by their place of employment only, from which we conclude they are employees.

Analyzing the occupation data along these lines demonstrates that the deceased population projects an upper- and upper-middle-class profile in all three cultures, if we accept Ibrahim's findings for Egypt and assume they hold for the other two cultures as well. If not, the decision would have to be made on the basis of an examination of occupations from the English and Persian obituaries to make a determination about the socioeconomic background from which their populations come. The Persian obituaries, for example, mention military officers, bankers, lawyers, teachers, architects, mayors, and other government officials and employees. The English obituaries mention presidents of companies, chairmen, executives, supervisors, foremen, directors, and court clerks, among others. Regardless of classification, original or modified, these types of occupations would fall under middle and upper strata of social organization in the United States and Iran. Adopting a uniform classification provides a systematic way to analyze the data in a comparative perspective.

Since in previous sections discrepancies based on Sex, Culture, and Time have already been discussed for the population identified with occupation, in this section we analyze the distribution by categories to see how the populations fare in relation to each other by sex and culture groups and how change may have taken place in the representation of occupation types in the obituary world. The results may then be compared with the world outside to determine the degree of correspondence or divergence between the two and to project specific directions in which the obituaries may be heading. I only address this latter point, leaving detailed comparisons with the world outside for future research.

Table D.1 provides the distribution of occupations by categories within each culture group and for the population as a whole. Three categories emerge with strong profiles in the overall distribution: categories I, II, and V, which make up 80 percent of the occupations mentioned in the obituaries. This means that 488 of 642 deceased whose families identified their occupations came from such background. The Arabic share of this population (316) is 65 percent, the English share (72) 15 percent, and Persian (100) 20 percent, corresponding closely to the overall cultural contribution of each. Naturally, some categories are missing from some culture groups: category III is peculiar to Arabic; Persian obituaries had no deceased with occupations from categories VI and VII; and English obituaries had no representation in the "Other" category. This category includes three groups: students (Arabic and Persian), presidents or leading officers of social (nonprofit) organizations (Arabic), and *ra'is al-khaṣa l-malakiyya* (chief executive of the royal estates), an occupation related to the monarchy (Arabic). All three are technically not occupations but are still used in the obituaries as a form of "respected" public identity, a professional role acquired during the deceased's lifetime and with which they have obviously been known. Students in both Egypt and Iran, particularly in the earlier part of the century, had important political roles. Three of the deceased in the "Other" category were Egyptian women who were officers in social organizations, one of whom was president of the Muslim Women Association in 1948. The group is, however, dominated by students in Iran and in Egypt.

The distribution by Sex and Culture in table D.2 shows interesting gender differences. In each culture about half the deceased women identified by occupation come from category I: Arabic, 44 percent; English, 53 percent; and Persian, 60 percent. Other interesting conclusions can be drawn from the data in this table: the only deceased women identified as business owners are American women; and the number of women identified as having administrative or managerial roles is very small: two Egyptian women, four American women, and no Iranian women. This comparison of occupational categories by sex of the deceased supports an idea suggested earlier that the identification of women in the public domain follows patterns previously established for men: the two categories within which women's occupations fall are among the three most commonly projected of men. Men's identification defines public space— its overall nature and specific characteristics. When women begin to share that space, they are defined by standards already set for men. Women's presence in public space outside the obituaries ultimately brings about change within that space as a result of their day-to-day interactions therein. The change resulting from their presence in the obituary pages is harder to assess because their identities are defined by their families, the writers of the obituaries. The presence of women in the obituaries and the changes in their identification therein are bound to trigger further change, if the obituaries are viewed as a genre that reproduces itself as obituary writers gain exposure and therefore experience in the writing of this genre.

The analysis of occupations over time has pointed to 1988 as an important year for Egyptian and American women. The distribution by occupational category (table D.3) shows that the nine occupations applied to American women in that year are equally divided among categories I, II, and IV. Thus for deceased American women, identification by occupation starts with the professional (category I), then the executive-managerial (category II) in 1978, and finally in 1988 business ownership is introduced, an interesting projection in itself and in its relation to other groups. Deceased Egyptian women begin their occupational identification in 1958,[6] also as professionals, and then they add on categories II and VI in 1978. In 1988 they add a fourth category (V) service. Iranian women's occupations also come first from category I, and in 1988 category V is added.

Change in men's occupational categories is different. Among the Egyptian group, only category III shows a decrease in representation over the years. This, as suggested earlier, is a true reflection of this group's history in the social reality outside the obituaries, as a result of the dismantling of this group and the perceived sociocultural devaluation of its power and status. The strongest increase is reflected in categories I, II, and IV, a result of movements within the upper and upper-middle classes in Egypt. An increase in category IV, for example, may be a reflection of change in policies more favorable toward business groups. This group has prospered in the world outside the obituaries as a result of various socioeconomic changes, such as the Open Door Policy adopted in the 1970s (Ibrahim 1982).

The results of the analysis of American men's occupations by category support many of the ideas presented thus far. Until 1978 category I has the strongest representation. In 1978 category II gains some strength, but only in 1988 do other categories emerge with any frequency (IV and V). Since men in the world outside the obituaries have occupied positions within all these categories, the change represented in 1978 and 1988 is not due to the world outside the obituaries but to changed perceptions among obituary writers as to how they should identify their deceased (a change in the value assigned to identification by occupation). As the perception of value in occupational identification increases, more deceased are identified as such; and when they are, they reflect the socioeconomic background from which the deceased come: upper- and middle-class America.

Iranian men's obituaries that mention identification by occupation congregate primarily in category V (especially in 1968 and 1978), followed by categories I and II. The steady representation from category I beginning in 1958 and continuing throughout the rest of the period is likely a reflection of social change in Iran. Professionals as a group (also known as technocrats) had begun to emerge in Iran earlier in the century (1920s). By mid-century they had gained enough prominence that their representation is increased in the obituary pages not only as a natural consequence of their eventual passage into the obituary world but also as a result of their increased overall prominence and status in the social order outside the obituaries.

Through their accomplishments in a changing social reality, the deceased can be said to bring about change in the obituary pages. This change is also facilitated by the obituary writers themselves as a result of change in their perceptions of value and mutual benefit to be realized from the occupational identification of the deceased.

Finally, recall in the analysis of professional titles in chapter 4 a question was raised regarding differences between Arabic and Persian obituaries in their representation of the deceased by military titles. Military titles were found to occur with a much higher frequency in the Persian obituaries than in the Arabic obituaries. Lutfi Elkholi (1997) suggests that a policy had been established by the military authorities in Egypt prohibiting the publication of military ranks and affiliations of active officers without prior authorization. The validity of such a claim can now be tested further in relation to occupations. In the Persian obituaries, seventeen deceased are identified as military professionals, constituting almost half of all professions listed under category I. In the Arabic obituaries only two deceased are identified with a military rank, in 1948. Four others are identified as pilots, one in 1938 and the three others in 1958. But pilots are not necessarily air force pilots; they could be civilian or commercial pilots as well. Either way, the number is so small that the overall results support the explanation offered for this cross-cultural difference.

4. PROFESSIONAL AND SOCIAL IDENTITIES

The results from the analysis of occupations in this chapter and of titles in chapter 4 turned out to be different from our earlier expectations, more so in some areas of the analysis than in others. Because professional identities (both titles and occupations) represent public identities, they were expected to be the strongest reflection in the obituaries of the realities in the world outside (assuming that the obituaries present factual accounts). But because the distribution proved to be the most biased against deceased women in all three cultures, we must consider what these results actually mean and what implications they may have for our understanding of this obituary world.

My discussion here will contrast social identities (social titles) and professional identities (both occupations and professional titles). To do so,

I view the results from a slightly different perspective: instances whereby women and men are identified by a professional and social identity. A total of 55 instances of professional identifications are applied to the 1,620 deceased women and 914 to the 2,180 deceased men[7] (3.4 percent and 42 percent, respectively). Thus deceased women can be said to have been professionally identified only 3.4 percent of the time, men 42 percent. Performing the same calculations for social identities, we find that women are socially identified 39 percent of the time, men only 29 percent.

Do these results mean that only 4 percent of women in these three cultures have had some form of professional identity during the period covered? Or is it 4 percent of the upper and upper-middle classes? Or are professional identities ignored for women, more likely than they would be for men? I indicated earlier difficulties in proving one or the other alternative. First, it would be necessary to compile statistics (if available) on the employment of women and men of the corresponding classes during the corresponding years. Second, it may not be possible to prove if professional identities of any of the deceased included in this research have been ignored. As a result, we may not be able to actually prove if indeed the obituaries are true representations of the world outside. We can, however, argue on the basis of our knowledge the likelihood that the picture projected in the obituaries may have been a true representation of the social realities. At times such knowledge may have to be personal.

We have assumed that social and professional identities as constructed in the obituaries are projections of the way the deceased have been identified during their lifetime and that these identifications are factual. However, sometimes events and truths are in fact not reflected in the obituaries. Consider, for example, the title *hajja* or *hajj* applied to Muslims who have performed the pilgrimage to Mecca. One would expect, as I have suggested, that such persons would be identified with such titles in the obituaries. But are they *always* so identified? The only feasible way to answer the question is by examining obituaries of personal acquaintances or through knowledge we may have of how such people have been identified.

I must report that within my family, immediate and somewhat extended, and within the circle of friends and acquaintances whose obituaries I have encountered in this research, there have been many women and men who had performed the pilgrimage but whose obituaries did not include the title *hajja* or *hajj* because they were not identified in this way during their lifetime.

This perspective, personal as it may be, suggests that the obituaries both reflect and omit truths. In this particular case, they reflect the way the deceased were known and identified during their lifetime, but they omit some facts (that the deceased had actually performed their religious duty, the pilgrimage). By contrast, I do not recall cases where professional identities were not mentioned.

If social identities are not always conveyed in the obituaries, why can we not conclude that professional identities may also be ignored at times? In fact there is evidence that they are omitted, based on the results of professional identification of deceased men in the obituaries. Consider again that the obituaries show that only 42 percent of deceased men were mentioned with a professional identity. Are we to conclude from this that the remaining deceased had no professional identity, that is, no occupation or applicable professional title? This is highly unlikely among the upper and upper-middle classes of these three cultures.

We must, therefore, conclude that the relationship between the obituaries and the world outside is determined by additional factors, by principles that allow them to reflect only at times the world outside. To the extent that data from earlier years may have been biased against all aspects of female representation, we turn in chapter 6 to an examination of additional data collected from 1998 as a final step in this argument. If these results are still as divergent as before, we would have to conclude that the obituary world is biased against the professional identification of its deceased women by comparison to its deceased men.

Part III

The Obituaries and Beyond

Chapter 6
The End of a Century: 1998 Obituaries

The end of the twentieth century leaves us with one final year, 1998, to assess. This chapter is devoted to the analysis of the 1998 obituaries, which when compared with the data from 1988, allows us to see the changes in the last decade of the century. Analyzing the obituary pages of this final year provides a sense of completeness. Since the volume surveys close to a century of obituaries, the analysis of this final decade also sets the stage for continued research into the new millennium. In addition, this chapter serves to test earlier predictions made through our obituary role and orientation model to determine, for example, if trends have been maintained (or reversed) at the end of the century and if explanations proposed earlier are supported by the results from the 1998 obituaries. A relatively smaller sample was collected for this chapter: a total of 600 obituaries, 200 from each language/culture. Except for the size of the corpus, all other principles of data collection and methodology developed for the main corpus have been followed in the collection and analysis of this final data set.

Compared to previous years, the overall number of obituaries has decreased in the Arabic and English newspapers in 1998 but increased dramatically in the Persian newspaper. The number of obituaries collected from *Ettela' at* (the long list) almost doubled from 248 in 1988 to 433 in 1998. *Al-Ahram*'s obituaries, on the other hand, decreased by about 9 percent from 742 to 678 and the *New York Times* obituaries by a much more dramatic 43 percent from 1,081 to 615. These changes might be attributed to interaction with two factors: an increase in obituary size and a change in newspapers' allotment of space to obituaries. The obituaries in *Al-Ahram,* for example, do not exceed one page in any of the thirty days collected, whereas in previous years they often extended into an additional half-page and at times a whole page. Likewise, in 1998 the family obituaries of the *New York Times* occupy a half-page most of the time when in previous years they often filled up a whole page.

I. THE SHARING OF OBITUARY SPACE

1.1 Obituary Size

The analysis of obituary size supports the observation that change in the overall number of obituaries can be attributed to interaction with obituary space allotment. The mean length of the 1998 obituaries is 19.49 lines, an increase of 2.3 lines over the 1988 mean of 17.19 lines. This increase proved to be significant in both Arabic and English obituaries, which posted increases of 4.17 and 2.19 lines, respectively. But in Persian obituaries, obituary size increased by only 0.52 lines, which is not statistically significant. The mean change posted during this final decade (2.3) is the second highest for any period, second to the (3.45) increase of the previous decade.[1]

The results in table 6.2 of the ANOVA test for variance (Bonferroni/Dunn) confirm earlier findings. No significant Sex effect is found on obituary size in 1998, but the effect of Culture is significant ($p < .0001$). Recall that the interaction of Sex and Time did not prove to be significant for the fifty-year period, although Sex had a significant effect on overall obituary size independent of Time. Thus 1998 is not different in this respect from previous years, and we can safely conclude that change in obituary size cannot be attributed to Sex alone.

Nor is 1998 different with regard to culture effects. The two-way interaction of Culture and Time proved to be significant in 1998 as it did in earlier years. Table 6.1 shows that the mean length of Arabic obituaries in 1998 is 29.34 lines, in English, 15.12, and in Persian, 14.02. The difference in size between Arabic obituaries and both English and Persian obituaries is significant, but the difference between English and Persian obituaries is not. Furthermore, a comparison with 1988 obituary size shows the most dramatic

Table 6.1. Change in Obituary Size

	Arabic	English	Persian	Overall
1988	25.17	12.93	13.5	17.49
1998	29.34	15.12	14.02	19.19
Difference	+4.17*	+2.19*	+0.52	+2.3

*p < .0001

Table 6.2. Analysis of Variance: Obituary Size (1998) by Sex and Culture (N = 600)

Source of Variation	Sum of Squares	df	Mean Square	F
Main effects				
Sex	297.819	1	297.819	.2523
Culture	29227.75	2	14613.875	81.774*
Two-Way Interactions				
Sex and Culture				
Arabic	268.738	1	268.738	.648
English	688.205	1	688.205	7.887**
Persian	298.786	1	298.786	9.785**

*p < .0001   **p < .01

increase is still in Arabic obituaries (4.17 lines), followed by English (2.19 lines). Change in Persian obituary size of 0.52 lines is the least dramatic (and also not significant). The change in the size of Arabic and English obituaries represents the second highest for any period. The highest increase in Arabic obituary size occurs in 1958–68 (5.09 lines), and for English obituaries, in 1978–88 (3.01 lines). For Persian obituaries, the increase during 1988–98 is the smallest for any time period, except 1968–78 when average obituary size dropped (figure 2.4).

These results, then, establish an inverse relationship between obituary size and number of obituaries collected from each of the three newspapers in 1998. Persian obituaries posted the highest increase in number of obituaries but the smallest increase in obituary size, whereas Arabic and English obituaries posted significant increases in size but reduction in the number of obituaries. That such an inverse relationship can be established is an interesting observation in itself, but it does not directly impact the results.

A more important finding, however, comes from the interaction effect of Sex and Culture on obituary size (table 6.2). Sex differences proved to be significant in two of the three cultures—English and Persian but not Arabic. This provides direct support for predictions made earlier by the obituary role and orientation model. Sex differences in obituary size tend to be least relevant when obituaries are not deceased oriented, as Arabic obituaries are. But in the more deceased-oriented English obituaries and to a lesser extent Persian obituaries, obituary size is impacted by sex.

The analysis of obituary size relative to the median produces interesting results as well. The median for 1998 is 15 lines. A total of 278 obituaries fall above that mark. These include 111 obituaries of women and 167 of men (40 percent and 60 percent, respectively) (figure 6.1). The distribution by culture (figure 6.2) shows that the number of Arabic obituaries above the median is still the highest (149, or 54 percent), double that of the English obituaries (68, or 24 percent) and Persian obituaries (61, or 22 percent). In each culture the number of women's obituaries above the median is still less than that of men. The discrepancy between the sexes in 1998 is most marked in the Persian obituaries, where only 15 obituaries of women (25 percent) fall above the median while 46 obituaries of men (75 percent) fall above that mark. The difference is smallest in Arabic obituaries, with 67 (45 percent) women's and 82 (55 percent) men's obituaries above the median. The ratio in English obituaries is almost the same as that obtained in Arabic obituaries: 29 women's obituaries (43 percent) and 39 men's obituaries (57 percent) obituaries above the median.

Compared to the results presented in chapter 2, the English obituaries have become significantly longer and consequently the number of obituaries above the median length has also increased. In 1998, English obituaries are second to Arabic obituaries on both counts (mean and median). The widest gap between the sexes remains in Persian obituaries.

1.2 Population Distribution

Some evidence emerges in the 1998 obituaries that the share of obituary space enjoyed by the sexes, measured as it is in terms of their numerical distribution, is becoming more equitable. The distribution of the deceased population by Sex (table 6.3) shows a 45 percent to 55 percent female-to-male representation, or occupation of obituary space, which represents an improvement over the 40 percent to 60 percent figures from 1988. But the analysis of the data by Sex and Culture does not achieve a level of statistical significance in 1998, just as it did not in previous years. The analysis of expected values predicts a sex-by-culture distribution of 90 women to 110 men in each culture. The actual distribution is not significantly different.

Overall, the population distribution results from 1998 maintain previous patterns of representation and hierarchical ranking of sex and culture groups. Among the female population, Iranian women (30 percent) continue

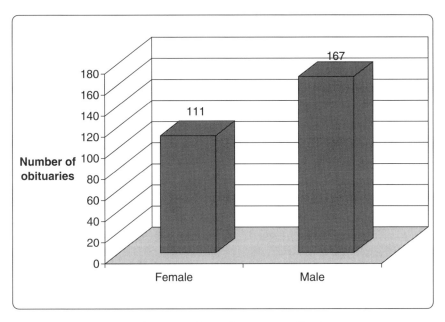

Fig. 6.1. Obituaries above the 1998 Median by Sex

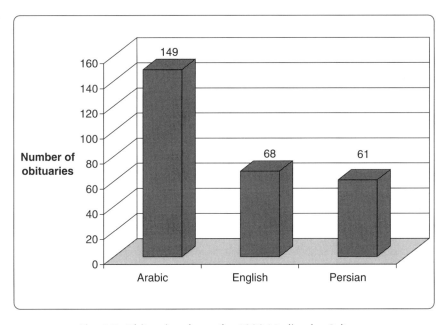

Fig. 6.2. Obituaries above the 1998 Median by Culture

Table 6.3: Population Distribution by Sex and Culture (1998)

	Arabic	English	Persian	Total
Female	88	100	82	270
	44%	50%	41%	(45%)
Male	112	100	118	330
	56%	50%	59%	(55%)
Total	200	200	200	600
	(100%)	(100%)	(100%)	(100%)

to be the least represented and American women the most (37 percent). The hierarchy among the male population puts the Persian male as most highly represented (36 percent) and the American male the least (30 percent).

2. LINGUISTIC VARIABLES AND OVERALL POPULATION

The distribution of the linguistic variables in 1998 maintains many of the trends established for 1988 as well as the overall population. A comparison with the results from 1988 shows little difference in overall representation with linguistic variables (table 6.4). In both years a same or very close level of representation is reached for all five linguistic variables with no dramatic change in percentage of deceased identified with any of them.

An analysis of the 1998 data for the independent effects of Sex and Culture for the overall population of 600 deceased is also given in table 6.4. A comparison of these results with those obtained earlier (table B.1) for the original 3,800 deceased reveals some differences, albeit minor. In the distribution by Sex, the results from Title do not achieve a level of statistical significance. The female population is underrepresented in all but Social Titles; women's acquired identity continues to be constructed through social categories significantly more so than does men's acquired identity.

The distribution by Culture continues to be statistically significant for all linguistic variables. Some differences emerge, however, in the relative contribution of each culture. For example, deceased identified by Name are again underrepresented in the Arabic obituaries, whereas the representation in English and Persian obituaries is almost identical. Identification by occupation

Table 6.4. Linguistic Variables in 1998 by Sex and by Culture

	Sex			Culture			
	Female n = 270	Male n = 330	χ^2	Arabic n = 200	English n = 200	Persian n = 200	χ^2
Name	260 44%	**330** 56%	12.4**	<u>*191*</u> 32%	**200** 34%	199 34%	14.8**
Title	120 42%	163 58%	1.5	**137** 48%	<u>*19*</u> 7%	**127** 45%	171.8*
Occupation	33 22%	**120** 78%	45.5*	**76** 50%	55 36%	<u>*22*</u> 14%	39*
Professional Title	4 5%	**82** 95%	67.2*	**51** 59%	<u>*13*</u> 15%	<u>*22*</u> 23%	62.7*
Social Title	**118** 57%	88 43%	18*	**88** 43%	<u>*6*</u> 3%	**112** 54%	179.4*

	Time		
	1988 (n = 718)	1998 (n= 600)	χ^2
Name	706 98%	590 98%	4.2
Title	344 48%	282 47%	0.109
Occupation	165 23%	153 26%	1.13
Professional Title	108 15%	86 14%	0.131
Social Title	249 35%	206 34%	0.017

*p < .0001   **p < .001

in the English obituaries is no longer underrepresented by comparison to the other two cultures; only Persian obituaries are underrrepresented along this variable. English obituaries continue to post the lowest figures for identification by social titles; both English and Persian obituaries demonstrate a decrease in identification by professional titles from their 1988 figures of 25 percent and 32 percent, respectively.

2.1 Interaction of Sex and Culture

Sex differentiation across cultures continues to be significant for most of the linguistic variables. A breakdown of the data by both Sex and Culture (table 6.5) shows the distribution by Name and by Professional Title is not significant in this cross-cultural comparison. The distribution is significant, however, for all other linguistic variables.

Furthermore, the analysis of expected values points to the divergent

Table 6.5. Sex Differentiation across Cultures in Linguistic Variables (1998)

	Arabic	**English**	**Persian**	χ^2
Name				4.3
Female	79	100	81	
	41%	50%	41%	
Male	112	100	118	
	59%	50%	59%	
Title				9.1**
Female	58	*2*	60	
	43%	11%	47%	
Male	78	**17**	67	
	57%	89%	53%	
Occupation				9**
Female	12	**19**	2	
	16%	35%	9%	
Male	64	*36*	20	
	84%	65%	91%	
Prof. Title				1.5
Female	3	1	0	
	6%	8%	0%	
Male	48	12	22	
	94%	92%	100%	
Social Title				9**
Female	55	*0*	63	
	62.5%	0%	56%	
Male	33	**6**	49	
	37.5%	100%	44%	

**p < .05

distribution from English obituaries. American women continue to be over-represented by comparison to the other sex-by-culture groups in identification by occupation, and American men in identification by both title and social title. The Arabic and Persian populations are not significantly divergent from the expected values; their distribution does not achieve the required level of statistical significance in any of their sex-by-culture groups.

2.2 The Effect of Time

To assess change during this last decade, results from 1998 and 1988 are presented in table 6.6 for comparative purposes. Percentages reported are of sex-by-culture groups in each of the two years. In 1998, for example, 90 percent of the deceased women in Arabic obituaries are identified by first name, an increase of 3 percent; in Persian obituaries 99 percent of deceased women appear with their first name, one percentage point less than in 1988. All deceased women in American obituaries are identified with a first name in both year groups.

By far the largest percentage increase (46 percent) occurs in the iden-tification of Egyptian women by social title; the next largest is a 33 percent increase in the identification of Egyptian men by professional title. The only decline in the Egyptian obituaries occurs in the identification of men with occupation (4 percent). In the English obituaries the two largest increases oc-cur in the identification of both women (10 percent) and men (6 percent) by occupation. The only measurable decline (6 percent) in the English obituaries occurs in men's identification with professional titles. In Persian obituaries the only increase (6 percent) appears in men's identification with occupation. Rep-resentation by title shows the strongest decline for both women (11 percent) and men (15 percent). Most of this decline is due to decreased identification by social title: 5 percent for women and 11 percent for men.

This comparison points to interesting changes within each culture that may also represent emerging trends. Degree of representation by occupation and professional title, for example, suggests a possible inverse relationship between the two variables. In both Arabic and English obituaries, increase in the representation of men in one coincides with a decrease in the other. In English obituaries they almost negate each other's effect (6 percent for both) but in Arabic obituaries the difference is much stronger (4 percent decrease in identification by occupation; 33 percent increase in identification by

Table 6.6. Change by Culture Group (1988–98)

	FEMALE		MALE	
	1998	1988	1998	1988
ARABIC				
Name	_79_	_83_	**112**	**144**
	90%	87%	100%	100%
Title	58	52	78	82
	66%	55%	70%	57%
Occupation	_11_	_8_	**64**	**88**
	14%	8%	57%	61%
Professional Title	_3_	_5_	**48**	**42**
	6%	5%	62%	29%
Social Title	**55**	**47**	_33_	_43_
	95%	49%	44%	30%
ENGLISH				
Name	100	100	100	100
	100%	100%	100%	100%
Title	_2_	_3_	**17**	**25**
	2%	3%	17%	18%
Occupation	_19_	_9_	**36**	**42**
	19%	9%	36%	30%
Professional Title	_1_	_2_	**12**	**25**
	1%	2%	12%	18%
Social Title	0	0	6	0
	0%	0%	6%	0%
PERSIAN				
Name	81	88	118	151
	99%	100%	100%	100%
Title	**60**	**74**	_67_	108
	73%	84%	57%	72%
Occupation	_2_	_2_	**20**	**16**
	2%	2%	17%	11%
Professional Title	_0_	_1_	**23**	**33**
	0%	1%	20%	22%
Social Title	**63**	**73**	_49_	_85_
	78%	83%	45%	56%

professional title). Because almost all the results from Persian obituaries reflect a decline, I am tempted to suggest that obituary style is being renegotiated (redefined or simplified). Dramatic changes such as those noted above in Arabic and English obituaries suggest change in obituary style as well, which is perhaps best described as renegotiation of saliency or value assigned to certain categories in the identification of the deceased. This conclusion is further supported by the analysis of actual titles and occupations mentioned in the obituaries.

3. ACTUAL TITLES AND OCCUPATION TYPES

Acquired identities as projected in 1998 obituaries are also similar to the overall profiles obtained earlier. Table 6.7 provides listings of the actual 1998 titles. The social identity these titles construct of Egyptian women is still relatively balanced (or split) between the religious and social respect categories (47 percent and 53 percent, respectively). Egyptian men's social identity in 1998 obituaries relies more on religious titles, with 19 of the 33 social titles (58 percent) falling within this category and 14 (42 percent) within the social status/respect category. This suggests a divergence from the trend established earlier for Egyptian men, in which the identification of deceased men with religious titles was on the decline. The picture in Persian obituaries remains unchanged. Deceased men continue to be identified with their religious status more so than their social status, although the differences are not as marked as they were earlier: 58 percent of all social titles applied to Iranian men in 1998 are religious, 33 percent project social status, and 8 percent are mixed. In English obituaries, social titles are included in men's obituaries only, with 6 deceased identified as *Mr.* None of the deceased women is mentioned with a social title (*Mrs.,* in particular).

In 1998, then, only the social identity of deceased men in the Egyptian obituaries has changed, reflecting an increased prominence of the religious (versus social) categories of social identity. Professional identity as projected through titles changes dramatically for some groups but not overall. The profile constructed of deceased women does not demonstrate a professional identity constructed through titles: no deceased Iranian women are identified with professional titles; only one deceased American woman is identified with a professional title; and three deceased Egyptian women are identified with

Table 6.7: Professional and Social Titles by Sex and Culture Group (1998)

			ARABIC		
Professional Titles	**Female**	**Male**	**Social Titles**	**Female**	**Male**
doctor	1	15	*hajj(a)*	26	12
engineer	1	8	*sayyid(a)*	22	1
accountant	1	2	ustadh	—	11
ustadh(a)	—	10	*muqaddis(a)*	3	4
military	—	3	sheikh	—	3
police	—	5	hanim	2	—
hajj, sheikh	—	2	*sayyida-hajja*	1	—
qiss, qummus	—	2	anisa	1	—
mustashar	—	1	sheikh-arab	—	1
			khawaga	—	1
Total	3	48		55	33

			ENGLISH		
Professional Titles	**Female**	**Male**	**Social Titles**	**Female**	**Male**
doctor	1	7	Mr.	—	6
reverend, DD	—	3			
judge	—	2			
Total	1	12		0	6

			PERSIAN		
Professional Titles	**Female**	**Male**	**Social Titles**	**Female**	**Male**
engineer	—	8	*hajj(eh)*	2	26
doctor	—	5	banu	25	—
military	—	5	khanum	11	—
ustath	—	3	agha	—	11
sayyid-hajj	—	1	*sayyid(eh)*	5	4
ayatullah	—	1	khanum-hajjeh	17	—
			banu-hajjeh	2	—
			dushizeh	1	—
			agha-hajj*	—	4
Total	—	23		63	45

Note: *4 more combinations: *agha-hajj-sayyid, agha-hajj-sheikh, hajj-sayyid, hajj-sheikh* such a title. Furthermore, professional titles applied to women are, as in previous years, all from the professions and none from the military or the clergy. For deceased men, the professions still dominate in the identification by professional titles: 75 percent of deceased American men; 73 percent of deceased Egyptian men; and 70 percent of deceased Iranian men. Less frequently mentioned titles include those from the military and the clergy. Thus, compared to 1988, the percentages for Egyptian and Iranian men are more comparable in 1998 and women's professional identity continues to be minimally constructed through the use of titles, if at all.

The professional profile of the deceased is also constructed through identification with occupation. The female group is still less diverse than the male in the types of occupations used to identify them (table 6.8). Only two deceased Iranian women are identified with an occupation; of the 18 deceased American women so identified, 78 percent belong to the professional and managerial category; of the 11 Egyptian women so identified, 91 percent are from the first two categories combined. Thus the vast majority (84 percent) of the 31 deceased women identified with occupation come from categories I and II, the top of the socioeconomic scale. The male group is more diverse, although the vast majority (75 percent) also come from categories I (39 percent) and II (36 percent). The Egyptian group differs from both the American and Iranian groups in the relative ranking of categories I and II. Only among the Egyptian group are there more deceased from category II. Almost 50 percent of Egyptian men identified with occupations belong to this group, but only 28 percent of American men and an even smaller 11 percent of Iranian men do.

The differences observed here may have cross-cultural implications in terms of the value assigned to managerial versus professional categories, reflecting differences in the social meaning (value, power, respect) associated with them. This might explain why in Arabic, the most status-oriented obituary culture of all three, more men are consistently identified with occupations belonging to category II than the expected category I.

Looking at men's obituaries over the fifty-year period reveals that more Egyptian deceased men are identified with occupations in category II than are American or Iranian men when the percentages of both categories are compared by culture. Out of 428 deceased Egyptian men identified with occupations, 29 percent of these occupations fall under category I; 26 percent fall under category II (table D.2). By comparison, in the obituaries of deceased

Table 6.8. Classification of Occupations by Sex and Culture (1998)

	Arabic		English		Persian	
	Female	**Male**	**Female**	**Male**	**Female**	**Male**
I Professional and technical	5 45.5%	15 23%	14 78%	23 64%	— —	8 44%
II Administrative and managerial	5 45.5%	31 48%	2 11%	10 28%	—	2 11%
III A'yan and representatives	—	1 2%	—	—	—	—
IV Business owners, merchants	—	9 14%	1 5.5%	1 3%	—	—
V Civil service and employees	1 9%	3 5%	1 5.5%	—	1 50%	8 44%
VI Clerical	—	—	—	—	—	—
VII Sales	—	—	—	2 5%	—	—
Other	—	5 8%	—	—	1 50%	—
Total	11 (100%)	64 (100%)	18 (100%)	36 (100%)	2 (100%)	18 (99%)

Note: Percentages do not always add up to 100% due to rounding.

American men identified with occupations (67 total), 51 percent are drawn from category I, while only 24 percent are drawn from category II. Likewise, 35 percent of deceased Iranian men identified with occupations (104 total) are identified with occupations from category I but only 15 percent from category II. So although the overall populations have shown consistent preference for the professional and technical category over the fifty-year period, the difference between the top two categories among the Egyptian male group is minimal, unlike the other two.

In 1998, however, the trend is reversed among the Egyptian male group, and for the first time the percentage of deceased men with occupations belonging to category II dramatically exceeds that of deceased men with occupations in category I (48 percent to 23 percent, respectively) (table 6.8).[2]

The trend is maintained among the other two male groups, however. Sixty-four percent of deceased American men identified with occupations fall under category I; 28 percent fall under category II. For deceased Iranian men, the figures are 44 percent and 11 percent, respectively.

The Egyptian male group then is consistently different over time in its occupational identification from both the American and Iranian groups. Since identification with occupation is only an option typically exercised by the family member(s) who author the obituaries, it is their perception of "importance" or "value" that determines their choices. The status orientation of Egyptian obituary culture would certainly encourage identification with occupations more highly valued on a scale based on perceptions of (socioeconomic) power.

For the most part, then, the trends observed earlier are continued in 1998, although some surprises do appear and new styles emerge. One interesting stylistic innovation appears in the Arabic obituaries, for example. We see for the first time in Muslim families' obituaries statements like the following appearing at the end of some obituaries: *wa nas'alukum al-faatiḥa* (and we ask you for *al-faatiḥa* [the opening surah in the *Quran*]), meaning that we ask you to read the *faatiḥa* for the soul of the deceased. The belief here is that the reading of this particular surah eases the way for the departing soul; it is also read every time one visits a cemetery, participates in a funeral procession, or even sees one.

The introduction of such a phrase suggests that the Arabic obituaries in 1998 are becoming more like the Persian obituaries in terms of their role in the funeralization process: soliciting spiritual support for the departed soul from among the living. It also gives more prominence to the religious frame, for these obituaries now start on a religious (spiritual) tone by quoting a Quranic verse and end with another religious (spiritual) reminder. More than 14 of the 119 Muslim families (over 12 percent) chose to adopt this format in writing obituaries for their deceased. In so doing, they evoke the religious frame more so than in earlier years since obituaries would now begin and end on a religious (spiritual) note.

Chapter 7

The Search for a Model, a Connection

We have seen three worlds, reflecting three realities, or perceptions thereof, interacting. One is the world outside the obituaries with its own rules, players, and attitudes. The other is the world of the obituaries with its own rules, players, and attitudes. The link between the two lies in the families who author the obituaries and their worlds. The players are shared; the values are shared. But to what extent? How do they all relate to each other? How do they connect, or perhaps disconnect?

In our search for a connection between the two worlds, the families as authors emerge as the best candidate. Their perceptions and decisions ultimately shape this relationship through the texts they create. Texts are never created in a vacuum; they need materials, factual or otherwise, for their content. They need an audience and a medium through which this audience is reached. And they need authorship to create text and a purpose for which text is created. The interaction of these forces in the production of obituaries as texts is ultimately responsible for variation across obituary cultures and styles as well as variation between the world as projected through the obituaries (via their authors) and the world outside as perceived by the audience as readers of these texts.

The material, or content, is provided primarily by the individuals who populate the obituaries, be they deceased or survivors, through activities they engage in during their lifetime: their achievements, networks, and family background. Authors select information they deem necessary to create a text and to serve best the purpose for which text is created, namely, the communication of the event appropriately situated within the funeralization process to satisfy the needs of surviving families and put the deceased to rest. As texts, however, the obituaries may differ from other types of texts or genres in that their representations of individuals and events should for the most part be based on "truth," or the realities of the world outside them. On that basis the obituaries are expected to reflect that sociocultural reality. But, as we have seen, they do not always do so. This discrepancy between expectations and results is what I address in this final chapter.

I begin by summarizing the major results of our analysis of obituaries and their deceased. These will be grouped into areas of convergence and divergence in relation to the social realities beyond the obituary pages in an attempt to model the results within a space-sharing conceptual framework. The summary I include in the next section is at times presented from a slightly different perspective, one that allows us to compare the identification of the deceased in terms of concepts of basic and acquired identities.

Recall that a distinction was made early in the volume between Name as representation of basic identity and Title and Occupation as representations of acquired identities. Data collection and analytical methods adopted for the research necessitated a distinction between identification by occupation and professional title despite their overlapping domains, both being symbolic representations of professional identities acquired by the deceased during their lifetime. This is because analyses in previous chapters were based on the actual linguistic terms used to identify the deceased in the obituary pages (corresponding to the five dependent variables posited for analysis). As a result, the distinction between social and professional identification of the deceased was not directly captured in earlier graphs. The three figures presented in this chapter (figures 7.1, 7.2, and 7.3) are designed to do that. I have combined the results obtained from the distribution of professional titles and occupations and used the combined figures to create a category corresponding to "professional" identification. I then use these (combined) figures to compare with figures obtained earlier on representations of social and basic identities of the deceased, that is, social titles and names, respectively. Percentages in these three figures are of sex group, culture group, and year group, respectively, and totals include figures obtained from the analyses of the 1998 obituaries.

I. THE WORLD OF THE OBITUARIES

The world constructed through the analysis of the obituary pages is a gender- and culture-differentiated one, in varying degrees. Sex differentiation, for example, could not be established for certain variables within certain culture groups (for example, names and social titles in English obituaries), but there are very few cases where culture does not differentiate among sex groups. (See Professional Title in table B.2.) Culture has a greater differentiating effect in change over time than does Sex. The change in obituary size and population distribution, for example, shows no significant Sex effects but strong effects from Culture. In the analysis of the population identified with the linguistic variables, the distribution for all five variables was significant for Culture over Time but not always for Sex over Time. The distribution of deceased identified with name and with professional title was not sex differentiated—not until the population was broken down by culture group.

Although differentiation has not always favored one sex group, one culture group, or one time period, clear patterns have emerged.

The world of the obituaries is for the most part a man's world—more so in some culture groups than in others—throughout the sixty years, 1998 included, despite some dramatic changes during the later years (beginning with 1968). The obituary world is overpopulated with men. This is true not only of the deceased population with its 57 percent males, but of the survivors as well. Consider, for example, that only 60 percent of the obituaries between 1938 and 1988 mention female survivors. Consider also the effect of culture on this distribution. In Arabic obituaries, 62 percent mentioned female survivors and relatives of the deceased, in English obituaries, 88 percent, and in Persian obituaries, 20 percent. English obituaries are clearly the least biased. They have the highest percentage of representation, which appears even stronger when viewed within the norm of listing only immediate family members in American obituaries. Likewise, the bias against female representation is stronger in Persian (and Arabic) obituaries, where obituary culture extends survivors' lists to blood relatives and in-laws.

1.1 The Gendered World of Obituaries

In the introduction we asked how one becomes a woman (or a man) in the obituaries. "Woman" in the obituary world is constructed in ways similar to those in the world outside. Women are less visible than men in both worlds. Their reduced visibility in the obituaries is primarily due to the smaller size of women's obituaries and of their representation in this public domain, and to the loss of first name (in some cultures). The image projected of women in the obituary world is differentiated, just as it is in the world outside, in its content from that of men: stronger in its "social" component with clear ties to the male family members, husband in particular, and with emphasis on piety (depending on culture), but weaker on the "professional" component (universally). Figure 7.1 illustrates this difference well. Whereas 45 percent of deceased men have some form of professional identification, only 5 percent of deceased women do. Furthermore, the difference between social and professional identification is stronger among the female group than it is among the male. The image of women projected in the obituary world does change over time, but not so much to deconstruct its gendered nature—at least not yet.

The numerical representation of deceased women, for example, has not significantly changed over time in relation to that of men, nor has the size of their obituaries. Women's obituaries remain significantly shorter over time, despite the fact that cross-culturally the average size of an obituary does increase significantly over time. Likewise, the ratio of women's and men's obituaries has not changed significantly despite an increase of 63 percent (179 to 285) in the former over the fifty-year period. The number of men's obituaries, by comparison, has doubled (217 to 433).[1]

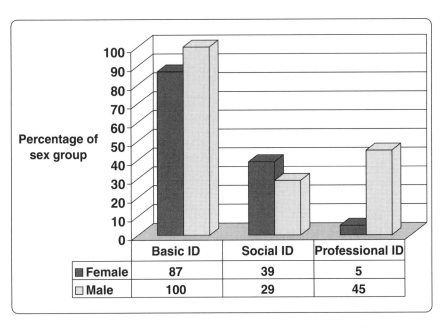

Fig. 7.1. Identification of the Deceased by Sex (1938–98)

Gender in the obituaries is constructed through the way the deceased are named. Name is a variable for women in the obituaries, as it is in the world outside although the details may differ. The absence of a deceased's first name in the obituaries is definitely a marker of woman's obituary, as is the presence of two last names and the word *née* after the deceased name (in English). Men's obituaries show no variation in first name. A woman's obituary very likely identifies her with a social title, as would a man's obituary. However, for a woman identified with a social title, the likelihood that it would be a marital title relating her to her husband is very high. This is not true for a man with a social title. Finally, obituaries of deceased women, unlike those of deceased men, rarely mention professional identity.

Thus a deceased woman's visibility and her status relative to those of a deceased man are severely hampered through reduced numerical representation, obituary size, and identification by name and professional capacity. They are enhanced by her social identity, the only aspect of acquired identity where both deceased women and men have almost equal representation.

1.2 The Culture-Differentiated World of Obituaries

Culture differentiation was strong in almost all areas, but hierarchical position of obituary cultures relative to each other varied depending on the variable, or measure of equity, in question (figure 7.2). Figure 7.2 demonstrates the cross-cultural similarities and differences. Some are attributed to obituary culture, such as the abundance of professional identifications for the deceased in Arabic obituaries. Some are attributed to the world outside the obituaries, for example, the high frequency with which the deceased are identified with social titles in Arabic and Persian obituaries as opposed to English obituaries. Some others are attributed to both, for example, differences in identification of the deceased by name (basic identity) where the status orientation of Arabic obituaries is responsible for the relatively low percentage obtained.

On the basis of the results, one can develop a characterization of what an obituary in an Arabic, English, or Persian newspaper may be. An Arabic obituary is the longest of the three and is filled with names, titles, and occupations. Its deceased are most likely identified with a social title and in a professional capacity. An English obituary is short and identifies only immediate family members. Its focus is the deceased, possibly identified in a professional capacity but always by name. A Persian obituary is also short and

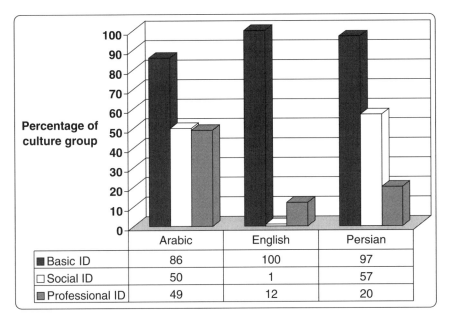

Percentage of culture group	Arabic	English	Persian
■ Basic ID	86	100	97
□ Social ID	50	1	57
▨ Professional ID	49	12	20

Fig. 7.2. Identification of the Deceased by Culture Group (1938–98)

includes individuals' and family names. Its deceased is almost always identified by name and very frequently (almost 60 percent of the time) by a social title.

Culture also has a differentiating effect in the changing world of twentieth-century obituaries, as we see in the next section.

1.3 Stability versus Change in the Obituary World

Overall, the world of the obituaries is "stable": change takes place, but over longer periods of time than had been anticipated. When undifferentiated by culture or gender, change in the identification of the deceased over these sixty years would look like figure 7.3.

The reanalysis introduced in this figure presents an interesting view of change during the century. Identification of the deceased in their professional capacities continues to increase throughout the century, but their identification in social capacities demonstrates two trend reversals: regression after 1948 and progression after 1978. But the overall picture that emerges at the end of the century is one equally weighted in its identification of the deceased in their social and professional capacities. Figure 7.3 also points to 1948, hence mid-century, as a turning point in all three aspects of identification. It represents

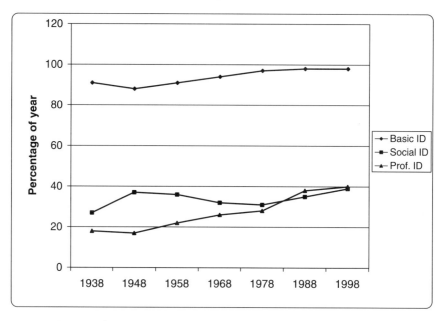

Fig. 7.3. Change in the Identification of the Deceased (1938–98)

the lowest point on the trajectories representing professional and basic identifications of the deceased and the beginning of a downward trend for the third trajectory, the social identification. Most impressive, however, is the change demonstrated by the trajectory representing professional identification. Starting in 1938 at a much lower point than the trajectory for social identification, in 1978 it crosses over and ends the century at about the same level as the trajectory for social identification, or slightly higher. Thus the century starts with the deceased perceived and represented in their social capacities more so than their professional capacities and ends with a representation of acquired identities balanced between the social and the professional.

Stability in the obituary world can be viewed as the result of the overall direction of change—consistent but relatively slow movement. In this view of the obituary world, undifferentiated as it is by culture, stability may also be due to compensatory cross-cultural effects. Dramatic change in one culture may be offset by less dramatic change in another, or a progression in one culture may be balanced against a regression in another. Furthermore if, as I have suggested, some of the most dramatic changes in the world outside the obituaries have taken place around mid-century, and if it is true that older people tend to populate the obituaries more so than younger, then we would expect changes affecting people's identities, perceived and projected, to appear in the obituary world much later than they would in the world outside.

The overall stability suggests that gender could not have been deconstructed in the obituaries, nor could equity have been reached in many of these measures. In two cases, however, significant sex differentiation could not be established over time for the population undifferentiated by culture: identification by name and by professional title (table B.3). In no time period was the distribution of the sexes relative to each other significantly different from normal variation. This, however, does not necessarily mean that the distribution is equitable, just that it is not different enough in any one of the twelve sex-by-year groups. Consider, for example, that in 1988 93 percent of professional titles were applied to deceased men and only 7 percent to deceased women. Equity in distribution cannot even be addressed in such a situation. Yet when that same difference is maintained over the years, the distribution does not change significantly, suggesting that stability does not necessarily imply equity.

Sex differentiation has, however, been deconstructed in one area—identification by social title. As of 1988, social titles are applied with nearly equal frequency to deceased women and men, 49 percent to 51 percent; in 1938 this ratio was 29 percent to 71 percent. Although quantitatively social titles may be equally divided between the sexes, qualitatively profiles constructed on the basis of women's and men's obituaries continue to be gendered. The category "social respect" continues to dominate in the identification of women by social title, and it also reflects different meanings in relation to the sexes (see chapter 4).

The obituary world has also been, and continues to be, strongly impacted by culture, viewed here as a amalgam of obituary culture itself, newspaper-as-medium effects, and realities outside the obituaries. The picture projected in the obituary world of culture groups relative to each other has not significantly changed, and much more so than in the case of gender. Culture groups continue to be significantly differentiated over time in their identification of the deceased along all measures of equity. The relative ranking of cultures does not change, for example, when the first and last years (1938 and 1988) are compared for obituary size and population distribution. Change does occur, however, in some of the linguistic measures of equity. In some cases the contribution from culture groups becomes evenly distributed—each culture contributes an equal share. For example, with regard to the variable Name, in 1938, 67 percent of all named deceased are from English obituaries, 31 percent from Arabic, and 2 percent from Persian; in 1998 these percentages are 32, 34, and 34 percent, respectively. The analysis of deceased identified by name across the three cultures does not achieve a level of statistical significance in 1998, suggesting that individual obituary cultures have sufficiently changed to make the cross-cultural distribution at the end of the century no longer different from normal variation.

None of the other linguistic variables demonstrates such a balanced distribution as to culture. They show instead improvements in the distribution, increasing the equity among the representations from the three cultures and at times changing the cultural rankings. Obituary cultures situated in title-oriented societies (Egypt and Iran) come closer to each other in their relative share of obituary title space. They continue to increase their shares until the space is almost equally divided between them, but they continue to differ in the value they assign to the social versus professional identification of the deceased. English, the only nontitled society in our sample, remains in 1998 outside that space with minimal (unmeasurable) contribution to social titles but a better share (15 percent) of professional title space.

The fact that the only variable that is represented equally among all three obituary cultures is Name gives further credence to the analytical distinction made between "basic" and "acquired" identities. Only in the former are cultural differences finally removed, despite the fact that the distribution in 1998 is still significantly sex differentiated in one culture (Arabic) independent of the others ($\chi^2 = 11.9$ and $p < .001$). One might conclude, as a result, that a view of the obituary world based on the cross-cultural analysis may differ from one based on each culture group independently of the others, since the cross-cultural analysis measures relative degrees of differences across individual groups.

Individual obituary cultures are all gendered, like the world outside them, some more so than others depending on which measure(s) are chosen for analysis and comparison.

The figures for identification by name for deceased Egyptian women are the lowest: only 66 percent had their names mentioned in their obituaries, compared to 100 percent of American women and 93 percent of Iranian women. Their effect is compounded, however, by what name symbolizes (basic identity). Egyptian women are also the only group who in 1998 still appear without a name, almost 10 percent of the time. Iranian women achieved a 100 percent representation with name since 1998.[2] (American women remain at 100 percent throughout the period.) Deceased Egyptian women fare very poorly in relation to deceased Egyptian men in all other measurements except social titles, where they occupy 48 percent of that space and men 52 percent. The picture in the Egyptian world of obituaries is quantitatively most gendered when it comes to occupation and professional titles. Professional space consistently belongs to men—94 percent of occupation space; 97 percent of professional title space. Social space remains the domain of women in Egyptian obituary culture—63 percent in 1998.

American obituary culture does not construct its gendered world on the basis of name, nor the occupation of social title space. In these two areas women and men are equal: both are always mentioned by name, and both are rarely mentioned with social titles. It is in professional space that strong gender differences emerge—women claim 18 percent of occupation and 4 percent of professional title space; the rest goes to men. By the end of the century, women occupy 36 percent of occupation space but only 8 percent of professional title space.

Iranian obituary culture is gendered in similar ways. Deceased women have only 5 percent of both the occupation and title components of professional space, but 53 percent of social title space. By 1998 their share of the latter is 56 percent.

Overall, then, obituary space in individual cultures is, and continues to be, gendered. All three women's groups post increased representation by professional identity, although men still have greater representation. Where the cultural context supports identification with social title, as it does in Egypt and Iran, the identification of deceased men by social title tends to decrease over time by comparison to that of deceased women of the respective culture.

Representations of deceased women and men based on their social and professional identifications change in different ways in individual culture groups. The profile constructed of Iranian women, for example, remains strong in the areas of marital status/social respect. For Egyptian women the picture changes dramatically, almost deconstructing the original. In 1938 the marital-as-social-respect aspect dominates the picture at the expense of the piety/religious component. In 1988 the piety component gains so much visibility that the overall picture is actually split between the two. The century ends in 1998 with a picture still balanced between the two but relatively higher (53 percent) in its marital status component. For men the situation is different in each culture. The profile constructed of Egyptian men is lower on the piety/religious component, which is higher for Iranian men. In 1998 a slight shift occurs in the profile of deceased Egyptian men, increasing the piety component to 58 percent.

Likewise, professional profiles constructed of deceased women and men continue to be different. It is much more diverse for men, reflecting occupations and titles from three areas (the clergy, the military, and the professions). Women's profiles, however, reflects only one of these areas, the professions. Thus the professional component of women's space is not only limited in its size by comparison to that of men, but also in its content. Women's professional profile improves over the years only in some cultures. It occupies more space in American and Egyptian obituaries and reflects more diverse types of occupations, but still within the one category of professions.

2. A SPACE-SHARING MODEL OF THE OBITUARY WORLD

The results summarized above have led us on many occasions to argue that the obituary world does not necessarily reflect the sociocultural realities outside it and that it may indeed be governed by principles of its own. Three such principles have been proposed: obituary role, obituary orientation, and the Principle of Mutual Benefit. These situate the obituaries through a principled connection with the world outside them, allowing the two worlds to converge at times and diverge at others. All three are conceived not as absolutes but as models for the analysis of obituaries within and across culture groups. The three principles address two major questions regarding obituary content and purpose: what fills up obituary space, and why is obituary space filled the way it is?

Before we turn our attention to "obituary space"—the principles that govern it and those that link it to the world outside—it is necessary first to understand what space means within the context of the obituaries, collected as they have been from three different continents. What justifies a model based on space-sharing, alternatively domination, when these obituaries have been created in geographically distant locations independent of each other and at times also disconnected from each other?

This question necessitates arguments for two specific positions. First is the concept of space itself and the construction of a space-based model within which to study the obituaries (and possibly other types of texts). Second is the appropriateness of such a concept as a model for comparative, cross-cultural analysis in general but of the obituaries in particular. A model based on space-sharing, I will argue, presents an analytical framework within which both local and cross-cultural (cross-location) data can be systematically studied and the results uniformly presented. The conceptualization of obituaries as space has the additional advantage of allowing for a view of the obituary world modeled on the world outside, of which it is after all only a part, thus providing a model within which the relationship between the two worlds is appropriately framed.

The conceptualization of physical space, textual or otherwise, is easier when it involves measurement of areas with clearly defined boundaries such as a piece of land or an obituary. It is more difficult to conceptualize space that is not so defined. Space occupied by linguistic items such as names of individuals, occupations, or titles (textual as this may be) is one such example. It is even more difficult to conceptualize measurements of cultures, sexes, and times in relation to that space since cultures, sexes, and times are not physically connected to this overall space. So in what sense, one might ask, can they then be part of it, let alone share or participate in it?

As I worked through this project, I developed a sense of space that is not related to any physical reality such as lines or land. It is rather based on numbers and categories related to each other by percentages, which I have interpreted as shares of this "conceptual" space. I can then talk about title space, for example, who occupies the most or the least of it, and how that occupation of title space may change over time. I can then compare between the occupants of that space, be they women or men, from one culture or another, or from one time or another. They all share that conceptual title space. The shares could be equally divided between the sexes and across the cultures and times that occupy that space. But they can also be unequally divided and, therefore, reflect potential bias in the distribution, hence the sharing, of that space.

Because space is typically finite, conflicts often arise over the occupation of space in both the obituary world and the world outside. Conflicts arise in the world outside the obituary pages as a result of domination of certain space by some group to the exclusion, total or relative, of some other group, and the other's perception of the exclusion as being an act of aggression. Such conflicts over space—for example, land as national space—have often turned into wars to regain losses, perceived as symbolic of survival, visibility, and power. National liberation movements, directed as they typically are against colonialists, wars between nation-states over boundaries, and wars between individuals and groups within a nation-state all qualify as being conflicts primarily over space as land. But conflicts also arise over other types of space. Movements for equal opportunities in employment, for example, constitute conflict over (occupational) space and are usually resolved by means other than actual wars.

Conflicts also emerge in the obituary world over the occupation of obituary space, and they are typically resolved through the accommodation of the other group(s). The exclusion of a family member's name from an obituary, for example, can create a conflict situation, more personal and less dramatic by comparison. Conflicts often arise as a result of the sense of loss, actual or perceived, an individual may experience. Exclusion from that space would symbolize not only a loss of visibility but also of family connection and by implication the sociocultural power associated with the connection. Families of the deceased often apologize publicly by publishing such announcements in the obituary pages, which serves to reinstate the individual into that space. Otherwise, the conflict may escalate and the family may lose its connection with the excluded party and his/her family.

I have chosen a model based on concepts of sharing, rather than domination, partly to reflect this difference. Concepts of power and domination are derived from interactions in the social realities of our world. They are inappropriate when applied to obituary texts, for obvious reasons, although they remain part of the perspective of an author, including myself as author of this text, and the families as authors of obituary texts. The author provides the link between different worlds, different space through the perspective from which s/the creates text. That perspective is often grounded in the author's experiences as individual and as member of a group, which explains difficulties encountered in excluding such concepts of power and domination from this particular text, despite their inappropriateness to the obituary world, and from obituary texts as well.

Two issues emerge from this attempt to conceptualize space in the obituaries and the world outside. One relates the obituary world viewed as newspaper space to the world outside, the physical and social realities within which the newspapers exist. The other constructs the obituary world as textual space filled with words from different languages representing different cultures. Words are symbolic of meanings, concepts, and representations. The amount of textual space such words occupy reflects shares not only of languages/cultures but also of concepts/representations that these words symbolize. Since these words are selected by the authors, the relationship between textual space and authorship or point of view determines what occupies that space.

I have attempted through the research design to create a world in which obituary space would be shared equally among the three cultures, by controlling for number of days from which to collect obituaries and number of obituaries selected from each culture per year. Despite such efforts, the total obituary space, representing 4,400 obituaries from 1938 to 1998, proved to be not equally shared by the three cultures (culturally differentiated), by the sexes (sex differentiated), or by all years (time differentiated). The cultures differed in their relative allotment of obituary space in both its physical (page space) and conceptual (numerical) sense. We have attributed such differences to cultural value or meaning associated with obituary space. When that relative cultural space changes over time toward a more equal distribution, we conclude a change must have occurred in individual obituary cultures to reduce, and eventually eliminate, differences that should not have been there from the start. Changes in cultural shares then allow us to hypothesize a change in the sociocultural meaning associated with the obituaries within and across cultures.

The space in my obituary world, physical and conceptual, is large enough to be filled with information from the obituaries of 4,400 deceased, divided on one axis among three languages (newspaper cultures) and over seven years (1998 included) on another. This space is filled with names of individuals, their titles (social and professional), and their occupations. When this space is organized, it can be viewed from different perspectives. It can, for example, be further divided into areas for each category. The space occupied by the 4,400 names of individuals differentiated between the sexes, allotting each sex an unequal share, a percentage, of that name space. The space occupied by English social titles, for example, is minimal by comparison to that same space in Arabic and Persian, again translating percentages of these titles from each language to shares of overall social title space. Finally, the share of that title space occupied by individual years can also change as, for example, the consistent reduction in the social title space filled by Arabic titles after 1952.

Attempts to create perfect worlds are bound to fail, as mine did, so long as these worlds are modeled on human societies in their everyday settings. They are likely to succeed only in fiction, provided the writer is able to transcend, even suspend, perceptions of actual social realities. But since obituaries are not fiction, they are bound to fail as perfect worlds. This I see as a genre effect, to which I return in the next section. My world of obituaries failed to be perfect because it inevitably reflects the social realities from which its population was drawn. But this is precisely why I chose the obituary world, populated as it is with the deceased, individuals who no longer belong to our social and physical realities and whose final profiles as projected in their obituaries should have been free of bias. But they were not. Our final tribute to our deceased continue to project them through our eyes, which see them as part of this world rather than free of it.

To my surprise, however, the obituary world constructed in the pages of this volume has not always been biased, and at times was different from the world outside it, hence the need for a connection between them. As a first step in connecting the two worlds through this model of space-sharing, I group the results into areas of convergence and divergence. This grouping is intended only as an overall assessment.

In two areas, occupations and professional titles, the results are classified as being both convergent and divergent, divergent in two areas, names and numerical representation, and convergent in one area, titles. Because comparisons with the world outside are based on our knowledge of it, which at times is not complete, some areas are considered both convergent and divergent for reasons explained below.

Table 7.1. The Results in Relation to the World Outside the Obituaries

	Names	Titles	Occupations	Prof. Titles	Social Titles	Numerical Rep.	OB size as visibility
Divergent	Yes	—	Yes	Yes	—	Yes	—
Convergent	—	Yes	Yes	Yes	Yes	—	Yes

Obituary size is unique to the world of the obituaries, hence it cannot be directly matched in a relationship of divergence or convergence with anything outside it. Only as a measure of visibility can it be related to the world outside, and as such it would be convergent with it insofar as women are less visible than men in both worlds, as argued in chapter 2. But it may also be divergent in that women's increased visibility over time did not translate to a corresponding increased visibility for deceased women in the obituaries.

Titles and social titles are convergent since the results confirm cross-cultural observations, for example, about the overall classification of societies along a title continuum—Egypt and Iran being more titled than the United States. They are also confirmed by events occurring in the world outside. Decline in identification by title in Egyptian obituaries as a whole but among men in particular and the different social and professional profiles constructed of women and men in Arabic and Persian obituaries are examples of this type (chapters 4 and 5). The relationship with outside events was at times not clearly established, although contradictions did not emerge either. Examples include increase in the social identification of deceased Iranian men in 1988 and its decrease among women, attributed to the impact of the Islamic Republic, and the decrease (versus increase) of the religious component in the respective social profiles constructed of deceased Egyptian men and women, attributed to effects of political Islam. None of these explanations, or connections with external events, can be proved or disproved. In the absence of contrary evidence, I have considered the connection supported, until proven otherwise, and therefore the results convergent.

Occupations and professional identities are classified as being convergent in that they confirm the background of the deceased as upper and upper-middle class, but also divergent in some important areas, particularly cross-cultural rankings (or space shares). Discrepancy in the distribution of occupational shares among the three cultures, if a reflection of the world outside, could imply that there are more people with occupations in Egypt than there are in the United States and Iran, a contradiction to available employment statistics.[3] Similar contradictions resulted from the ranking of women cross-culturally by occupation. In that sense, occupational and professional identities in the obituary world appear to be both divergent and convergent.

The most obvious divergent results emerged from naming the deceased and population distribution by sex. The case for population distribution has been made on the basis of earlier comparison with mortality rates in the world outside, specifically in Egypt (chapter 2). That comparison showed the obituary world to be divergent in four of the six years. Naming the deceased is divergent on almost all counts. The only obituaries without the deceased's first name are those of women; in the world outside there are times when both women and men are identified without their first names. The results are also cross-culturally divergent. In the United States, women's names are often legally linked to their husbands, but in Egypt and Iran they are not. Yet in the obituary world it is the Egyptian or Iranian woman who loses her name in favor of her husband's; in her death woman as wife is finally linked to man as husband (see chapter 3).

At times it has been difficult to make decisions due to insufficient information about the world outside (for example, availability of information on sex differentiation in social titles); other times because the information was not easily accessible (for example, employment statistics on the upper and upper-middle classes in Egypt, the United States, and Iran).

3. OBITUARIES AS GENRE

A space-sharing model such as that outlined above provides a framework within which the two worlds may be related: both consist of space, physical and conceptual, one occupied by individuals in their physical everyday settings and the other by words on a page constructed by authors to symbolically represent others. As a result of this difference (social reality versus text), the two worlds cannot be identical. Nor can one uniquely determine the other. The link between them is based on a relationship of mutual benefit and is constructed through the eyes of their authors, who ultimately convey a point of view or perspective. The three principles—role, orientation, and mutual benefit—represent connections between the two worlds, the core being mutual benefit. Each provides a link, but to a different aspect of the world outside. Together they can explain why the obituaries as texts and as genre would have to differ from the world outside, and why they would have to conform to, and thus reflect, aspects of it as well.

Obituary role is defined on the basis of the communicative function, or purpose, of the obituaries: announcement versus announcement-plus, the plus being a cultural variable ranging from status (Arabic) to feeling (Persian) to accomplishments (English). Within the same culture, obituaries can vary, but they are expected to remain within the relative boundaries of each culture group. Obituary orientation defines the focus of the obituary, and therefore its content—as deceased oriented or family oriented. Again, individual obituaries in the same culture may vary, although the overall cultural orientation is expected to prevail. The interaction of role and orientation allows for additional types of obituary cultures beyond our sample of three.

The Principle of Mutual Benefit provides a direct link by situating the obituary world as a whole within the funeralization process, which is situated in the world outside and linked to the family and the deceased, to the authors who write the obituaries, and to the newspapers that publish them. Mutual benefit is based on the idea that obituaries satisfy the need of the families to do right for the deceased and their need for support through the participation of others in death ceremonies. It highlights communication as the link between the obituaries and the world outside through their role in publicizing the event and attracting participants to it, which can only be accomplished when these texts are written (authorship) and published, hence the connection to the newspapers and their role in providing physical space and readership for obituaries.

These first two principles are obituary based. They relate aspects of obituary form and content to obituary cultures, themselves situated in the cultural space and time of the social realities outside them. Inevitably they reflect these realities, perhaps indirectly as well. But it is through this third principle that the obituary world is allowed to have "a life of its own," interacting with the world outside it for the benefit of both. Mutual benefit is also an organizing principle, as I explain later, that can be further generalized and made part of analytical models based on concepts of space-sharing, or just "sharing" since the concept itself implies mutual benefit.

As part of this theoretical model of space-sharing, these principles taken together relativize information obtained from the obituary world, that is, content of obituaries, as to their purpose, the cultures that support them, and the perceptions of their writers as individuals and as members of specific communities and cultural networks. If we assume these principles, both sex and culture differentiation would follow. Cultures where obituaries have acquired, or are in the process of acquiring, a role in addition to their being death announcements, will have longer obituaries accordingly. Their population distribution and their representation of the deceased will also reflect this role in accordance with the Principle of Mutual Benefit, assigning higher value to those aspects of representation perceived to be of higher benefit for their overall purpose. Thus if men are perceived to be more important in public space, more of them will be mentioned. If occupations and professional identities are perceived as reflecting extended networks and thus valuable in publicizing the event, they would be mentioned in obituaries regardless of orientation, although the reasons may differ. Social identities, when perceived as being valuable in promoting respect and status for the deceased, will also be mentioned regardless of orientation but in accordance with the Principle of Mutual Benefit. Basic identities are no exception in the obituaries. Naming the deceased (that is, identifying them with their names) may or may not be beneficial to the deceased and their memory, to the families, and to the event as a whole.

All such decisions are primarily the result of authorship, since the writers select the materials based on their perceptions of value relative to the purposes at hand. The choices and decisions writers make often produce constructions of identities not favorable to the memory of the deceased, recorded as part of a legacy left for posterity.

Mutual benefit affects obituary space as a result of other decisions, made by the newspapers, for example, and by the families. Overall obituary space, situated as it is within individual newspapers, is determined by the newspapers through the allotment of space and their continued support of that space. Such decisions are motivated by the newspapers' assessment of value to the community (secondary) and benefit to the newspapers (primary). Obituary space bought by individual families is determined, at times, by financial considerations. In both cases, families and newspapers, decisions are made in accordance with perceptions of importance, hence benefit, to both. Consequently, space is shared, or filled, by content perceived to be of mutual benefit to the families, the deceased (or their memory), the participants, and naturally to the newspapers.

Even the fact that obituaries are expected to be "truthful" can be seen to follow from the Principle of Mutual Benefit, which links them to the outside world. Misrepresentation (of the deceased's occupation, for example) is not beneficial since it could mislead potential participants. Likewise identifying women with their names at a time and place when women's names and their physical identities are hidden from public view, as they were in Egypt and Iran earlier in the twentieth century, could have brought embarrassment to the family. Thus the Principle of Mutual Benefit is also a principle of economy whereby space is shared in the best possible way to benefit all (although at times benefits to the deceased, to their memory, appear to have been ignored.) As a result, obituaries viewed as public space are governed by principles of space-sharing. The interaction of sex, culture, and time within this space is likewise governed by principles of economy and space-sharing mediated through mutual benefit.

This interpretation makes the relationship between the two worlds relative rather than absolute. The results are expected to converge or diverge depending on how effective and beneficial they are for the obituary world: its writers, its deceased, its survivors, and the newspapers that publish the obituaries. The model as presented above reverses the roles of the two worlds relative to each other, at least as we had originally perceived them. It has the effect, even the advantage, of placing the two worlds within their appropriate perspectives in relation to each other. The world of obituaries is no longer viewed only as a "subspace" where the world outside replicates itself: obituaries do not exist simply to reflect the world outside but to contribute to it as well. The obituary world has its own reasons for existence, which at times require that it reflect aspects of the world outside, other times they do not.

The model proposed above is just that, a conceptual framework within which the obituary world is to be analyzed and related to the world outside. Based on concepts of sharing and mutual benefit, it represents an ideal or a perfect world, free of bias, one where conflicts are resolved through negotiated mutually beneficial means. How do bias and inequity intrude into such a world and how can they be measured? We have already indicated that perfect worlds do not exist, particularly when modeled on human societies. By the same token, we do not expect this perfect model of space-sharing to exist either. As a model, it represents an ideal state, an abstract theoretical construct, against which bias, variation, equity, and the like can be identified, measured, and attributed to their sources: the obituary writers, whose perceptions and decisions determine content and style; the newspapers, who provide the physical space; and the deceased, whose lives provide the content. All are part of social realities of time and culture space full of imperfections and biases that creep into this model of a perfect world primarily through the writers, whose perceptions are part of the human collective consciousness and that of their own cultural space, and the deceased, whose lives may have been hampered by the imperfections of their time and space, its biases and inequities.

The deceased, due to limitations imposed on them by the social realities of their time and place, may have been unable to provide content—life achievements—appropriate for the obituary world as texts and as a genre, defined by the newspapers and the cultural contexts that support them. The writers may have been unable, or unwilling, to transcend cultural (mis)perceptions and overcome the barriers imposed on them. The strong effect of time, however, proves that some deceased have provided content and some writers have overcome the boundaries. As agents and active participants during their lifetime, the deceased have been able to bring about change in their place and time. Likewise, as agents and active participants in the construction (and maintenance) of the obituary world, the writers have been able to bring about change in its time and place as well.

It follows from this model, and correctly so, that the world of obituaries we have constructed is biased against its own deceased. Bias comes from two sources: the writers and the social realities of time and place. As a result, the representation of the deceased in their own obituaries often deprives them of their names and their acquired identities. Neither is beneficial to their memory (since they themselves can no longer be affected). Ironically, the writers emerge as a source of bias and, therefore, divergence from this ideal model.

Are we to conclude, then, that writers of family obituaries are biased against their own deceased? Hard as this may be to accept, it is true. Without knowing it, they reproduce in the texts they create profiles of deceased women and men that conform not to a model of sharing, as we would have expected, but to a model of dominance as constructed in the social realities outside the obituaries. In fact, profiles created in the obituaries are at times worse than those in the world outside, as when deceased women are deprived of their basic identities, the names with which they should have been publicly identified and remembered, or when motherhood no longer counts for a woman who has lost her child, or when a woman's identity is merged into another male's and she becomes "the mother of the wife of John Doe."

Obituary writers select information about the deceased and their families they deem important and beneficial to their purpose in writing the obituaries. Their decisions affect the texts they write, and by implication the obituary world as a whole, but they are also affected by the obituaries as genre within a specific time and place. Understanding the relationships involved in authorship (the creation of a text), the nature of the genre within which text is written, and the expectations of its audience provide yet another perspective on the role of obituary writers.

The term "genre" is typically applied in literature and the arts to distinguish one art form, or subtype, from another primarily on the basis of its content and form. Content distinguishes, for example, between fiction and nonfiction. Form distinguishes between, say, poetry and the novel. Thus for a text to qualify as being of a certain type, or genre, it has to conform to its content and form since it is the relationship between the two that often defines a particular genre. The boundaries are at times not clear, at other times consciously deconstructed by writers.

Within this broad definition of genre the obituaries must be viewed as nonfiction, on the basis of their content. As such they are expected (by their readers) to be "truthful" to the events they report. Obituary writers are expected not to use their imagination in constructing identities and events, nor to create an imaginary world but a real one where content matches the realities of the world outside. In short, they are expected not to falsify information; they are bound to be truthful. But they are not expected to provide all information about the deceased either.

The obituary is not a biography; it is an announcement of death. Obituary writers, like other writers, must be selective in the information they include, and their decisions determine the content of the obituaries. Through this selection process, their point of view comes to determine text since point of view includes attitudes, values, perceptions, and biases as well. These all affect the writers' (and the readers') relationship with text, shaping both its content and its form. By definition, then, a writer's decision to include or exclude information cannot be totally free of bias, nor can it be totally independent of genre effects, which by definition include audience and their expectations.

A difference emerges, then, between information included and information excluded. Information included about the deceased and the event must be factual, otherwise the obituary fails in its primary role as a death announcement (in addition to other possible implications). Obituary writers do not affect this aspect of content, but the deceased and the event itself do. If the deceased, for example, did not have an occupation or some form of professional identity, the writers, bound as they are to be truthful, cannot change the situation. Excluded information, however, is the direct result of decisions made by obituary writers. Decisions to exclude are filtered through the eyes of the writer and are, consciously or unconsciously, based on their attitudes, perceptions, and biases or lack thereof. These are mostly shaped by the writers and the sociocultural context of their time and place (a collective consciousness of which most are unaware). It is through exclusion of information, then, that bias affects content, contributing to what we as analysts eventually consider inequitable distributions, not beneficial by our standards to projections of the deceased. As analysts, possibly from a different time and place, we cannot determine what information has been excluded; thus we rely on statistical measures and methodologies of data collection and analysis that establish strong probabilities that the distribution we find is different from normal variation, as explained in earlier chapters; and we also rely on comparative research to relate the results obtained from the obituary world to available information from the world outside them.

The obituaries as genre should not be expected to conform literally to the principles of the world outside them. Like other genres, they convey a point of view, mostly of their authors, with the purpose of communication, using linguistic style that conforms to but may diverge from expected norms, and relying on materials factually true to the realities of the world outside them but selected by the authors to reflect their perceptions of what may be of value to them as authors and to their families from whom they receive authority, to the deceased as subject, and to their readership as audience. Through the creativity of their authors, or their potential divergence from accepted norms of obituary style and representations, obituaries may change over time, and we have seen examples of such changes. Insofar as authors conform to established traditions of textuality, obituaries remain stable. The same can also be said of the deceased: the more conforming their lives may have been to accepted societal norms as they have been defined for them, the more likely would their obituaries conform to established traditions of obituary style and representations.

Obituary writers are not expected to intentionally construct biased profiles of the deceased. This contradicts their position as family members, their role as writers, as well as the role obituaries have in the funeralization process with its focus on family needs to do right for the deceased. Yet decisions they make in excluding information can have the effect of creating profiles sufficiently biased to constitute significant deviation from a norm (or natural variation). This is because obituary writers are not always aware of their biases, and their decisions are not all made on a conscious level.

Because many factors are involved in the writers' decisions and choices, variation continues and change occurs in obituary style and in the ways the deceased are identified. Just as obituary writers, in this analysis, have been made responsible for maintaining the status quo in the obituaries as a genre, they must also be credited for being agents of change. Consider in this respect the innovation in the 1998 Arabic obituaries in the form of the phrase *wa nas'alukum al-faatiḥa* "we ask you for *al-faatiḥa* [to read the opening surah of the *Quran* for the deceased's soul]." Somewhere between 1988 and 1998 some obituary writer(s) must have found this phrase appealing, for whatever reason, and decided to use it in the obituaries. Other writers must have found it equally appealing and followed suit. The reasons why a family would choose such a phrase are many. The phrase reinforces religious (Islamic) identity due to its Quranic reference, which the family may wish to assert and find solace in. Its spiritual appeal and connection to the deceased's soul may be another. Consider, on a different note, change in identification by occupation, name, or any of the other variables. Such changes are more likely to have been generated not by obituary writers who conform to the status quo and maintain accepted norms of obituary style and conventions, but by innovative writers, who could have seen a woman's identification with her job and the pride she and her family may have derived from such an accomplishment as worthy of mention in her obituary as a final tribute to her and as part of her identity. Such an innovation would then encourage others to follow suit. Change would begin to emerge and with it the reconstruction of our collective memories of how identities of the deceased are to be represented in the obituary pages.

Viewed as genre, then, obituaries as a whole are no longer expected to reflect exactly the outside world, for they are not replicas of it. The random selection procedure adopted for the collection of the data was intended to guarantee that the selection would be a true representation of the world outside, and maybe it has been. But it cannot guarantee that when the obituaries themselves are not.

This research began with the assumption that the obituaries would reflect the world outside and that studying the obituaries would teach us something about that world—its people, their attitudes, their perceptions and representations of each other—and how this can all be conveyed through linguistic texts of which the obituaries are only one type. In fact, and despite discrepancies noted, this research has accomplished all that. The obituary world is now seen as gendered and culture differentiated, reflecting the attitudes of its creators and aspects of the social realities of their worlds. But it is also seen as somewhat independent, sometimes for the better but other times for the worse. Worst of all is that we may have shown that bias is carried over from the living onto the dead. But we have also shown that the living are the agents of change. Through their lives they change their conditions and those of their time and place, and through their deaths they force us to change ours.

Epilogue

Respectfully dedicated to the people of the obituaries,
whose paths have crossed mine, if only for a while, to
teach me about the world of the obituaries, where one
path ends for another to begin.

This has been a journey I have taken with the deceased who populate
the obituary world, and with their families as well. I wish to thank them for the
opportunity I have had to be with them in that world for more than ten years.

I remember their names, except those women who lost theirs in the
world of the obituaries. I remember their faces, particularly those of the
martyrs in the Persian newspapers (whom I did not study but whose presence
was so clear) and of the women in black (chador). I will always remember
the joy I felt every time I found more Egyptian women with their names,
American women with their professions, and Iranian women mentioned at
all. I will always remember Mrs. Richardson as she was identified in the *New
York Times* staff-written announcement of her death, whose story I wanted to
include in the text but could not find an appropriate context for it until now.

On March 14, 1938, the *New York Times* obituary page included the
following headline: "Mrs. Richardson's Funeral," with the subhead, "Special to
the *New York Times*." The obituary makes the usual announcements of location
and time of services, even the name of the clergy conducting the service. It
identifies the deceased as Mrs. Charles F. P. Richardson, and then describes
the time and place of her death. The obituary, written by the newspaper staff,
announces the arrival to Newport of her survivors: Mrs. Townsend Phillips of
New York, a niece; Mrs. Herbert C. Pell of Tuxedo Park, New York, her sister-
in-law; and Mr. and Mrs. Clarence C. Pell of Westbury, Long Island, the latter
a nephew. The family obituary of Mrs. Richardson appears a day earlier in the
New York Times. From that we find out her name and identity. She is actually
Charlotte Lathrope Pell, widow of Charles P. Richardson. We get to know
more about her here. She was the last surviving member of her immediate

family, but her nephew Herbert C. Pell Jr. was at the time U.S. minister to Portugal and a former member of Congress. Mr. Richardson, her husband, was a member of the U.S. diplomatic corps during the administration of President Theodore Roosevelt, when he served as secretary of the embassy at Berlin and in Brazil. Later he was chargé d'affaires in Denmark.

I felt sorry for Mrs. Richardson but happy I found her family obituary. I found out her name and was grateful to her family for that. More important is that her family identified her with her maiden, not married, name. They retained her identity for her in her death, unlike the *New York Times* staff.

I will always remember the disappointment, perhaps even anger, I felt every time I realized that the world of the obituaries, too, is gendered and culture differentiated. It did not seem fair, and it still does not. We, the living, have created it; there is no one else to blame. Have we created it in our own image? Perhaps, then, we can examine ourselves through the world of obituaries we have created and ask what it all means. What does it say about us, as individuals and as culture groups? What legacy do we leave behind? What does the *New York Times*' obituary of Mrs. Richardson mean? What does the family obituary of Charlotte Lathrope Pell mean?

This has also been a personal journey for me. My father became part of the obituary world in 1993, when I was halfway through this project and while he was in the United States. He had asked to stay in Minneapolis, a city he had grown to love. And we let him be. But I will always remember the story behind his obituary and the cultural differences that emerged between the part of the family in the United States and the other part in Egypt as we wrote his obituary. The part of the family in the United States wrote an obituary announcing the death. The obituary was written within the appropriate religious frame, but after some discussion among the younger group, it was decided to include only immediate family, perhaps also aunts and uncles I cannot recall, but not jobs or titles. This, it was said, would be too much. The obituary was faxed to Cairo, but was totally rejected, irritating everybody. It was a joke, we were told. This was an American, not an Egyptian, obituary. To publish it in this form would be a disgrace to the memory of our beloved father and to the family. An alternative Egyptian obituary was faxed back, and it certainly was an Egyptian obituary identifying every relative anybody could remember, even some of whom we may have never seen all our lives, at least as adults. Older women in the family such as aunts were identified as *ḥaram* so-and-so without their names, but in all fairness women's professional identities were acknowledged and they were identified appropriately with names, titles, and occupations. The part of the family in the United States rejected the alternative, arguing it did not make sense to include all these people most of whom we did not even know. After all, the deceased person himself would not have cared for all this, and so on.

My mother finally got into the picture and made the final decisions. She identified us and all other women in the family with our names, titles, and occupations (those of us who had acquired professional identities). She identified my father's mother and father. She identified spouses with their names, titles, and occupations, if they had them. Women without professional identities she identified with their names but also with their fathers' names and professional identity. They, it seemed, needed an identity of their own, too, but since they did not have one she assigned to them the public identity of the closest male, their fathers—which she also did with her own identification. But she did not mention each and every relative as the Egyptian part of the family had wanted. She restricted the survivors portion of the obituary to a more limited family circle: his parents, herself as his wife, his children and their spouses, his siblings, his grandchildren and their spouses, his immediate cousins, and her siblings, in that order. The revised version was faxed to Cairo—a better version we were told. The obituary appeared in *Al-Ahram*, top right-hand corner of the page, but in larger-than-usual type, occupying over half the length of the newspaper column. That was an Egyptian obituary. The debate, as I look back on it, reflected the need to do what was right for the deceased, to give him the respect the family felt was due to him within the cultural context in which he was known and in which the family lived. Everybody was satisfied.

I was proud of my mother, and I still am, for she was much more in tune with Egyptian obituary culture than the part of the family in the United States. I could see in her the change in Egyptian obituary culture. I could see in her the sociocultural shifts that have taken place in the construction of gender identity in public space. In the early 1960s, for example, she would not have written such an obituary. Perhaps she would not have had the opportunity in the presence of a stronger male authority. But perhaps she would have, for she is a woman to contend with. We cannot know what could or would have happened some thirty years ago. We do know, however, that the majority of

Egyptian families would not have written such an obituary at the time, but they would have in 1988.

In concluding this volume, and perhaps the stage of my life devoted to it, I add to my gratitude list the people of the obituary world whose lives, or perhaps whose deaths, have become part of my life for over ten years. They have traveled with me through two sabbaticals, one to Chicago and another to St. Louis. I thank them for their lives and thank their families for writing obituaries for them.

Will I let them go? Only time can tell.

Appendix A

Definitions of Arabic and Persian Social Titles

Arabic

The following definitions of titles found in the obituaries are from Badawi and Hinds's 1986 *Dictionary of Egyptian Arabic.*

effendi Turkish. Egyptian man in western clothes; title of, and form of address or reference to, an Egyptian man from the middle class. (27)

basha Turkish *pasha;* formerly a title of, and form of address and reference to, highest ranking officers and officials, now commonly used in respectful address to high officials (particularly police officials); term of address used for both men and women to indicate familiarity. (49)

bek, beh Turkish *bey. Bey,* formerly a title of, and form of address and reference to, second highest ranking officers and officials, now used loosely to indicate respect or to flatter. (118)

sayyida title of, and form of address or reference to, a married woman; title of a Muslim female saint. (440)

sayyid title of, and polite form of address and reference to, a man. (40)

sheikh title of, and form of address or reference to, a man who is of the Islamic professions (e.g., reciter of the Koran, head of a Sufi order) and to whom some religious status is attributed; title of respect to an older man; leader of a group *sheikh ilbalad* = appointed government official in charge of a section of a village (formerly, the elected deputy to the ʿ*umda*); acknowledged mentor or master. (489)

sitt lady, woman; mistress [of a house] *sitt ilbeet;* respectful form of address or reference to a grandmother; title of, and form of address or reference to, a woman *sitt hanim* = madam. (198)

ḥagg a pilgrim, one who has performed the Meccan pilgrimage; title of, and form of address or reference to, a pilgrim; polite form of address to an older man. (191)

ḥagga	female *ḥagg*
khawaga	European or western foreigner; [obsolete] Christian. (268)
ʿumda	headman of a village and its dependencies, mayor. (598)
qarinat	formal term of reference to a wife (697). (In popular belief, one's spiritual double, one's counterpart in the spirit world.)
muqaddis	a Christian who has made a pilgrimage to Jerusalem. (688)
qassis, qiss	formal term of reference to a priest or minister of the church. (699)
qummus	archpriest, hegumen (Christian). (718)

*In Egyptian Arabic, /g/ corresponds to Standard Arabic /j/, hence the discrepancy in the transcription of *ḥagg(a)* and *khawaga* in relation to *ḥajj(a)* and *khawaja* in the text.

Persian

The following titles and relational terms are from Haïm's 1968 *New Persian-English Dictionary.*

agha	a gentleman; a lord; *aghay* (Mr.); title of a father or elder brother. (22)
ayatullah	a title of the highest ecclesiastical order. Lit. the sign of God. (37)
banu	a lady, a gentlewoman; a princess; a woman of high rank. (220)
dushizeh	a maiden; a virgin. (874)
hajj	a pilgrim (to Mecca). (612)
hajjeh	a woman who has made a pilgrimage (to Mecca). (613)
hujatul-Islam	a spiritual title: His Reverence, Eminence. Argument or plea of Islam. (625)
karbalai	a native of Karbala; one who has made a pilgrimage to Karbala (site of the martyrdom of Iman Hussein). (624)
khanum	a lady; a wife; a mistress. Note: as a title of honor, the word is placed after the name. (692)
mashadi	Title of one who has visited sepulcher of Emam Rza at Meshed; a native of Meshed. (909)
mutaʿaliqeh	a dependency; family, esp. a wife. (809)
sayyid	a descendant of the Prophet; a lord, master, chief; prince. (127)
sayyideh	a female descendant of the Prophet; a lady; a princess. (127)

sheikh   an old man; a venerable man. A learned man, a teacher or professor. Note: used as a title of respect. (236)

sheikhul-Islam a title of highest degree given in Islam. (236)

I have retained the Arabic transliteration system for Arabic words in Persian, using the vowels *i* and *u* instead of *e* and *o,* repectively, and the *q* instead of *gh* (which is how these sounds would be pronounced in Persian). The only exception is the feminine ending, where I have retained *eh* instead of the Arabic *a(h).* The two Persian titles *hajj* and *hajjeh* also appear in the obituaries as *hajji* and *hajjieh,* respectively. I have opted to use one version of each for accuracy of the count.

Appendix B

Tables of Statistics

Table B.1 has been discussed in the overview (part 2). The remaining tables report results of the two-way interactions of Sex and Culture (B.2), Sex and Time (B.3), and Culture and Time (B.4), and the three-way interaction of Sex, Culture, and Time (B.5). The terms sex and culture differentiation are used in reference to analyses that measure sex and culture differences, respectively.

In table B.2 the distribution of the sexes relative to each other within each culture and across all three is measured on the basis of populations identified with the linguistic variables. The analysis proved to be statistically significant for all linguistic variables except Professional Title. Thus no statistical significance can be established in this case for sex differentiation across cultures.

Table B.3 reports results of the analysis of sex differences over time for the population identified with the linguistic variables. A level of statistical significance is established for all linguistic variables except Name and Professional Title. For these two, then, the distribution of the sexes is not significantly different from normal variation at any time period.

Table B.4 reports results of the interaction of Culture and Time on populations identified with the linguistic variables, comparing results from the three cultures to determine if change is culture differentiated. The chi-square analysis establishes statistical significance for each linguistic variable, suggesting the change is strongly culture differentiated.

Table B.5 reports results of the three-way interaction of Sex, Culture, and Time. The analysis measures cross-cultural differentiation over time for each linguistic variable within each sex group. Among the female population, no culture differences could be established for Occupation and Professional Title since no statistical significance could be obtained for the distribution across cultures and over time. The results for the male population differ. Statistical significance is established for all linguistic variables, suggesting that the distribution over time for this group is different from normal variation.

Table B.1. Distribution of Linguistic Variables by Sex, Culture, and Time (N = 3800)

	Sex			Culture			
	Female	Male	χ^2	Arabic	English	Persian	χ^2
Name	1379	**2178**	339.3*	_1128_	**1439**	990	305*
	39%	61%		32%	40%	28%	
Title	634	**925**	4.1***	**843**	_57_	659	1315.5*
	41%	59%		54%	4%	42%	
Occupation	43	**599**	407.3*	**451**	_82_	_109_	426.9*
	7%	93%		70%	13%	17%	
Prof. Title	12	**315**	222*	**182**	_51_	94	98.9*
	4%	96%		56%	16%	29%	
Social Title	**624**	640	35*	**675**	_4_	585	1146.6*
	49%	51%		53%	0.3%	46%	

	Time						
	1938	1948	1958	1968	1978	1988	χ^2
Name	_359_	_507_	_622_	670	**694**	**706**	75.8*
	10%	14%	17%	19%	20%	20%	
Title	_122_	231	287	281	294	**344**	32.5*
	8%	15%	18%	18%	19%	22%	
Occupation	_56_	_77_	_97_	128	119	**165**	29.9*
	9%	12%	15%	20%	19%	26%	
Prof. Title	_14_	_21_	49	56	**79**	**108**	76*
	4%	6%	15%	17%	24%	33%	
Social Title	_108_	**215**	242	227	223	249	15.6**
	9%	17%	19%	18%	18%	20%	

*p < .0001   **p < .01   ***p < .05

Table B.2: Sex Differentiation across Cultures (Sex and Culture)

	Arabic	English	Persian	χ^2
Name				81.2*
Female	_339_ 30%	**679** 47%	361 36%	
Male	**789** 70%	_760_ 53%	629 64%	
Title				36.3*
Female	_317_ 38%	_6_ 11%	**311** 47%	
Male	**526** 62%	**51** 89%	348 53%	
Occupation				20.2*
Female	_23_ 5%	**15** 18%	5 5%	
Male	**428** 95%	_67_ 82%	104 95%	
Prof. Title				1.2
Female	5 3%	2 4%	5 5%	
Male	177 97%	49 96%	89 95%	
Social Title				9.2**
Female	_312_ 46%	**4** 100%	**308** 53%	
Male	**363** 54%	_0_	_277_ 47%	

*p < .0001   **p < .01

Table B.3: Sex Differentiation in Distribution of Linguistic Variables over Time

	1938	1948	1958	1968	1978	1988	Total	χ^2
Name								2.3
Female	142	191	231	258	284	273	1379	
	40%	38%	37%	39%	41%	39%		
Male	217	315	391	412	410	433	2178	
	60%	62%	63%	61%	59%	61%		
Title								17.4**
Female	*31*	95	123	123	131	121	634	
	25%	41%	42%	44%	45%	37.5%		
Male	**91**	136	164	158	161	215	925	
	75%	59%	57%	56%	55%	62.5%		
Occupation								11.7***
Female	1	2	4	10	7	**19**	43	
	2%	3%	4%	8%	6%	12%		
Male	55	75	93	118	112	*146*	599	
	98%	97%	96%	92%	94%	88%		
Prof. Title								8.8
Female	0	1	0	0	3	8	12	
		5%			4%	7%		
Male	14	20	49	56	76	100	315	
	100%	95%	100%	100%	96%	93%		
Social Title								30.9*
Female	*31*	95	123	123	**131**	121	624	
	29%	44%	51%	54%	59%	49%		
Male	**77**	120	119	104	*92*	128	640	
	71%	56%	49%	46%	41%	51%		

*p < .0001 **p < .01 ***p < .05

Table B.4. Culture Differentiation in Distribution of Linguistic Variables over Time

	1938	1948	1958	1968	1978	1988	χ^2
Name							228.6*
Arabic	113	**181**	193	197	217	227	
	31%	36%	31%	29%	31%	32%	
English	**239**	**240**	240	_240_	_240_	_240_	
	67%	47%	39%	36%	35%	34%	
Persian	_7_	_85_	189	**233**	**237**	**239**	
	2%	17%	30%	35%	34%	34%	
Title							168.7*
Arabic	**109**	**270**	142	143	145	_134_	
	89%	74%	49%	51%	49%	39%	
English	8	_0_	8	_3_	10	**28**	
	7%		3%	1%	3%	8%	
Persian	_5_	_61_	**137**	**135**	139	**182**	
	4%	26%	48%	48%	47%	53%	
Occupation							90.2*
Arabic	**52**	**64**	66	91	82	_96_	
	93%	83%	68%	71%	69%	58%	
English	3	_3_	_6_	_6_	13	**51**	
	5%	4%	6%	5%	11%	31%	
Persian	_1_	10	**25**	**31**	24	_18_	
	2%	13%	26%	22%	20%	11%	
Professional Title							29.9**
Arabic	7	14	29	**38**	47	_47_	
	50%	67%	59%	68%	59%	44%	
English	**6**	_0_	6	_2_	10	**27**	
	43%		12%	4%	13%	25%	
Persian	1	7	14	16	22	34	
	7%	33%	29%	29%	8%	31%	
Social Title							162*
Arabic	**103**	**160**	116	_106_	_100_	_90_	
	95%	74%	48%	47%	45%	36%	
English	1	0	1	1	0	1	
	1%		0.4%	0.4%		0.4%	
Persian	_4_	_55_	125	**120**	**123**	**158**	
	4%	26%	52%	53%	55%	63%	

*p < .0001   **p < .001

Table B.5.: Culture Differentiation in Sex Groups over Time (Sex, Culture, and Time)

WOMEN	1938	1948	1958	1968	1978	1988	χ^2
Name							113*
Arabic	_21_	51	52	61	71	**83**	
	15%	27%	23%	24%	25%	30%	
English	**120**	**109**	108	114	126	_102_	
	85%	57%	47%	44%	44%	37%	
Persian	_1_	_31_	71	**83**	87	**88**	
	1%	16%	31%	32%	31%	32%	
Title							61.6*
Arabic	**30**	**67**	58	56	_58_	_52_	
	97%	71%	47%	46%	41%	40%	
English	3	0	1	1	0	2	
	3%		1%	1%		2%	
Persian	_0_	_28_	64	66	**79**	**74**	
		29%	52%	54%	59%	57%	
Occupation							9.6
Arabic	0	1	2	7	5	8	
		50%	50%	70%	71%	42%	
English	1	0	1	2	2	9	
	100%		25%	20%	29%	47%	
Persian							
Prof. Title							8.4
Arabic	0	0	0	0	0	5	
						62.5%	
English	0	0	0	0	0	2	
						25%	
Persian	0	1	0	0	3	1	
		100%			100%	12.5%	
Social Title							61*
Arabic	**30**	**67**	58	56	_54_	_47_	
	97%	71%	47%	46%	41%	39%	
English	1	0	1	1	0	1	
	3%		1%	1%		1%	
Persian	_0_	_28_	64	66	**77**	**73**	
		29%	52%	54%	59%	60%	

*p < .0001

Table B.5. Continued

MEN	1938	1948	1958	1968	1978	1988	χ^2
Name							133.3*
Arabic	92	**130**	141	136	146	144	
	42%	41%	36%	33%	36%	33%	
English	**119**	**131**	132	_126_	_114_	138	
	55%	42%	34%	31%	28%	32%	
Persian	_6_	_54_	118	**150**	**150**	**151**	
	3%	17%	30%	36%	36%	35%	
Title							109.8*
Arabic	**79**	**103**	84	87	91	_82_	
	87%	76%	51%	55%	57%	38%	
English	7	_0_	7	2	10	**25**	
	8%		4%	1%	6%	12%	
Persian	_5_	_33_	**73**	69	60	**108**	
	5%	24%	45%	44%	37%	50%	
Occupation							86.1*
Arabic	**52**	**63**	64	84	77	_88_	
	95%	84%	69%	71%	69%	60%	
English	2	_3_	5	_4_	11	**42**	
	4%	4%	5%	3%	10%	39%	
Persian	_1_	9	**24**	**30**	24	_16_	
	2%	12%	26%	25%	21%	11%	
Prof. Title							30.9***
Arabic	7	14	29	38	47	_42_	
	50%	70%	59%	68%	62%	42%	
English	**6**	0	6	_2_	10	**25**	
	43%		12%	4%	13%	25%	
Persian	1	6	14	16	19	33	
	7%	30%	29%	29%	25%	33%	
Social Title							102*
Arabic	**73**	**93**	58	50	46	_43_	
	95%	77.5%	49%	48%	50%	34%	
English	0	0	0	0	0	0	
Persian	_4_	_27_	61	54	46	**85**	
	5%	22.5%	51%	52%	50%	64%	

*p < .0001   ***p < .001

Appendix C

Social and Professional Titles as Applied to Women and Men

Table C.1. Women's Social and Professional Titles

	SOCIAL TITLE			PROFESSIONAL TITLE		
Title	**#**	**Meaning**	**Title**	**#**	**Meaning**
Arabic					
sayyida	208	married/older	*doktora*	3	doctor
hajja	58	pilgrimaged, Muslim	*muhandisa*	1	engineer
anisa	18	Miss	*ustadha*	1	professor
muqaddisa	13	pilgrimaged, Christian			
sitt	10	lady, Ms.			
hanim	3	lady, Ms.			
amira	1	princess			
ukht	1	sister			
Total	312			5	
English					
Mrs.	4		Dr.	1	
			Ph.D.	1	
Total	4			2	
Persian					
banu	238	married woman	*doktor*	4	doctor
khanum	22	Ms.	*muhandis*	1	engineer
hajjeh	11	pilgrimaged, Muslim			
dushizeh	8	Miss			
banu-hajjeh	17				
khanum-hajjeh	12				
Total	308			5	

Table C.2. Men's Social and Professional Titles

	SOCIAL TITLES			PROFESSIONAL TITLES		
Title	#	Meaning	Title	#	Meaning
Arabic						
hajj	91	pilgrimaged, Muslim	muhandis	45	engineer
sheikh	65	religious/older	doktor	38	Dr.
ustadh	55	Mr.	ustadh	35	professor/Mr.
effendi	52			28	military
beh	32		sheikh	8	sheik
muqaddis	21	pilgrimaged, Christian	hajj	3	pilgrimaged, Muslim
khawaga	18		fadilat ustadh	3	reverend, Muslim
sayyid	17	Mr.	mustashar	6	consultant
basha	6		qummus	4	archpriest, Coptic
sheikh-ʿarab	4		qiss	1	priest
wagih	1		safir	2	ambassador
miʿallim	1		muhami	1	attorney
			jeoloji, kimai	2	geologist, chemist
			muʿalim	1	educator
Total	363			177	
English						
			Doctor	30	
			Religious	10	reverend 9, rabbi 1
			Military	3	
			Ph.D.	3	
			D.D.S.	3	
Total	0			49	
Persian						
agha	86	Mr.		36	military
hajj	76	pilgrimaged	muhandis	20	engineer
sayyid	26	Mr.	doktor	15	doctor
agha-hajj	31		ayatulla-sheikh	4	religious
agha-sayyid	18		hujatul-Islam	10	
hajj-sayyid	6		ustaz sheikh	1	
agha-sheikh	4		ustaz	1	
sayyid-hajj	2		ustaz doktor	2	professor doctor
mirza	5				
hajj-mirza	6				
family title	5				
ustaz	2				
agha-mashadi	2				
karbalai	2				
sheikh	1				
agha-hajj-sheik	2				
agha-hajj-mirza	1				
agha-hajj-sayyid	2				
Total	277			89	

Table C.3. Women's Titles over Time

SOCIAL TITLES	1938	1948	1958	1968	1978	1988	Total
English							
Mrs.	1		1	1		1	4
Arabic							
sayyida	14	52	49	40	30	23	208
	47%	78%	84%	71%	56%	49%	(67%)
hajja	1	5	5	10	17	20	58
	3%	8%	9%	18%	32%	43%	(19%)
anisa	5	4	4	4	—	1	18
	17%	6%	7%	7%		2%	(6%)
muqaddisa	—	2	—	1	7	3	13
		3%		2%	13%	6%	(4%)
sitt	10	—	—	—	—	—	10
	33%						(3%)
hanim	—	2	—	1	—	—	3
		3%		2%			(1%)
amira	—	1	—	–	—	—	1
ukht	—	1	—	—	—	—	1
Total	30	67	58	56	54	47	312
	(100%)	(100%)	(100%)	(100%)	(100%)	(100%)	(100%)
Persian							
banu	—	22	59	57	61	39	238
		79%	92%	86%	79%	53%	(78%)
khanum	—	3	2	4	5	8	22
		11%	3%	6%	7%	11%	(7%)
banu-hajjeh	—	—	1	2	6	8	17
			2%	3%	8%	11%	(6%)
khanum-hajjeh	—	—	—	—	3	9	12
					4%	12%	(4%)
hajjeh	—	1	—	2	—	8	11
		4%		3%		10%	(4%)
dushizeh	—	2	2	1	2	1	8
		7%	3%	2%	3%	1%	(3%)
Total	—	28	64	66	77	73	308
		(100%)	(100%)	(100%)	(100%)	(100%)	(100%)

Table C.3. Women's Titles over Time — Continued

PROFESSIONAL TITLES	1938	1948	1958	1968	1978	1988	Total
English							
Ph.D.	—	—	—	—	—	1	1
doctor	—	—	—	—	—	1	1
Total	—	—	—	—	—	2	2
Arabic							
doktor	—	—	—	—	—	3	3
muhandis	—	—	—	—	—	1	1
ustadh	—	—	—	—	—	1	1
Total	—	—	—	—	—	5	5
Persian							
doctor	—	1	—	—	3	—	4
muhandis	—	—	—	—	—	1	1
Total	—	1	—	—	3	1	5

Table C.4. Men's Titles over Time

SOCIAL TITLES	1938	1948	1958	1968	1978	1988	Total
English	—	—	—	—	—	—	—
Arabic							
hajj	7	16	14	22	18	14	91
	10%	17%	24%	44%	39%	33%	(25%)
sheikh	15	19	14	9	5	3	65
	20%	20%	24%	18%	11%	7%	(20%)
ustadh	1	—	11	13	14	16	55
	1%		19%	26%	30%	38%	(15%)
effendi	24	28	—	—	—	—	52
	32%	30%					(14%)
beh	15	13	2	—	1	1	32
	20%	14%	3%		2%	2%	(9%)
muqaddis	—	2	7	3	4	5	21
		2%	12%	6%	9%	12%	(6%)
khawaga	8	8	—	1	1	—	18
	11%	9%		2%	2%		(5%)
sayyid	3	2	6	2	1	3	17
	4%	2%	10%	4%	2%	7%	(5%)
basha	—	2	3	—	1	—	6
		2%	5%		2%		(2%)
sheikh-ʿarab	—	3	1	—	—	—	4
		3%	2%				(1%)
wagih	1	—	—	—	—	—	1
miʿallim	—	—	—	—	1	—	1
Total	74	93	58	50	46	42	363
	(100%)	(100%)	(100%)	(100%)	(100%)	(100%)	(100%)
Persian							
agha	1	13	27	16	9	18	84
	25%	48%	44%	30%	20%	21%	(30%)
hajj	—	6	8	12	16	34	76
		22%	13%	22%	35%	40%	(27%)
agha-hajj	—	1	5	7	4	14	31
		4%	8%	13%	9%	16%	(11%)
sayyid	—	2	5	6	6	7	26
		7%	8%	11%	13%	8%	(9%)
agha-sayyid	—	1	6	4	3	4	18
		4%	10%	7%	7%	5%	(7%)
hajj-sayyid	—	—	2	1	—	3	6
			3%	2%		4%	(2%)

TITLES	1938	1948	1958	1968	1978	1988	Total
hajj-mirza	—	—	—	1 2%	4 9%	1 1%	6 (2%)
family title	—	1 4%	2 3%	2 4%	—	—	5 (2%)
mirza	—	—	2 3%	1 2%	1 2%	1 1%	5 (2%)
agha-sheikh	—	—	1 2%	0	2 4%	1 1%	4 (1%)
sheikh	—	—	—	1 2%	—	—	1
karbalai	—	—	1 2%	1 2%	—	—	2 (1%)
ustaz	1 25%	—	—	—	—	1 1%	2 (1%)
agha-mashadi	—	1 4%	1 2%	—	—	—	2 (1%)
agha-hajj-sheikh	—	—	—	1 2%	1 2%	—	2 (1%)
agha-hajj-sayyid	0	0	1 2%	1 2%	—	—	2 (1%)
agha-family title	—	2 7%	—	—	—	—	2 (1%)
sayyid-hajj	2 50%	—	—	—	—	—	2 (1%)
agha-hajj-mirza	—	—	—	—	—	1 1%	1
Total	6 (100%)	14 (100%)	36 (100%)	38 (100%)	37 (100%)	67 (100%)	277 (100%)

PROFESSIONAL TITLES	1938	1948	1958	1968	1978	1988	Total
English							
doctor	2 33%	—	4 67%	1 50%	9 90%	14 52%	30 (59%)
reverend	3 50%	—	1 17%	1 50%	—	4 15%	9 (18%)
Ph.D.	—	—	—	—	1 10%	3 11%	4 (8%)
DDS	—	—	—	—	—	3 11%	3 (6%)
MD	—	—	—	—	—	1 4%	1 (2%)

TITLES	1938	1948	1958	1968	1978	1988	Total
rabbi	—	—	—	—	—	1 4%	1 (2%)
lt-colonel	—	—	—	—	—	1 4%	1 (2%)
captain	1 17%	—	—	—	—	—	1 (2%)
colonel	—	—	1 17%	—	—	—	1 (2%)
Total	6	0	6	2	10	27	51
Arabic							
muhandis	—	1 7%	5 17%	13 34%	16 34%	10 34%	45 (25%)
doktor	3 50%	4 29%	8 28%	2 5%	9 19%	12 28%	38 (22%)
ustadh	1 17%	1 7%	10 35%	9 24%	5 11%	9 21%	35 (20%)
"military"	1 17%	4 29%	5 17%	6 16%	6 13%	6 14%	28 (16%)
sheikh	—	1 7%	1 3%	2 5%	4 9%	—	8 (5%)
mustashar	—	—	—	1 3%	4 9%	1 2%	6 (3%)
fadilat ustadh	—	—	—	2 5%	1 2%	—	3 (2%)
ḥajj	—	—	—	1 3%	1 2%	1 2%	3 (2%)
muʿallim	—	1 7%	—	—	—	—	1
muḥami	1 17%	—	—	—	—	—	1
safir	—	—	—	1 3%	—	—	1
jeoloji	—	—	—	—	—	1 2%	1
qummus	—	2 14%	—	1 3%	1 2%	—	4 (2%)
kimai	—	—	—	—	—	1 2%	1
safir-doktor	—	—	—	—	—	1 2%	1
qiss	—	—	—	—	—	1 2%	1
Total	6 (100%)	14 (100%)	29 (100%)	38 (100%)	47 (100%)	43 (100%)	177 (100%)

TITLES	1938	1948	1958	1968	1978	1988	Total
Persian							
"military"	1	6	7	6	8	8	36
	100%	100%	50%	37%	42%	24%	(40%)
muhandis	—	—	1	5	3	10	19
			7%	31%	16%	30%	(21%)
doktor	—	—	4	4	3	4	15
			29%	25%	16%	12%	(17%)
hujatul-Islam	—	—	1	1	2	6	10
			7%	6%	11%	18%	(11%)
ayatullah-sheikh	—	—	1	—	2	1	4
			7%		11%	3%	(5%)
ustaz-doktor	—	—	—	—	—	2	2
						6%	(2%)
ustaz-sheikh	—	—	—	—	1	—	1
					5%		(1%)
ustaz	—	—	—	—	—	1	1
						3%	(1%)
doktor-muhandis	—	—	—	—	—	1	1
						3%	(1%)
Total	1	6	14	16	19	33	89
	(100%)	(100%)	(100%)	(100%)	(100%)	(100%)	(100%)

Appendix D

Classification of Occupations

Table D.1. Classification of Occupations by Culture Group

	Arabic	**%**	**English**	**%**	**Persian**	**%**	**Total**
I Professional and technical	132	29	42	51	39	36	213
II Administrative and managerial	110	25	20	24	15	14	145
III A'yan and representatives	24	5	—	—	—	—	24
IV Business owners, merchants	60	13	7	9	4	4	71
V Civil service and employees	74	17	10	12	46	42	130
VI Clerical	18	4	1	1	—	—	19
VII Sales	2	0.4	2	2	—	—	4
Other	31	7	—	—	5	5	36
Total	451	70	82	13	109	17	642

Table D.2. Classification of Occupations by Culture and Sex

	Arabic		English		Persian	
	Female	Male	Female	Male	Female	Male
I Professional and technical	10 44%	122 29%	8 53%	34 51%	3 60%	36 35%
II Administrative and managerial	2 9%	108 26%	4 27%	16 24%	0	15 15%
III *A'yan* and representatives	—	24 5%	—	—	—	—
IV Business owners, merchants	—	60 14%	3 20%	4 6%	—	4 4%
V Civil service and employees	2 9%	72 17%	—	10 15%	1 20%	45 43%
VI Clerical	1 0.4%	17 7%	—	1 2%	—	—
VII Sales	0	2 3%	—	2 3%	—	—
Other	8 35%	23 5%	—	—	1 20%	4 47%
Total	23	428	15	67	5	104

Table D.3. Occupations by Culture and Sex of the Deceased over Time

		1938	1948	1958	1968	1978	1988	Total
Arabic								
I Professional	F	—	—	1	2	2	5	10
	M	8	15	23	29	27	20	122
II Administrative	F	—	—	—	—	1	1	2
	M	14	11	10	20	23	30	108
III A ʿyan	F	—	—	—	—	—	—	0
	M	10	5	4	2	0	3	24
IV Business	F	—	—	—	—	—	—	0
	M	6	10	6	12	8	18	60
V Civil	F	—	—	—	—	—	2	2
	M	7	12	12	17	15	11	74
VI Clerical	F	—	—	—	—	1	—	1
	M	3	4	5	2	1	2	17
Other	F	—	1	1	5	1	—	8
	M	4	6	4	2	3	4	23
Total		52	64	66	91	82	96	451
English								
I Professional	F	1	0	1	2	1	3	8
	M	1	2	3	3	5	20	34
II Administrative	F	—	—	—	—	1	3	4
	M	—	—	1	—	4	11	16
IV Business	F	—	—	—	—	—	3	3
	M	—	—	—	—	1	3	4
V Civil	F	—	—	—	—	—	—	—
	M	—	1	—	—	2	7	10
VI Clerical	F	—	—	—	—	—	—	—
	M	—	—	1	—	—	—	1
VI Sales	F	—	—	—	—	—	—	—
	M	1			1			2
Total		3	3	6	6	14	50	82
Persian								
I Professional	F	—	1	1	—	—	1	3
	M	—	1	10	8	9	8	36
II Administrative	F	—	—	—	—	—	—	—
	M	—	2	6	3	2	2	15
IV Business	F	—	—	—	—	—	—	—
	M	1	—	—	3	1	—	4
V Civil	F	—	—	—	—	—	1	1
	M	—	5	7	14	12	6	44
Other	F	—	—	—	1	—	—	1
	M	—	1	1	2	—	—	4
Total		1	10	25	31	24	18	109

Notes

Introduction

1. Huda Shaarawi (1879–1947) is one of Egypt's early feminist leaders. She is quoted in Badran 1995:73 as she recalls the early death in 1918 of Bahithat al-Badiya (Malak Hifni Nasef), another feminist leader and friend who had preceded her in making public demands for women's rights. In her recollection, she acknowledges the impact Bahithat al-Badiya has had on her. The eulogy she presented in the commemoration of Malak's death was the first public speech she had ever given, thus one path ends for another to begin.

2. I here acknowledge Jane (Roxie) Beyle, one of the students in that class who also worked in the obituary section of the *Salt Lake Tribune* and whom I credit with bringing the obituaries back into my life by asking if they would be an appropriate topic for a research paper.

3. Beeman, for example, notes effects from Arabic on conversational styles in Iran: "The proportion of Arabic-origin words increases dramatically in formal speech situations and oratory, lending some additional support to the proposition that movement from more to less determined style (Style A to Style B) may proceed on a continuum: greater to less Arabicization in all linguistic features" (1986:130).

4. Quoted from his *Language, Truth and Politics* in Graddol and Swann 1989:143.

5. See, for example, Nilsen et al. 1977, Friedl 1978, Miller and Swift 1977, Schulz 1990, Martyna 1983, among others.

Chapter 1

1. Quoted in Badran 1995:73.

2. A possible extension of this research would compare family- and staff-written obituaries of prominent figures.

3. "The Obituarist's Art Lives after Death," 64–66, quote on p. 64.

4. The article ends quoting George Eliot's words used to introduce this chapter and paying tribute to ordinary dead people. "In acknowledging for a moment the passage of such lives, we remind ourselves that our world is shaped and colored not only by the actions of great leaders and the interplay of economic forces, but by countless lesser contributors, be they dancers, airmen, inventors, doctors, entertainers, architects, batsmen, thinkers, villains or mere players of walk-on parts in the scenes of history" (68).

5. These eleven categories are administrative skills, quantitative emphasis, creativity/innovation, leadership, intellectual achievement, chief authority, civic activities, war service, personal virtues, selfless service, and family emphasis.

6. I checked with the staff of the *New York Times* obituary section regarding editorial policy on content and style of family-written obituaries. I found that the only restriction involves information that could be legally problematic for the newspaper, such as information pertaining to the cause of death, particularly if it involved an accident. They also require verification of the person's death by calling at least one person other than the writer (the funeral home, for example). As far as style, they had no restrictions, although they recommended looking at other obituaries before writing, something people do anyway if unfamiliar with obituaries and their formats.

7. The Arabic and Persian newspapers examined are more similar to the *Salt Lake Tribune* in this respect than they are to either the *New York Times* or the *Chicago Tribune.*

8. In this sample I have used boldface to highlight relationships (deceased to survivor) and italics for titles. Commas separate individual lists of relatives within the same relationship, and a semicolon separates different relationships. Items in brackets are not in the actual texts, but have been added for clarification.

9. According to Badawi and Hinds, the title *bek* or *beh* is derived from Turkish *bey.* It is "formerly [pre-1952 Egyptian Revolution] a title of, and form of address and reference to, second highest ranking officers and officials, now used loosely to indicate respect or to flatter" (1986:118).

10. Compare with "mother of the wife of" in obituary 1. In both the relationship is actually "mother-in-law." They have been translated differently to capture a difference in the Arabic text. Only in obituary 2 is the Arabic word for mother-in-law, *hamat,* used. In obituary 1 the Arabic text has *walidat haram,* literally "mother of the wife of."

11. The same is true for adopted children. This is an Islamic tradition attributed to the Quranic verse *'ud 'uuhum li 'aabaa' ihim*—"Call them [by names] of their fathers." Quranic Sura 33 (Al-Ahzab), verse 5 (Ali:1103).

12. Marriage between first cousins is allowed in Egypt (and the rest of the Arab world) and Iran.

13. *subhaan allathi biyadihi malaakuutu kulla shay' in wa ilayhi turja'uun.* Quranic Sura 36 (Yasin), verse 83 (Ali:1188). This and all translations of Quranic verses are from Ali's translation.

14. The Arabic text is not clumsy. A more idiomatic English translation of *ibnat karimat* is "daughter of Mahrous Aggag's daughter."

15. *Raqadat 'ala rajaa' al-qiyaama.* This phrase is typically used in Christian obituaries.

16. Translation for *kulliyyat al-i'lam,* probably equivalent to Department of Communication.

17. *inna lillaahi wa inna ilayhi raaji'uun.* Quranic Sura 2 (Al-Baqara), verse 156 (Ali:62).

18. Translation for Persian *aghay,* plural of *agha* (Mr.).

19. Three terms are used in the Persian obituaries to refer to memorial ceremonies

(*majlis fatiha, majlis khatm,* and *majlis tazakur*). These are discussed later (pp. 53–54).

20. Islamic law and tradition allow cousins, paternal and maternal, to marry each other. Cf. note 12 above.

21. "Kullu man ʿalayha faani." Quranic Sura 55 (Al-Rahman), verse 26 (Ali:1475).

22. "Thick" refers to the material from which the chador is made. It cannot be a see-through material.

23. I am indebted to my colleague Soheila Amirsoleimani for this information and for help with the translation of these two obituaries.

24. The 1988 Persian obituaries actually start in December 1987 and continue into January 1988. This is because I started data collection in 1988, and these were the only issues available to me at the time.

25. Some reasons are given in section 3.2.3.

26. Data collection was based on editions published for local circulation. Internet editions have been available only recently, and international editions were certainly not available in the earlier part of the century.

27. In the *New York Times* about 536 (67 percent) of identified locations are from New York, in *Ettelaʾat* 990 (97 percent) from Tehran, and in *Al-Ahram* 536 (45 percent) from Cairo, suggesting that *Al-Ahram* has the broadest local geographical coverage, *Ettelaʾat* the most localized, and the *New York Times* in between.

28. *Al-Akhbar* was first published in 1952.

29. I am grateful to the late Nawal El-Mahalawi, Al-Ahram Center for Translation and Publishing, for providing me with policy information included in this section regarding the obituary pages.

30. During these three days, unless otherwise specified, people are free (in fact are obligated) to visit and console the family of the deceased. After the three days are over, close family and friends continue to visit.

31. Islamic tradition requires the body to be buried as soon as possible, usually within twenty-four hours of death. Thus, depending on time of death, it may not always be possible for an obituary to appear before the funeral.

32. The language of that *shukr* uses the feminine plural forms, used exclusively in reference to female groups. Arabic distinguishes that from masculine plural, which is used in reference to both exclusively masculine as well as mixed groups.

33. Majidian 1981 gives the following circulation estimates for 1978: *Keyhan,* 350,000, followed by *Ettelaʾat* with 200,000.

34. Information about the cost of running an obituary or an ad in *Ettelaʾat* is not available.

35. The analysis of survivor data will not be reported in this volume but will be published separately at a later time.

36. The survivors' file includes the same information as the deceased and will not be reported on here.

37. The *New York Times,* however, boldfaces the last names of all the deceased (see section 2).

38. To be listed in a person's obituary is an important matter among Egyptian

families. Individuals and families may feel slighted if they are not mentioned in a relative's obituary, or if a person they consider to be more distant than themselves is mentioned when they are not. In many cases the feelings are so strong that the family of the deceased has to put another announcement in the obituary pages indicating the names and relationship of those people to the deceased. They would announce as an oversight that in the obituary of X the names of A, B, etc. were not mentioned, then list them with all the information that would have been included in the original obituary.

39. Ambiguity did arise in some cases in determining the sex of survivors, where kinship terms did not clearly establish one gender or the other.

40. This may be due to their Turkish origin.

Chapter 2

1. Quoted in Milani in commenting on Iranian women's rebellion against the stereotypical "feminine ideal that condemned them to *Sokut-o-Sokun* 'silence and immobility'" (1992:53).

2. Badran and Cooke 1990:232.

3. This may be related to the direction of the writing system: English is left to right, Arabic and Persian right to left. If so, then visibility is related to initial position.

4. The use of boldface was first coded during the collection of the Arabic data, but was later ignored when no variation in this area was found in the English and Persian obituaries.

5. It is understood somehow within the Egyptian "obituary-page culture" that the upper right-hand location is usually reserved for "important" families, perhaps those with "status" or "connections." No proof or support has been or will be given for such a claim.

6. Maximum and minimum length is another aspect of size that can shed some light but it is not very reliable. The difference between minimum and maximum length of Arabic, English, and Persian obituaries is 97, 43, and 51 lines, respectively. The discrepancy here is due to divergence in maximum length. Minimum length is set by the newspaper, which may explain the absence of dramatic variation across cultures (Arabic 4, English 2, Persian 3) and over time. This is not true of maximum length, where the differences are quite divergent and the variation quite extensive (Arabic 101, English 45, Persian 54). To think that a family would write a 101-line obituary for its deceased listing relatives and survivors indicates an importance attached to obituaries and their length, which turns them into something more than a death announcement, perhaps a status symbol, in some cultures, here Egypt. Maximum length, however, is not reliable: it is random and is based on one obituary (the longest). It is reported here simply as an indication of potential cultural differences and, if read in conjunction with the texts of the longest obituaries from each culture, could add more "cultural meaning" to content and size.

7. Increase in obituary size achieves a level of statistical significance (p < .0001) for the 1978–88 and the 1958–68 decades.

8. This trend is maintained in the 1998 obituaries, as shown in chapter 7. Furthermore, the difference in obituary size is statistically significant in two of the six decades (1958–68, 1978–88) and in the 1988–98 decade.

9. A more literal translation would be "the weight death carries" for the Arabic *alwazn allathi yaḥtalluhu almawt.*

10. This framework may also explain differences among newspapers. In the United States in particular, local newspapers tend to be more deceased oriented in the sense that obituaries tend to give a brief biographical sketch of the deceased: place and date of birth and of marriage, education, residence, and sometimes the cause of death. Other personal information such as hobbies may also be included. An example here is the *Salt Lake Tribune,* where obituaries on the whole appear to be much longer than the those in *New York Times,* the *Chicago Tribune,* or even the *St. Louis Dispatch* and very often include pictures of the deceased.

11. In Arabic it is 17.6 lines for women versus 18.9 lines for men; in Persian 10 versus 10.6; and in English 8.4 versus 8.8.

12. Middle Eastern women have acknowledged through their writings the effects their exclusion from the public domain has had on them as women and as writers. Fadwa Tuqan, a Palestinian poet, writes in her memoirs, *Difficult Journey, Mountainous Journey* (Nablus, 1984): "I was unable to compose poetry; my inner voice was weak in protest against everything that had caused my silence. I was expected to create political poetry while the corrupt laws and customs insisted that I remain secluded behind a wall, not able to attend assemblies of men, not hearing the recurrent debates, not participating in public life" (Badran and Cooke 1990:27). This theme recurs in women's writings in all three cultures.

13. Lee L. Bean (personal communication).

14. The ratio of Muslims and Christians in the Egyptian obituaries is another case where the distribution within the obituary pages is divergent from that in the world outside them. Whereas the Christian population represents a "significant" minority in Egypt (claimed to be somewhere between 10 and 13 percent), the ratio in the obituary pages is much higher than reported in government or other statistics: 39 percent Christian to 61 percent Muslim.

15. A better, more formal representation would assign numerical values to categories instead of the +/- system, which does not formally capture this concept of "relative degree."

16. The focus on this group is essentially justified on the basis that it is this group that populates the obituary pages, as will be shown in chapter 5.

17. See, for example, Hymowitz and Weissman 1978, McDonagh 1989, and Scott 1984, among others.

18. This refers to laws that regulate marriage, divorce, custody, etc.

19. In Egypt this dates back to 1892, the publication of Hind Nawfal's monthly newspaper *al-Fatah.*

20. Recall in this respect Milani's analysis of a veiled society and her reiteration of cultural taboos on women's public voice.

Statistical Analyses and Results

1. Percentages reported in this overview, unless otherwise specified, reflect the distribution of linguistic variables over the total population, taken from table B.1. The distribution, figures, and percentages, as applied to other segments of the population such as sex or culture groups, are found in discussions of individual variables in subsequent chapters and in appendix B.

2. There is a discrepancy in our perception of what "work" means in relation to women and to different socioeconomic groups, which is why I use the term "employment." Although most people would now acknowledge women's activity at home as work, it is still not considered employment since no pay is involved.

Chapter 3

1. Quoted in Miller and Swift 1977:12.

2. These observations have been inspired by observing play patterns of my granddaughter, Danya, and her playmates.

3. Alford analyzes nicknames, teknonyms, and name changes as instances of "emergent identity" and "identity transformations" (1988:81–96).

4. Alford notes two instances in his sample of societies with nameless individuals. In both cases the nameless are women. "Many Quarani women were reported [probably in Murdock 1945] to have no names at all, and Korean women, once married, lack personal names" (1988:52).

5. "In nine of the sixty sample societies (15 percent), naming serves to signal and announce legitimate parenthood, and in twenty three of the sixty societies (38 percent), the bestowal of a name signals the child's membership in the society. . . . Naming the child often symbolically brings him or her into the social sphere, and naming is often accompanied by other acts with similar symbolic significance" (Alford 1988:30).

6. Choice of names may also be impacted by religious affiliation as well as political and sociocultural change. A study of naming in Iran during the period 1963–88 (Habibi 1992) suggests that increase (or decrease) of Arabic versus Persian names among various socioeconomic groups may be explained as a reaction to two trends: one secular and promoted by the Pahlavi regime, the other religious and promoted by the postrevolution Islamic regime. The reaction among certain socioeconomic groups is contrary to the predominant discourse of the regime, but is supportive among others.

7. The convention in Arabic of using *ibn/ben* (son of) or *bint* (daughter of) may be the origin of this tradition. Perhaps in modern times these terms were dropped in favor of leaving the father's name attached.

8. Again the issue of last name is interesting from the historical perspective. In early Islamic texts, for example, people are identified with their (paternal) lineage (son or daughter of X who is son of Y, and so on). Also in modern times the first three names are sometimes taken arbitrarily so that "last name" turns out to be the third name in the series of names.

9. See Nancy Jabbra 1980 and Richard Antoun 1968 for aspects of naming in two different small Lebanese communities.

10. In all three cases individuals may legally change their name, but the number of such changes is most likely very small.

11. Obituaries 11 and 13 (1958).

12. Out of 90,133 names, 12,253 are not sex exclusive and apply to both women and men.

13. For the most part, however, major city newspapers follow the same format as that of the *New York Times*. Thus to test this hypothesis, comparisons with more local newspapers should be made. This was ignored here since it would contradict the parallelism argument necessary for the comparative purpose of this research, although it would answer the question of newspaper effect.

14. One potential for variation here involves the use of a middle initial, shown in a 1990 study by Rasold et al. to correlate with both gender and status in newspaper reporting. Middle initials were not considered during the data collection stage, partly because they are not used in the naming systems of Arabic and Persian.

15. The actual percentage for Iranian men is 99.7 percent. Two men (0.3 percent) were identified by their father's name.

16. A similar situation occurs in colloquial Egyptian Arabic where the term ʿela, derived from the same (root) source for ʿaʾila (family), can be used as a euphemism for "wife." Persian ayal is also derived from this root.

17. Another word derived from this same root is ḥurma. In Egyptian Arabic it also means "woman" or "wife," but is associated more with slang usage and possibly groups from lower socioeconomic backgrounds with less education and of more popular orientation.

18. The *Hans Wehr Dictionary of Modern Written Arabic* lists the feminine counterpart as another word for "wife." I have never heard it used, although I have heard the masculine version used mostly in anecdotal contexts (satires and comedies, for example), perhaps because of its extreme rarity.

19. The only possible "grammatical" reading for this sentence involves an interpretation of *armal* as a verb, hence a causative reading where Mohammed is understood to have brought about the state of Nadia's being a widow (he is somehow responsible for her husband's death).

20. More such proverbs can be found in Taymour's 1986 collection of colloquial (Egyptian) proverbs.

21. This last point is probably more universal than one thinks. In Arabic, for example, referring to a man or a young male adult as *ibn umm-u* (his mother's son) is derogatory just as it is in English. It connotes dependency and an inability to make decisions—emasculation of a sort. Referring to a daughter as *bint abuu-ha* (her father's daughter) is much less so. It simply means she takes after him, and the wording can have positive or negative connotations depending on how the father and the qualities in question are seen. If so, then the identification in the Arabic obituaries of women through men but not vice versa could be viewed as a reflection of such social values and the gendered social realities within which the obituaries are written.

22. The total here (1,344) excludes 17 other obituaries with nonmajor relationships and 78 others where the deceased is listed as being "survived by X" instead of the usual identification of the deceased with a certain relationship to a family member (X is mother of Y) The figures in table 3.4 reflect only the first type because the classification is based on the actual linguistic terms used in the obituary. The seventeen relationships beyond the four major ones are: twelve aunts, two nieces, one cousin, and one grandmother for women, and one uncle for men. Thus relationships identifying deceased women are more diverse, reflecting a broader family network. Results from the Persian obituaries are different (see note 24).

23. Arabic obituaries also provide lists of families related to the deceased by blood or marriage.

24. To make the results parallel with the Arabic obituaries, the figures in table 3.5 exclude thirty-two women and two men identified without names (a total of 397). Twenty other obituaries were excluded, where the relationship was expressed in the list of signatures. The reasons are similar to those justifying the exclusion of the English obituaries' "survived by."

25. Relationships beyond the four major ones include for women two *naveh* (grandchildren) and one *valedeh hamsar* (mother-in-law). They are more diverse for men: two *amu zadeh* (paternal cousins), one *pedar zan* (father-in-law), one *hafid* (grandson), one *ibn am* (paternal cousin), one *amu* (paternal uncle), and one *damad* (son-in-law).

26. The reader may wish to recall the earlier discussion on the role of obituaries in the funeralization process (chapter 2, section 1.1.3).

27. I suggested earlier the possibility that editorial policies dictate the last-name-first order. There could also be a legal basis for this policy.

28. The distribution by religious affiliation is as follows: Muslims 971 (95 percent), Zoroastrians 16 (2 percent), Christians 13 (1 percent), and indeterminable affiliation 24 (2 percent).

29. The percentages here are based on the obituaries of 197 deceased women with locations identified. The remaining 12 of the 209 Egyptian women without names either had no location identified or the specific location could not be determined for some reason.

30. Recall that naming practices in Iran also often assign two names to a child, one Arabic and one Persian.

31. For this reason, the analysis by Culture and Time is not discussed further.

32. One might also attribute the difference to the way Islam is practiced in Egypt and Iran (Sunna versus Shi'a). This argument will not be pursued, however, since neither suggests that women not be identified by name. In fact, I argue later that this is more an obituary- than culture-based phenomenon.

33. This is not to say that these lists are not biased.

Chapter 4

1. See, for example, Adler 1978, Alford 1988, and Braun 1988.
2. Further research is needed to substantiate this possibility, based on the time

and social context within which *ḥaram* originated and possible correspondences to the time *madame* was borrowed in Egyptian Arabic.

3. In Egypt the use of the word *madaam* (borrowed from *madame*) has introduced the missing possibility, which is to use a term of address with the last name only.

4. See, for example, the quote introducing chapter 5 from Lipset and Zeterberg.

5. The idea introduced in this section that obituaries can be viewed as a (universal) space shared by the various cultures, sexes, and other units of analysis will be further developed in the concluding chapter.

6. A third domain may be suggested here—the personal, which corresponds to basic identity as symbolized by names and family relationships used in identifying people, deceased included, as covered in chapter 3. On some level, this can be construed as a component within the "social," everyday domain.

7. Social status can also be viewed along the same lines as professional status to mean status acquired by a person through involvement in activities deemed valuable within a community and as such worthy of recognition through the symbolic act of title bestowal.

8. These numbers add up to more than the earlier figure of 1,559 deceased identified with title. Some deceased are mentioned with both professional and social titles, hence the discrepancy between the total figure 1,591 obtained here and the earlier 1,559.

9. Percentages here are calculated based on the number of titles (in table B.1) in relation to the total population from each culture group: Arabic, 1,337; English, 1,439; and Persian, 1,024.

10. References to women here are not intended to apply to all women since diversity among women as a group must be acknowledged as it is among other social and ethnic groups.

11. Dictionaries (for example, the *Hans Wehr Dictionary of Modern Written Arabic*) sometimes list it as applicable to Christians' participation in Holy Mass. No instances are found in the obituaries where it is applied to non-Muslims.

12. Other single-term religious titles (*karbalai* and *sheikh*) also appear in the data which, when added to this category, produce a figure of 29 percent for religious titles.

13. The title *sayyid* may have an additional religious connotation indicating the deceased (or family) as descendants of the Prophet Mohammad (see appendix A). This reading has been ignored since it could not have been established from the obituaries alone.

14. The title *khawaga* may fit into this category as well. It has not been included because its use may be restricted to certain groups, currently to "foreigners" (see appendix A).

15. *Mrs.* may not be as much of a title as a relational term.

16. I am indebted to Nawal El-Mahalawi for bringing this to my attention.

17. This exclusion may be responsible for the decrease since title combinations appear with some frequency as of 1978.

18. An alternative explanation would attribute this result to the changing social realities outside the obituaries—the change in socioeconomic class structure in Egypt. This would be reflected in the obituaries insofar as obituary writers would then

come from socioeconomic groups that value the usage of such titles and apply them frequently to the living and the deceased as well.

19. I have consistently interpreted *sheikh* as a religious title since this is the more likely interpretation within the more formal context of the obituaries. *Sheikh* may also have a nonreligious interpretation as leader or head of a group or community. This may explain its divergent behavior by comparison to other religious titles.

20. There is a sense in which combinations of this type (both terms are religious, or both are titles of respect) may still be interpreted as being "mixed." Since some titles are ambiguous as to whether they are solely religious or social, only the actual context in which they have been applied can clarify the reading.

Chapter 5

1. Translated in Badran and Cooke 1990:231.

2. For an interesting analysis and portrayal of leadership roles among rural communities (the *ʿumda* and the *aʿyan* (rural notables, among others) and the impact of post-1952 sociopolitical changes on such communities and their leadership, see Ansari 1986.

3. If the situation changes whereby women come to occupy such positions, grammatical feminine agreement would be used as it is now used in reference to women mayors outside of Egypt.

4. Instances where this different ranking was obtained include population distribution and, naturally, names.

5. See, for example, Badran 1995.

6. I here ignore the category "Other."

7. These figures are obtained by adding the number of deceased identified with professional titles and occupations for each sex (table B.1).

Chapter 6

1. Technically speaking, the increase is the third-highest change for any decade. The increase in 1958–68 was 2.4 lines, which is 0.1 higher than the 2.3 posted in 1998. I ignore this difference, however, and consider the increase in 1998 second highest as well.

2. Technically, the percentage of occupations from category II exceeded the percentage from category I in 1938 also, but the difference is minimal (only four percentage points).

Chapter 7

1. I have avoided comparisons of overall population distribution with 1998 because of additional limits I put on the total number of obituaries from that year.

2. Technically, only 99 percent of Iranian women are mentioned by name in 1998 (see table 6.6).

3. Some may disagree with the line of argumentation used here, and in other parts of the volume, whereby I compare statistics from the obituaries to those from the world outside, claiming, for example, no direct connection between identification with occupation and employment figures of any one space or time. Be this as it may, the line of argumentation I adopted is intended to establish that. I first assume that there is a connection between the two worlds (here in terms of occupation figures obtained from the obituaries and those of their respective culture groups). If the assumption leads to a form of contradiction, then I would have established that the original assumption is not true (hence the results from the two worlds are not connected).

References

Abdel Fadil, Mahmoud. 1982. "Educational Expansion and Income Distritution in Egypt, 1952–1977." In *The Political Economy of Income Distribution in Egypt,* ed. Gouda Abdel Khalek and Robert Tignor, 351–74. New York: Holmes and Meier.

Abdel Khalek, Gouda, and Robert Tignor, eds. 1982. *The Political Economy of Income Distribution in Egypt.* New York: Holmes and Meier.

Abdel Kader, Soha. 1987. *Egyptian Women in a Changing Society, 1988–1987.* Boulder, CO: Lynne Rienner Publishers.

Abu-Lughod, Janet. 1971. *Cairo: 1001 Years of the City Victorious.* Princeton: Princeton University Press.

Adler, Max K. l978. *Naming and Addressing: A Sociolinguistic Study.* Hamburg: Buske.

Alford, Richard D. l988. *Naming and Identity: A Cross-Cultural Study of Personal Naming Practices.* New Haven, CT: Human Relations Area Files.

Ali, Abdullah Yusuf. [198?.] *The Glorious Kur᾽an,* Translation and commentary. Beirut: Dar al-Fikr.

Al-Kholi, Lutfi. 1997. "*Ijtihadat.*" *Al-Ahram,* October 4 and 5, 1997.

al-Sayyid Marsot, Afaf Lutfi. 1978. "The Revolutionary Gentlewomen in Egypt." In *Women in the Muslim World,* ed. Lois Beck and Nikki Keddie, 261–76. Cambridge, MA: Harvard University Press.

———. 1985. *A Short History of Modern Egypt.* Cambridge: Cambridge University Press.

Andreasen, Tayo, Annette Borchorst, Drude Dahlerup, Eva Lous, and Hanne Rimmen Nielson, eds. 1991. *Moving On: New Perspectives on the Women's Movement.* Aarhus, Denmark: Aarhus University Press.

Ansari, Hameid. 1986. *Egypt, The Stalled Society.* Cairo: American University Press.

Antoun, Richard T. 1968. "On the Significance of Names in an Arab Village." *Ethnology* 7:158–70.

Arasteh, Reza. *Education and Social Awakening in Iran, 1850–1968.* 2nd ed. Leiden: E. J. Brill, 1969.

Ayalon, Ami. 1995. *The Press in the Arab Middle East.* Oxford: Oxford University Press.

Badawi, El-Said, and Martin Hinds. 1986. *A Dictionary of Egyptian Arabic: Arabic-English.* Beirut: Librairie du Liban.

Badawi, El-Said M., Mahmoud F. Hegazi, Ali El-Din Hillal, and Farouk Shousha, comps. 1991. *Dictionary of Arab Names.* Vols. 1 and 2. Muscat, Oman: Sultan Qaboos University.

Badran, Margot. 1995. *Feminism, Islam, and Nation: Gender and the Making of Modern Egypt.* Princeton: Princeton University Press.

Badran, Margot, trans. and ed. 1986. *Harem Years: The Memoirs of an Egyptian Feminist.* London: Virago Press.

Badran, Margot, and Miriam Cooke, eds. 1990. *Opening the Gates: A Century of Arab Feminist Writing.* London: Virago Press.

Bahramgeyqui, H. 1977. *Tehran: An Urban Analysis.* Tehran: Shabat Books Industry.

Bayat-Philipp, Mangol. 1978. "Women and Revolution in Iran, 1905–1911." In *Women in the Muslim World,* ed. Lois Beck and Nikki Keddie, 295–308. Cambridge, MA: Harvard University Press.

Beck, Lois, and Nikki Keddie, eds. 1978. *Women in the Muslim World.* Cambridge, MA: Harvard University Press.

Beeman, William O. 1976. "Status, Style and Strategy in Iranian Interaction." *Anthropological Linguistics* 18:305–22.

———. 1986. *Language, Status, and Power in Iran.* Bloomington: University of Indiana Press.

Braun, Friederike. l988. *Terms of Address: Problems of Patterns and Usage in Various Languages and Cultures.* New York: Mouton Der Gruyter.

Butler, Christopher. 1985. *Statistics in Linguistics.* Oxford: Basil Blackwell.

Chatty, Dawn, and Annika Rabo, eds. 1997. *Organizing Women: Formal and Informal Women's Groups in the Middle East.* New York: Berg.

Cowan, J. Milton, ed. 1976. *The Hans Wehr Dictionary of Modern Written Arabic.* New York: Spoken Language Services.

Dunnett, Peter J. S. 1988. *The World Newspaper Industry.* New York: Methuen.

Eakins, B., and G. Eakins. 1978. *Sex Differences in Human Communication.* Boston: Houghton Mifflin.

Early, Evelyn. 1993. *Baladi Women of Cairo: Playing with an Egg and a Stone.* Cairo: American University in Cairo Press.

Ehrlich, Susan, and Ruth King. 1994. "Feminist Meaning and the (De)politicization of the Lexicon." *Language in Society* 23:59–76.

Eid, Mushira. 1994a. "Hidden Women: Gender Inequality in 1938 Egyptian Obituaries." In *Investigating Arabic: Linguistic, Pedagogical, and Literary Studies in Honor of Ernest N. McCarus,* ed. Raji Rammuny and Dilworth Parkinson, 113–36. Columbus, OH: Greyden Press.

———. 1994b. "'What's in a Name?': Women in Egyptian Obituaries." In *Arabic Sociolinguistics: Issues and Perspectives,* ed. Yasir Suleiman, 81–100. Richmond, Surrey: Curzon Press.

———. 2000. "Women and Men in Egyptian Obituaries: Language, Gender, and Identity." In *Hearing Many Voices,* ed. Anita Taylor and M. J. Hardman, 41–57. Creskill, NJ: Hampton Press.

Fasold, Ralph, Haru Yamada, David Robinson, and Steven Barish. 1990. "The Language-Planning Effect of Newspaper Editorial Policy: Gender Differences in *The Washington Post.*" *Language in Society* 19:521–39.

Fernea, Elizabeth Warnock. 1985. *Women and the Family in the Middle East: New Voices of Change.* Austin: University of Texas Press.

Friedl, Erika. 1978. "Women in Contemporary Persian Folktales." In *Women in the Muslim World,* ed. Lois Beck and Nikki Keddie, 629–50. Cambridge, MA: Harvard University Press.

Göçek, Fatma Müge, and Shiva Balaghi, eds. 1994. *Reconstructing Gender in the Middle East: Tradition, Identity, and Power.* New York: Columbia University Press.

Graddol, David, and Joan Swann. 1989. *Gender Voices.* Oxford: Basil Blackwell.

Habenstein, Robert W., and William M. Lamers. 1963. *Funeral Customs the World Over.* Milwaukee: National Funeral Directors Association of the United States.

Habibi, Nader. 1992. "Popularity of Islamic and Persian Names in Iran before and after the Islamic Revolution." *International Journal of Middle East Studies* 24:253–60.

Haïm, S. 1969. *New Persian English Dictionary.* Tehran: Librairie-Béroukhim.

Halpern, Manfred. 1963. *The Politics of Social Change in the Middle East and North Africa.* Princeton: Princeton University Press.

Hymowitz, Carol, and Michaele Weissman. 1978. *A History of Women in America.* New York: Bantam Books.

Ibrahim, Saad Eddin. 1982. "Social Mobility and Income Distribution in Egypt, 1952–1977." In *The Political Economy of Income Distribution in Egypt,* ed. Gouda Abdel Khalek and Robert Tignor, 375–434. New York: Holmes and Meier.

Jabbra, Nancy. 1980. "Sex Roles and Language in Lebanon." *Ethnology* 19, no. 4:459–74.

Jarboe, Betty. 1989. *Obituaries: A Guide to Sources.* Boston: G. K. Hall.

Kandiyoti, Deniz. 1996. "Contemporary Feminist Scholarship and Middle East Studies." In *Gendering the Middle East,* ed. Deniz Kandiyoti, 1–28. New York: Syracuse University Press.

———, ed. 1996. *Gendering the Middle East.* New York: Syracuse University Press.

Kaplan, Justin, and Anne Bernays. 1997. *The Language of Names.* New York: Simon and Schuster.

Karam, Azza M. 1998. *Women, Islamisms, and the State.* New York: St. Martin's Press.

Kaufman, Debra R., ed. 1989. *Public/Private Spheres: Women Past and Present.* Boston: Northeastern University Custom Book Program.

Key, Mary R. 1975. *Male/Female Language.* Metuchen, NJ: Scarecrow Press.

Knutson, Gunnar S. l981. *Content Analysis of Obituaries of Prominent Librarians in the New York Times, 1884–1976.* Master's thesis, University of Chicago.

Le Page, Robert B., and Andrée Tabouret-Keller. 1985. *Acts of Identity: Creole-Based Approaches to Language and Ethnicity.* Cambridge: Cambridge University Press.

Lakoff, Robin. 1975. *Language and Woman's Place.* New York: Harper and Row.

Mabro, Judy, ed. 1996. *Veiled Half-Truths: Western Travellers' Perceptions of Middle Eastern Women.* New York: I. B. Tauris.

Majidian, Mina. 1981. *Ettela' at: A Descriptive Study of a Major Iranian Daily Newspaper, 1951–1978.* Ph.D. diss., University of Utah, Salt Lake City.

Martyna, Wendy. l983. "Beyond the He/Man Approach: The Case for Nonsexist Language." In *Language, Gender and Society,* ed. Michael Thorne, Cheris Kramarae, and Nancy Henley, 25–37. Rowley, MA: Newberry House.

McDonagh, Eileen Lorenzi. 1989. "An Oppressed Elite: Educational Patterns of

Notable American Women." In *Public/Private Spheres: Women Past and Present,* ed. Debra R. Kaufman, 43–77. Boston: Northeastern University Custom Book Program.

McFadden, Tom Johnston. 1953. *Daily Journalism in the Arab States.* Columbus: Ohio State University Press.

McIntire, Marina L. 1972. "Terms of Address in an Academic Setting." *Anthropological Linguistics* 14:286–91.

Measures, Howard. *Styles of Address: A Manual of Usage in Writing and in Speech.* New York: St. Martin's Press.

Merrill, John C. 1968. *The Elite Press: Great Newspapers of the World.* New York: Pitman Publishing Corp.

Merrill, John C., and Harold Fischer. 1980. *The World's Great Dailies: Profiles of Fifty Newspapers.* New York: Hastings Publishers.

Metz, Helen Chopin, ed. 1991. *Egypt: A Country Study.* Washington, DC: Library of Congress, Federal Research Division.

Milani, Farzaneh. 1992. *Veils and Words: The Emerging Voices of Iranian Women Writers.* Syracuse: Syracuse University Press.

Miller, Casey, and Kate Swift. 1977. *Words and Women: New Language in New Times.* New York: Anchor Press/Doubleday.

Moghadam, Valentine M. 1993. *Modernizing Women: Gender and Social Change in the Middle East.* London: Lynne Rienner.

Neft, Naomi, and Ann D. Levine. 1997. *Where Women Stand: An International Report on the Status of Women in 140 Countries, 1997–1998.* New York: Random House.

Nilsen, Alleen Pace, Haig Bosmajian, H. Lee Gershuny, and Julia P. Stanley, eds. 1977. *Sexism and Language.* Urbana, IL: National Council of Teachers of English.

"The Obituarist's Art Lives after Death." *The Economist,* December 24, 1994–January 6, 1995:64–66.

Paidar, Parvin. 1995. *Women and the Political Process in Twentieth-Century Iran.* Cambridge Middle East Studies I. Cambridge: Cambridge University Press.

———. 1996. "Feminism and Islam in Iran." In *Gendering the Middle East,* ed. Deniz Kandiyoti, 51–67. New York: Syracuse University Press.

Parkinson, Dilworth. l985. *Constructing the Social Context of Communication: Terms of Address in Egyptian Arabic.* Amsterdam: Brill.

Pine, L. G. 1969. *The Story of Titles.* Rutland, VT: Charles E. Tuttle.

Reiter, Ranya. l975. "Men and Women in the South of France: Public and Private Domains." In *Toward an Anthropology of Women,* ed. Ranya Reiter, 252–83. New York: Monthly Review Press.

Roman, Camille, Suzanne Juhasz, and Cristanne Miller, eds. 1994. *The Women and Language Debate: A Sourcebook.* New Brunswick, NJ: Rutgers University Press.

Rugh, William A. 1979. *The Arab Press: News Media and Political Process in the Arab World.* Syracuse: Syracuse University Press.

Sanasarian, Eliz. 1982. *The Women's Rights Movement in Iran: Mutiny, Appeasement, and Repression from 1900 to Khomeini.* New York: Praeger.

Schulz, Muriel R. 1990. "The Semantic Derogation of Woman." In *The Feminist Critique of Language*, ed. Deborah Cameron, 134–47. London: Routledge.

Scott, Anne Firor. 1984. *Making the Invisible Woman Visible*. Urbana: University of Illinois Press.

Shaarawi, Hoda. 1879–1947. *Mudhakarat Hoda Shaarawi, raidat al-marʾa al-arabiyya al-haditha* (Memoirs of Hoda Shaʿrawi, leader of contemporary Arab women). Cairo: Dar al-hilal. 1981.

Smith, Philip M. 1985. *Language, the Sexes and Society*. Language in Society, 8. New York: Basil Blackwell.

Spiro, Socrates. 1895. *Qamus al-lahja al-ʿamiya al-misriya* (An Arabic English dictionary of colloquial Egyptian Arabic). Cairo: al-Moqattam Printing Office. (Reprinted 1980 by Librairie du Liban, Beirut.)

Stilo, Donald L., and Jerome W. Clinton. 1988. *Modern Persian: Spoken and Written*. Princeton: Princeton University Press.

Subki, Amal. 1986. *al-ḥaraka al-nisaʾiya fi misr* (The women's movement in Egypt). Cairo: al-Hayʾa al-misriya al-ʿama li-lkitab.

Sullivan, Earl L. 1986. *Women in Egyptian Public Life*. Syracuse: Syracuse University Press.

Taymour, Ahmad, ed. 1986. *al-Amthal al-ʿamiyya* (Colloquial proverbs). 4th ed. Cairo: Al-Ahram Center for Translation and Publishing.

Thorne, Michael, Cheris Kramarae, and Nancy Henley, eds. 1983. *Language, Gender and Society*. Rowley, MA: Newberry House.

Treichler, Paula A. 1989. "From Discourse to Dictionary: How Sexist Meanings Are Authorized." In *Language, Gender and Professional Writing: Theoretical Approaches and Guidelines for Nonsexist Usage,* ed. Francine Wattman Frank and Paula A. Treichler, 51–79. New York: Commission on the Status of Women in the Profession, Modern Language Association of America.

Valaoras, Vasilios G. 1972. *Population Analysis of Egypt, 1935–1970 (With Special Reference to Mortality)*. Cairo: Cairo Demographic Center.

Vreeland, Herberd, ed. 1957. "Iran." *Country Survey Series*. New Haven: Human Relations Area File.

Wilber, Donald N. 1976. *Iran: Past and Present*. 8th ed. Princeton: Princeton University Press.

Woods, Anthony, Paul Fletcher, and Arthur Hughes. 1986. *Statistics in Language Studies*. Cambridge: Cambridge University Press.

Zartman, I. William, ed. 1980. *Elites in the Middle East*. New York: Praeger.

Index